P9-DFR-088

First Reading of the Emancipation Proclamation by Francis Bicknell Carpenter, United States Capitol Art Collection. Photograph by the Architect of the Capitol.

The Inner Life
of Abraham Lincoln

Six Months at the White House

F. B. CARPENTER

Introduction by Mark E. Neely Jr.

University of Nebraska Press
Lincoln and London

⊖ The paper in this book meets the minimum requirements
of American National Standard for Information Sciences—
Permanence of Paper for Printed Library Materials, ANSI
Z39.48-1984.

First Bison Books printing: 1995
Most recent printing indicated by the last digit below:
10   9   8   7   6   5   4   3   2   1

Library of Congress Cataloging-in-Publication Data
Carpenter, F. B. (Francis Bicknell), 1830–1900.
[Six months at the White House with Abraham Lincoln]
The inner life of Abraham Lincoln: six months at the White
House / F. B. Carpenter; introduction by Mark E. Neely, Jr.
p.   cm.
Originally published: Six months at the White House with
Abraham Lincoln. New York: Hurd and Houghton, 1866.
Includes bibliographical references.
ISBN 0-8032-6365-1 (pbk.: alk. paper)
1. Lincoln, Abraham, 1809–1865—Anecdotes.   2. Presi-
dents—United States—Anecdotes.   I. Title.
E457.15.C316   1995
973.7′092—dc20
95-20127   CIP

Originally published as *Six Months at the White House with
Abraham Lincoln* in 1866 by Hurd and Houghton, New York.
Reprinted from the 1880 edition, titled *The Inner Life of
Abraham Lincoln: Six Months at the White House,* by
Houghton, Osgood and Company, Boston.

No material has been omitted from this Bison Books edition.
As with the 1880 edition, chapter 1 begins on arabic page 9.

INTRODUCTION

Mark E. Neely Jr.

Francis B. Carpenter was in the right place at the right
time. Through visionary foresight—and good antislavery
connections in New York and Washington—this portrait
painter from New York arranged to camp out in the White
House from February through July 1864 and was thus
on hand to quiz President Abraham Lincoln and his cabinet about the origins of the Emancipation Proclamation
while their memories were fresh. These were times
fraught with dangerous incidents for the republic. Events
moved so fast, through shockingly bloody military cam-
paigns and with a hotly contested presidential election
canvass as well, that few thought to interview administration officials about the past; most were absorbed in
the present and fearfully trying to discern the future.
Apparently, no one except Carpenter asked Lincoln about
the Emancipation Proclamation's history! Doubtless most
journalists and historians thought they could ask him
after the war was over, but as it turned out, Lincoln did
not survive the war, and the opportunity was lost forever.

When other sources permit us to check up on him, Carpenter proves to have been an accurate observer with a
reliable memory for what he saw and heard while painting portraits in the executive mansion. It may well be
that Lincoln and the other usually wary politicians in
the administration responded less guardedly to Carpenter than they might have to a probing journalist. As Carpenter relates, Lincoln once said to a White House caller

who had come to discuss a delicate political matter and
noticed the artist working in the same room with them,
"Oh, you need not mind him; he is but a painter" (30).

Carpenter questioned Lincoln in order to paint accurately a giant canvas depicting the *First Reading of the
Emancipation Proclamation of President Lincoln*. As a
history painter, Carpenter also offers readers in the twentieth century, with their heightened awareness of visual
matters in history, the single most important source for
understanding the assumptions behind the photographs,
paintings, and popular prints of that era (he had a role in
producing all three). Carpenter does not offer as much as
we want or need, but sources of information on such matters are scarce, and what he offers is crucial.

The book's original subtitle should not be ignored—as
it often is and as Carpenter himself, or the publisher did—
in editions of the book from 1868 on; they carried the title
*The Inner Life of Abraham Lincoln: Six Months at the
White House*. The book was, as its original subtitle announced, in part "The Story of a Picture." That picture,
as Carpenter so disarmingly allowed it to be called, remains one of the few American historical paintings of any
significance in American visual memory, ranking only a
little behind the art works of John Trumbull, who created our image of Bunker Hill and the signing of the Declaration of Independence, and of Emanuel Leutze, who
created the unforgettable image of George Washington
crossing the Delaware. (Fred B. Perkins's *The Picture and
the Men,* a book about Carpenter's painting published in
1867, in no way supersedes Carpenter's own account).

Carpenter's personal origins were almost as humble
as those of his most famous presidential subject. He was
born in Homer, New York, in 1830; his father was a farmer.
The only formal art instruction he had came in some five
months' apprenticeship to a portrait painter in Syracuse.
He established a studio in New York City in 1852 and
gained important commissions. He remained deeply reli-

gious. Raised as a Congregationalist, he never adopted the trappings of Bohemian lifestyle commonly associated with painters. Along with serious religious interests came attachment to moral reform, and Carpenter's antislavery enthusiasm led him to the great artistic work of his life, visualizing the origins of the Emancipation Proclamation. An old friend acted as his financial patron for the project, and another, a newspaperman, made connection with the Republican politicians, Schuyler Colfax and Owen Lovejoy, who had access to the president. Lovejoy apparently persuaded Lincoln to let the painter work in the White House. From that opportunity came important visual images of Lincoln and this important book.[1]

Before discussing the contributions of the volume in more detail, the reader should be forewarned that *Six Months at the White House* is not without faults. First, and most important, Carpenter's personal religious zeal considerably exceeded Lincoln's, and his absorbing interest in Lincoln's religious life, the source, no doubt, of the second and misleading title of the book, *The Inner Life,* serves to distort his word portrait of the sixteenth president. This was obvious even at the time, an age more fervently evangelical than our own, and the reviewer of the book in the *Atlantic Monthly* rightly observed that "goody-goody dwells in the spirit and letter of all his attempts to portray the religious character of the President."[2]

The reader, therefore, is put on guard to give searching test to any anecdotes that stress Lincoln's religiosity, especially when derived from persons who were not his intimates. For example, Carpenter says that after the death of William Wallace Lincoln, the president's eleven-year-old son, on Thursday, 20 February 1862, Lincoln was for a time inconsolable and for a much longer time than that given to shutting himself away from all society on each Thursday and giving way to his feelings. "He would see no one, and seemed a prey to the deepest melancholy."

Enter the Reverend Francis Vinton, a New York clergyman who was "an acquaintance of Mrs. Lincoln and of
her sister, Mrs. Edwards, of Springfield." He "was requested by them to come up and see the President." The
grief-stricken Thursdays had alarmed Mrs. Lincoln, and
she and her sister had told Vinton about them. Lincoln
received Vinton in the parlor and the minister told him:

> To mourn the departed as *lost* belonged to heathenism—not
> to Christianity. "Your son," said Dr. Vinton, "is *alive,* in Para-
> dise. Do you remember that passage in the Gospels: 'God is
> not the God of the *dead* but of the living, for *all* live unto
> him'"? The President had listened as one in a stupor, until
> his ear caught the words, "Your son is alive." Starting from
> the sofa, he exclaimed, "Alive! *alive!* Surely you mock me."
> "No, sir, believe me," replied Dr. Vinton; "it is a most com-
> forting doctrine of the church. . . ." Mr. Lincoln looked at
> him a moment, and then, stepping forward, he threw his
> arm around the clergyman's neck, and, laying his head upon
> his breast, sobbed aloud. "*Alive? alive?*" . . . Through a mem-
> ber of the family, I have been informed that Mr. Lincoln's
> views in relation to spiritual things seemed changed from
> that hour. (117–19)

No one who has read many books about Lincoln can easily picture him putting his arms around a Protestant minister previously unknown to him and blubbering. Mary
Todd Lincoln commented to an early biographer, "There
are some very good persons, who are inclined to magnify
conversations & incidents, connected with their slight
acquaintance, with this great & good man . . . it was not
his nature, to commit his griefs and religious feelings so
fully to words & that with an entire stranger." Nor was
the hysterical Mrs. Lincoln in any condition to be taking
care of her husband's sanity after the death of Willie; it
was more likely the other way around.[3]

Besides, the story cannot be squared with the record.

On the first Thursday after Willie's death, Lincoln met with Congressman William D. "Pig Iron" Kelley of Pennsylvania and had a long discussion into the night with Secretary of War Edwin M. Stanton and with General George B. McClellan's chief of staff. On the second Thursday after Willie's death he had a meeting in his office about patronage in Hawaii, he met also with General McClellan to discuss military strategy, and he went to the residence of Assistant Secretary of the Navy Gustavus V. Fox. On the following Thursday he met in his office with William Dennison of Ohio and with Senator James A. McDougall of California. He calculated the daily expense of the war and figured out that eighty-seven days' cost would pay for all the slaves in the Border States at $400.00 each.[4]

Unfortunately, a substantial part of the book, especially from page 236 on, contains little more than cheap anecdotes clipped from the topical sources available at the time, rather than the priceless words Carpenter was privileged to hear in person. Toward the end, the book degenerates into that unfortunate genre: a compilation of the "wit and wisdom of Abe Lincoln." These anecdotes were popular at the time, but are worthless as history and useful only as revealing the popular mind of the era. Not all the stories before page 236 come from firsthand observation, by any means, and all that are not should be scrutinized closely. The book ends as a cut-and-paste job, with the reprinting of much of a lecture about Lincoln delivered by his old law partner, William H. Herndon. That makes a rather undistinguished conclusion to a book that begins with great promise.

One other warning is perhaps necessary: Carpenter wrote and painted from a secure antislavery outlook. His enterprise was not to criticize the Emancipation Proclamation or its origins but to glorify them. Taking that into consideration, a reader will find the account surprisingly sober and innocent of practiced political ideology. The history of the document appears rather mundane and straightforward. But Carpenter may have been inclined to accept evidence that made Lincoln seem as principled and advanced in his antislavery thinking as possible. One hint of this attitude is the reprinting of a spurious letter from Lincoln to General James Wadsworth. The letter, the original text of which has never been found, has been a matter of dispute for years, but at least two of its paragraphs were not likely written by Lincoln, including this one quoted by Carpenter:

> How to better the condition of the colored race has long been a study which has attracted my serious and careful attention; hence I think I am clear and decided as to what course I shall pursue in the premises, regarding it a religious duty, as the nation's guardian of these people, who have so heroically vindicated their manhood on the battlefield, where, in assisting to save the life of the Republic, they have demonstrated in blood their right to the ballot, which is but the humane protection of the flag they have so fearlessly defended. (270–71)

Historian Ludwell Johnson has pointed out that this paragraph certainly "does not sound like Lincoln, who was not given to talking of his 'religious duty' or to describing himself as the 'nation's guardian' of the Negro." Carpenter cites no source for the letter, but it was widely printed in newspapers at the time.[5]

Keeping these warnings in mind, readers will be able to enjoy and savor the lively information supplied in Carpenter's book. The fact remains that Carpenter provides vital witness to the views of Lincoln and his cabinet on the origins of the Emancipation Proclamation. He also witnessed and described believably, as a contemporary reviewer put it, Lincoln "in consultation with his Cabinet, at play with his children, receiving office-seekers of all kinds, granting many favors to poor and friendless

people, snubbing secession insolence, and bearing patiently much impertinence from every source."[6]

In our century, when historian Paul M. Angle assembled
A Shelf of Lincoln Books (1946), he included on it Francis
B. Carpenter's *Six Months at the White House with
Abraham Lincoln: The Story of a Picture.* That put Carpenter in rather distinguished historical company, for
Angle chose only eighty-one works out of some four thousand written about Abraham Lincoln. But Carpenter's
reputation was to fall soon afterward, when the only book
to deal with the vast biographical literature on Lincoln
was published in 1947. Benjamin Thomas's *Portrait for
Posterity: Lincoln and the Biographers* classed
Carpenter's book with other early ones on Lincoln that
were "replete with anecdotes and folklore, . . . [and with]
eulogy . . . unadulterated."[7] Avoiding the folkloristic and
eulogizing approach was the hallmark of serious Lincoln
scholarship in the modern era, and such words branded
Six Months at the White House as an unreliable source.
It is in fact an indispensable source, though replete with
folklore, eulogy, and anecdote. All Lincoln sources must
be used with care, but, unlike many of them, Carpenter's
book *must* be used.

If Carpenter sometimes betrayed a tin ear in retelling
Lincoln anecdotes, he possessed an unfailingly accurate
and perceptive eye. Few people realize that to Carpenter
should go much of the credit for the indelible visual image of Lincoln. As he prepared to make his painting,
though given access to the subjects themselves, Carpenter could not make such busy men sit still for long and
had ultimately to rely on photographic models. Therefore, soon after his arrival in the White House, he persuaded Lincoln to head to Mathew Brady's Washington
gallery to have photographs made for his purposes. From
this one remarkable sitting, 9 February 1864, came the
photographic model for the five-dollar bill portrait, the
profile used for the Lincoln penny many years later, and

one of the most beloved domestic images from nineteenth-century American photography, the portrait of Lincoln and his son, Tad, looking at an album of photographs in Lincoln's lap. The photographer on that occasion was a Brady employee named Anthony Berger, who supplied the lens, but the eye was surely supplied by Carpenter.[8]

Carpenter's major contribution to Lincoln's lasting visual image, the great painting of the first reading of the Emancipation Proclamation, was a triumph more of opportunity and restraint than painterly genius. He and a few other painters recognized history when it was being made, but Carpenter alone understood that the event needed no embellishment. Postmaster General Montgomery Blair told the painter, "In your great picture you have succeeded in bringing out and making the faces show their thoughts. You have not sunk the natural in the heroic, a fault so common that it must be difficult for an artist to avoid it."[9] Paul Angle referred to the painter's "transparent sincerity" and to that trait should be added his lack of pretension—something that must have been difficult to rein in when he knew as surely as he knew his own name, that the scene he was allowed to paint was the most important in American history since the signing of the Declaration of Independence. But by restraining his impulse to glorify the historical occasion falsely, Carpenter created a lasting image of republican government at work.

What Carpenter managed to resist was the desire to decorate the scene. He thus avoided the major mistakes of his contemporary artists in depicting the Civil War administration. To try to lend to the Lincoln administration some of the imperial embellishments of European state occasions, coronations, the ceremonies surrounding the signing of treaties, and scenes at court, led some artists astray. Formal receptions at the White House, replete with military and diplomatic finery, gilded White House furnishings and decoration, and a gallery of famous personages became the subject of paintings and prints, but they did not endure to be displayed, year after year, in the halls of public schools and in courthouses across the land well into the twentieth century, as Carpenter's scene did.[10] To reject that subject matter for one more comporting with republican simplicity threatened to rob the work of art of any sense of grand theme. Other portraitists of the Great Emancipator relied on *symbols* rather than decoration, but their problem was that the symbols available in the lingering neoclassical vocabulary of art were timeworn if not obsolete. The insertion in the background of a painting of a fragment of a classical column to suggest republican statesmanship on the Greek and Roman model and a broken chain to remind viewers of the liberation of a race seemed incongruous in a photographic age (though Civil War photographers, including Mathew Brady, did it). Art, as Carpenter announced on the very first page of his book, "cannot dwell always among classic forms, nor clothe its conceptions in the imagery of an old and worn-out world." This son of the photographic era added:

> I had resolved to discard all appliances and tricks of picture-making, and endeavor, as faithfully as possible, to represent the scene as it actually transpired; room, furniture, accessories, all were to be painted from the actualities. It was a scene second only in historical importance and interest to that of the Declaration of Independence; and ... it need borrow no interest from imaginary curtain or column, gorgeous furniture or allegorical statue. Assenting heartily to what is called the "realistic" school of art, when applied to the illustration of historic events, I felt in this case, that I have no more right to depart from the facts, than has the historian in his record. (24–25)

Neoclassical setting was the strategem mostly of high art. For the masses, the popular art of lithography supplied less subtle celebrations of emancipation. Portraits of Lincoln standing above a grateful kneeling slave, his chains having been broken by the president himself, however improbable, entered Currier & Ives' inventory of political prints (neither painters nor sculptors were exempt from the temptation thus to depict emancipation too literally). Also immensely popular in that age when language still held a considerable edge over the pictorial in importance were actual presentations of the text of the proclamation—facsimiles of the handwritten document with decorative borders, texts embellished with special lettering and other graphic flourishes, and reproductions of the text in calligraphy with certain letters thickened to delineate a portrait of Lincoln. Carpenter dismissed such productions in the book by describing a scene in the White House when President Lincoln, receiving a gift of one of these elaborate calligraphic portraits, afterward in private characterized it as "ingenious nonsense" (158).

Carpenter avoided all of these pitfalls of embellishment consciously. But it was for good reason that he referred to the "realistic" school of art in quotation marks. Art provides only the illusion of reality, and Carpenter had no desire to create a monumental canvas with no message for the age. "There was a curious mingling of fact and allegory in my mind," he noted. "The general arrangement of the group, as described by the President, was fortunately entirely consistent with my purpose, which was to give that prominence to the different individuals which belonged to them respectively in the Administration." In Carpenter's antislavery view of things, prominence stemmed also from enthusiasm for the cause. "There were two elements in the Cabinet, the radical and the conservative. Mr. Lincoln was placed at the head of the official table, between two groups, nearest that representing the radical, but the uniting point of both." The cabinet members may have sat and stood in the order Carpenter described, but they surely did not sit so that none turned his back to a viewer or steadily in such stiff poses (27).

Carpenter offers modern readers a rare insight into the conscious assumptions and purpose behind a nineteenth-century American painting. Despite his lack of formal education in art, Carpenter had considerable, well-articulated sophistication about his art. The conscious manipulation of these ideas and vocabulary offers reassuring evidence that the categories of interpretation of art have not been imposed by overthoughtful critics on unsophisticated and intuitive American painters.

Carpenter thought in terms of visual images, and that makes his ideas accessible to our age, while explaining the often unstated assumptions behind the works of his own age. Describing the president's agitated state during the bloody Battle of the Wilderness in 1864, for example, Carpenter recalls meeting him "clad in a long morning wrapper, pacing back and forth a narrow passage leading to one of the windows, his hands behind him, great black rings under his eyes, his head bent forward upon his breast,—altogether such a picture of the effects of sorrow, care, and anxiety as would have melted the hearts of the worst of his adversaries, who so mistakenly applied to him the epithets of tyrant and usurper." To think that a "picture"—an image—could combat such serious political charges was not an idea common in the age, and in truth Carpenter seems to speak metaphorically here. Yet he could create "pictures," as he stubbornly called them, without adorning even the products of his trade with their higher-sounding names, paintings, portraits, canvases. On another occasion, Carpenter quotes Congressman Kelley's eulogy on Lincoln, "The President never seemed grander in my sight than when, stealing upon him in the evening, I would find him with a book open before him, as he is represented in the popular photograph, with little Tad beside him." Relating yet another anecdote in which the president asks an officer on a naval ship to get a couple of his men to pick some flowers for Tad, Carpenter added himself: "The Commander-in-Chief of the Army and Navy of the United States,—with almost unlimited power in his hands,—the meekness and simplicity with which Mr. Lincoln bore the honors of his position, is a spectacle for all time" (30–31, 93, 94–95).

What Carpenter did not say was (1) that he was in large part responsible for the photograph on which Kelley commented and (2) he was himself working on a family parlor scene based on it and other individual pictures of the Lincolns. In the end it proved to be but one among many such scenes reproduced as popular engravings or lithographs, but the modern viewer can glimpse in the book the contemporary message such images carried: here was no tyrant and merciless wielder of power. Here was someone meek and simple in a scene that properly melted hearts.

For all his thoughtful approach, careful preparation, and painstaking execution of the Emancipation Proclamation painting, Carpenter's image of Lincoln and his cabinet reached the American people mainly through another artistic medium, the steel engraving. A New York book publisher, J. C. Derby, paid Scotland-born engraver Alexander Hay Ritchie $6,000 to engrave the plate, on which this meticulous craftsman labored for some eighteen months. The result was a beautiful mezzotint engraving so popular that eventually nearly 30,000 prints were pulled from the plate and it was worn out.[11] In a sense, Ritchie engraved the image on the American heart.

Carpenter owned the original painting for a long time, much longer than he wanted to. All the while he fiddled with it, altering the portraiture significantly from what one can see in the print; the artist did not really improve on his original work, and the prints are therefore especially desirable. Eventually, a philanthropist named Elizabeth Thompson purchased the painting for $25,000 and donated it to Congress in 1878. It hangs in the capitol to this day.

Sadly, Carpenter's skills somehow declined after the

great painting, the print, and the book. He never wrote another book or painted a canvas of note, or provided the source of a popular engraving of such power despite considerable effort and opportunity. He never had another inspired vision of a great historical moment, and if he had, his skills in handling brush and palette declined so alarmingly that he would have been unequal to the occasion. He died in New York City in 1900.

But once, in 1864, Carpenter had been presented with a truly great occasion, and he rose to it. Readers should keep that in mind as they look at this artful old book.

NOTES

1. Harold Holzer, Gabor S. Boritt, and Mark E. Neely Jr., "Francis Bicknell Carpenter (1830–1900): Painter of Abraham Lincoln and His Circle," *American Art Journal* 16 (spring 1984), 67–69.

2. *Atlantic Monthly* 18 (November 1966): 645.

3. Justin G. and Linda Levitt Turner, *Mary Todd Lincoln: Her Life and Letters* (New York: Random House, 1972), 293.

4. Earl Schenck Miers, ed., *Lincoln Day by Day: A Chronology* (Washington DC: Lincoln Sesquicentennial Commission, 1960), 3:97, 98, 101; Roy P. Basler, ed., *The Collected Works of Abraham Lincoln* (New Brunswick NJ: Rutgers University Press, 1953–1955), 5:160–61.

5. Basler, ed., *Collected Works* 7:101–2; Ludwell H. Johnson, "Lincoln and Equal Rights: The Authenticity of the Wadsworth Letter," *Journal of Southern History* 32 (February 1966): 85.

6. *Atlantic Monthly,* 644.

7. Paul M. Angle, *A Shelf of Lincoln Books: A Critical Selective Bibliography of Lincolniana* (New Brunswick NJ: Rutgers University Press, 1946), 101; Benjamin P. Thomas, *Portrait for Posterity: Lincoln and the Biographers* (New Brunswick NJ: Rutgers University Press, 1947), 7.

8. Lloyd Ostendorf and Charles M. Hamilton, *Lincoln in Photographs: An Album of Every Known Pose* (Dayton OH: Morningside, 1985), 172–83.

9. Holzer, Boritt, and Neely, "Francis Bicknell Carpenter," 77.

10. The painting illustrated on page 83 of "Francis Bicknell Carpenter," which defies Carpenter's "republican style," was at the time of the article's writing misattributed to Carpenter by the White House Historical Association. For its proper attribution to Peter F. Rothermel, see Harold Holzer and Mark E. Neely Jr., *Mine Eyes Have Seen the Glory: The Civil War in Art* (New York: Orion, 1993), 222–26, 224n.

11. J. C. Derby, *Fifty Years among Authors, Books and Publishers* (Hartford CT: M. A. Winter & Hatch, 1886), 489.

PREFACE.

In offering this volume to the public I shall attempt no apology for its shortcomings, other than to say that its production is the result of the unexpected popularity of the series of articles, relating to the illustrious subject of whom it mainly treats, which were commenced in the New York " Independent " soon after the assassination.

Written in a spirit of enthusiasm and affection, which there has been no effort to disguise, the book is, nevertheless, a simple matter-of-fact record of daily experience and observation, fragmentary, but *true*, in all essential particulars. There has been no disposition to select from, embellish, or suppress, any portion of the material in my possession. The incidents given were not in any sense isolated exceptions to the daily routine of Mr. Lincoln's life. My aim has been throughout these pages to portray *the man* as he was revealed to me, without any attempt at idealization

In addition to my own reminiscences, I have woven into the book various personal incidents, published and unpublished, which bear intrinsic evidence of genuineness, — attaching in these instances, where it seemed necessary and proper, the sources of such contributions.

I am not one of those inclined to believe that Mr. Lincoln, in the closing months of his career, reached the full measure of his greatness. Man may not read the future : but it is my firm conviction, that, had he lived through his second term, he would have continued to grow, as he had grown, in the estimation and confidence of his countrymen ; rising to a grander moral height with every emergency, careful always to weigh every argument opposed to his convictions, but, once mounted upon those convictions, grounded in righteousness, as immovable as one of the giant ranges of our own Rocky Mountains !

Aspiring in no sense to the dignity of a biography, this volume will fulfil its object if it helps to any better knowledge of one, who, apart from the reverence with which he ever will be regarded for his connection with the cause of human Freedom, was the best product and exemplar which the world has yet seen of American soil and institutions ; the

study of whose character, illustrating as it did the
highest form of statesmanship, founded upon truth,
justice, and solid integrity, combining the deepest
wisdom with a child-like freshness and simplicity,—
will be of perpetual interest and value.

                                            F. B. C.

96 *West 45th Street*, NEW YORK.

The Inner Life of Abraham Lincoln

SIX MONTHS AT THE WHITE HOUSE.

I.

I LEAVE to other and abler pens the proper estimate of ABRAHAM LINCOLN as a ruler and statesman, — his work and place in history. Favored during the year 1864 with several months of personal intercourse with him, I shall attempt in these pages to write the story of that association ; not for any value which the record will have in itself, but for the glimpses it may afford of the person and character of the man, — every detail of whose life is now invested with enduring interest for the American people.

II.

That Art should aim to embody and express the spirit and best thought of its own age seems self-evident. If it fails to do this, whatever else it may accomplish, it falls short of its highest object. It cannot dwell always among classic forms, nor clothe its conceptions in the imagery of an old and worn-out world. It must move on, if it is to keep pace with that "increasing purpose which through the ages runs," and its ideals must be wrought out of the strife of a living humanity.

It has been well said by a recent writer: "The record of the human family to the advent of CHRIST, was the preparation of the photographic plate for its image. All subsequent history is the bringing out of the divine ideal of true manhood." Slowly, but surely, through the centuries, is this purpose being accomplished. Human slavery has been the material type or expression of spiritual bondage. On the lowest or physical plane, it has symbolized the captivity and degradation of our higher nature; with the breaking in of new light, and the inspiration of a deeper life, it is inevitably doomed. That man, to attain the full development of the faculties implanted in him, must be in spiritual and physical freedom, is a principle which lies at the foundation of all government; and the enfranchisement of a race to-day thus becomes the assertion and promise of a true and coming Emancipation for all men.

III.

When ABRAHAM LINCOLN, called from the humblest rank in life to preside over the nation during the most momentous period of its history, uttered his Proclamation of Freedom, — shattering forever the chains which bound four millions of human beings in slavery; an act unparalleled for moral grandeur in the history of mankind, — it was evident to all who sought beneath the surface for the cause of the war that the crisis was past, — that so surely as Heaven is on the side of Right and Justice, the North would triumph in the great struggle which had assumed the form of a direct issue between Freedom and Slavery.

In common with many others, I had from the beginning of the war believed that the government would not be successful in putting down a rebellion based upon slavery as its avowed corner-stone, without striking a death-blow at the institution itself. As the months went on, and disappointment and disaster succeeded one another, this conviction deepened into certainty. When at length, in obedience to what seemed the very voice of GOD, the thunderbolt was launched, and, like the first gun at Concord, " was heard around the world," all the enthusiasm of my nature was kindled. The " beast " Secession, offspring of the " dragon " Slavery, drawing in his train a third part of our national stars, was pierced with the deadly wound which could not be healed. It was the combat between Michael and Satan of Apocalyptic vision, reënacted before the eyes of the nineteenth century.

IV.

To paint a picture which should commemorate this new epoch in the history of Liberty, was a

dream which took form and shape in my mind towards the close of the year 1863, — the year made
memorable in its dawn by the issue of the final de-
cree.   With little experience to adapt me for the
execution of such a work, there had nevertheless
come to me at times glowing conceptions of the true
purpose and character of Art, and an intense desire
to do something expressive of appreciation of the
great issues involved in the war.   The painters
of old had delighted in representations of the birth
from the ocean of Venus, the goddess of love.
Ninety years ago upon this Western continent had
been witnessed — no dream of fable, but a substantial fact — the immaculate conception of Constitutional Liberty ; and at length through great travail
its consummation had been reached.   The long-
prayed-for year of jubilee had come ; the bonds of
the oppressed were loosed ; the prison doors were
opened.   " Behold," said a voice, " how a Man
may be exalted to a dignity and glory almost divine,
and give freedom to a race.   Surely Art should
unite with Eloquence and Poetry to celebrate such
a theme."

I conceived of that band of men, upon whom
the eyes of the world centred as never before upon
ministers of state, gathered in council, depressed,
perhaps disheartened at the vain efforts of many
months to restore the supremacy of the government.   I saw, in thought, the head of the nation,
bowed down with his weight of care and responsi-

bility, solemnly announcing, as he unfolded the prepared draft of the Proclamation, that the time for
the inauguration of this policy had arrived; I endeavored to imagine the conflicting emotions of
satisfaction, doubt, and distrust with which such an
announcement would be received by men of the
varied characteristics of the assembled councillors.

For several weeks the design of the picture was
slowly maturing, during which time, however, no
line was drawn upon paper or canvas. Late one
evening, absorbed in thought upon the subject, I
took up an unframed photograph lying carelessly in
my room, and upon the blank side of this, roughly
and hastily sketched, was embodied the central idea
of the composition as it had shaped itself in my
mind.

To one disposed to look for coincidences in daily
life, and regard its events as no mere succession of
accidents, there must often come those which wear
a deep significance. In seeking a point of unity
or action for the picture, I was impressed with the
conviction that important modifications followed the
reading of the Proclamation at the suggestion of
the Secretary of State, and I determined upon such
an incident as the moment of time to be represented. I was subsequently surprised and gratified
when Mr. Lincoln himself, reciting the history of
the Proclamation to me, dwelt particularly upon
the fact that not only was the time of its issue decided by Secretary Seward's advice, but that one

of the most important words in the document was
added through his strenuous representations.

The central thought of the picture once decided
upon and embodied, the rest naturally followed:
one after another the seven figures surrounding the
President dropped into their places. Those supposed to have held the purpose of the Proclamation
as their long conviction, were placed prominently in
the foreground in attitudes which indicated their
support of the measure; the others were represented
in varying moods of discussion or silent deliberation.

A few evenings after the completion of the design I went to see a friend who I knew was intimate with the Hon. Schuyler Colfax and Hon.
Owen Lovejoy, through whom I hoped to obtain
Mr. Lincoln's assent to my plan. I revealed to
him my purpose, and asked his assistance in carrying it into effect. During the following week he
went to Washington, and in company with Mr.
Colfax called upon the President, and laid before
him my project. He kindly listened to the details,
and then said : " In short, if I understand you,
you wish me to consent to sit to this artist for the
picture ? " My friends acknowledged this to be the
object of their errand. Mr. Lincoln at once, with
his accustomed kindness, promised his coöperation.

The last day of the year the Hon. Mr. Lovejoy,
whom I had never met, but who had become warmly
interested in the execution of the work, being in
New York, called at my studio with the wife of my

friend, who had been my earnest advocate. At the close of the interview he remarked, in his quaint way, taking me by the hand, "In the words of Scripture, my good friend, I can say now I believe, not on account of the saying of the woman, but because I have seen for myself."

V.

Impracticable as my scheme had at first seemed, the way was thus opened for its execution. When fairly committed to the purpose, however, the want of means and the magnitude of the undertaking almost disheartened me. My original plan embraced a canvas sufficiently large for a life-size group of the President and entire Cabinet; to paint such a picture would consume many months, perhaps years. Enthusiasm alone would never accomplish the work. The few friends to whom I should have felt at liberty to apply for help were not wealthy. Who outside of these could be persuaded that a work of the character and proportions contemplated, undertaken by an artist of no experience in historical studies, would not end in utter failure?

I had left my home at the usual hour one morning, pondering the difficulty which, like Bunyan's lions, seemed now to block the way. As one alternative after another presented itself to my mind and was rejected, the prospect appeared less and less hopeful. I at length found myself in Broadway at the foot of the stairs leading up to my studio.   **A** gentleman at this moment attracted my attention, standing with his back towards me, looking at some pictures exposed in the window of the shop below. Detecting, as I thought, something familiar in his air and manner, I waited until he turned his face, and then found I was not mistaken ; it was an old acquaintance who five years before lived near me in Brooklyn, engaged in a similar struggle for a livelihood with myself, though his profession was law instead of art.

We had both changed our residences and had not met for years.   After a cordial greeting, he accepted my invitation to ascend to the studio.   I had heard that he had been successful in some business ventures, but the matter made but little impression upon me, and had been forgotten.   Suddenly there seemed to come into my mind the words : " This man has been sent to you."   Full of the singular impression, I laid before him my conception.   He heard me through, and then asked if I was sure of President Lincoln's consent and coöperation.   I informed him of the pledge which had been given me.   " Then," said he, " you shall paint the picture.   Take plenty of time, — make it the great work of your life, — and draw upon me for whatever funds you will require to the end." *

---

* To Mr. SAMUEL SINCLAIR, of the *New York Tribune*, for the introduction to Mr. Lincoln, and to FREDERICK A. LANE, Esq., of New York, for the generous aid thus extended, I shall ever be indebted for the accomplishment of my work.

VI.

On the evening of February 4th, 1864, I went to Washington. Shortly after noon of the following day, I rang the bell at Mr. Lovejoy's residence on Fifteenth Street. To my sorrow, I found him very ill; but it was hoped by his friends that he was then improving. Though very feeble, he insisted upon seeing me, and calling for writing materials, sat up in bed to indite a note introducing me to the President. This, handed to me open, I read. One expression I have not forgotten, it was so like Mr. Lincoln himself, as I afterward came to know him. " I am gaining very slowly. — It is hard work drawing the sled up - hill." And this suggests the similarity there was between these men. Lovejoy had much more of the agitator, the reformer, in his nature, but both drew the inspiration of their lives from the same source, and it was founded in sterling honesty. Their modes of thought and illustration were remarkably alike. It is not strange that they should have been bosom friends. The President called repeatedly to see him during his illness; and it was on one of these occasions that he said to him, " This war is eating my life out; I have a strong impression that I shall not live to see the end." Mr. Lovejoy's health subsequently improved, and for a change he went to Brooklyn, N. Y., where, it will be remembered,

2

he had a relapse, and died, universally mourned as one of the truest and most faithful of our statesmen. Mr. Lincoln did not hear from him directly after he left Washington. Through a friend I learned by letter that he was lying at the point of death. This intelligence I communicated to the President the same evening, in the vestibule of the White House, — meeting him on his way to the War Department. He was deeply affected by it. His only words were, " Lovejoy was the best friend I had in Congress."

To return from this pardonable digression, — I took the note of introduction at once to the White House ; but no opportunity was afforded me of presenting it during the day. The following morning passed with the same result, and I then resolved to avail myself of Mrs. Lincoln's Saturday afternoon reception — at which, I was told, the President would be present — to make myself known to him. Two o'clock found me one of the throng pressing toward the centre of attraction, the " blue " room. From the threshold of the " crimson " parlor as I passed, I had a glimpse of the gaunt figure of Mr. Lincoln in the distance, haggard-looking, dressed in black, relieved only by the prescribed white gloves ; standing, it seemed to me, solitary and alone, though surrounded by the crowd, bending low now and then in the process of handshaking, and responding half abstractedly to the

well-meant greetings of the miscellaneous assemblage. Never shall I forget the electric thrill which
went through my whole being at this instant.   I
seemed to see lines radiating from every part of
the globe, converging to a focus at the point where
that plain, awkward-looking man stood, and to hear
in spirit a million prayers, " as the sound of many
waters," ascending in his behalf. Mingled with
supplication I could discern a clear symphony of
triumph and blessing, swelling with an ever-increas-
ing volume. It was the voice of those who had
been bondmen and bondwomen, and the grand
diapason swept up from the coming ages.

It was soon my privilege, in the regular succession, to take that honored hand. Accompanying
the act, my name and profession were announced
to him in a low tone by one of the assistant private
secretaries, who stood by his side. Retaining my
hand, he looked at me inquiringly for an instant,
and said, " Oh yes ; I know ; this is the painter."
Then straightening himself to his full height, with
a twinkle of the eye, he added, playfully, " Do
you think, Mr. C——, that you can make a handsome picture of *me ?* " emphasizing strongly the
last word. Somewhat confused at this point-blank
shot, uttered in a tone so loud as to attract the
attention of those in immediate proximity, I made
a random reply, and took the occasion to ask
if I could see him in his study at the close of

the reception.   To this he responded in the peculiar vernacular of the West, " I reckon," resuming meanwhile the mechanical and tradi- tional exercise of the hand which no President has ever yet been able to avoid, and which, se- vere as is the ordeal, is likely to attach to the position, so long as the Republic endures.

VII.

The appointed hour found me at the well-remem- bered door of the official chamber, — that door watched daily, with so many conflicting emotions of hope and fear, by the anxious throng regularly gathered there.   The President had preceded me, and was already deep in Acts of Congress, with which the writing-desk was strewed, awaiting his signature.   He received me pleasantly, giving me a seat near his own arm-chair; and after having read Mr. Lovejoy's note, he took off his spectacles, and said, " Well, Mr. C——, we will turn you in loose here, and try to give you a good chance to work out your idea."   Then, without paying much attention to the enthusiastic expression of my am- bitious desire and purpose, he proceeded to give me a detailed account of the history and issue of the great proclamation.

" It had got to be," said he, " midsummer, 1862. Things had gone on from bad to worse, until I felt that we had reached the end of our rope on the plan of operations we had been pursuing; tnat we had about played our last card, and must change our tactics, or lose the game! I now determined upon the adoption of the emancipation policy; and, without consultation with, or the knowledge of the Cabinet, I prepared the original draft of the proclamation, and, after much anxious thought, called a Cabinet meeting upon the subject. This was the last of July, or the first part of the month of August, 1862." (The exact date he did not remember.) "This Cabinet meeting took place, I think, upon a Saturday. All were present, excepting Mr. Blair, the Postmaster-General, who was absent at the opening of the discussion, but came in subsequently. I said to the Cabinet that I had resolved upon this step, and had not called them together to ask their advice, but to lay the subject-matter of a proclamation before them; suggestions as to which would be in order, after they had heard it read. Mr. Lovejoy," said he, "was in error when he informed you that it excited no comment, excepting on the part of Secretary Seward. Various suggestions were offered. Secretary Chase wished the language stronger in reference to the arming of the blacks. Mr. Blair, after he came in, deprecated the policy, on the ground that it would cost the Administration the fall elections. Nothing, however, was offered that I had not already fully anticipated and settled in my own mind, until Secretary Seward spoke. He said in substance: 'Mr. President, I approve of the proclamation, but I question the expediency of its issue at this juncture. The depression of the public mind, consequent upon our repeated reverses, is so great that I fear the effect of so important a step. It may be viewed as the last measure of an exhausted government, a cry for help ; the government stretching forth its hands to Ethiopia, instead of Ethiopia stretching forth her hands to the government.' His idea," said the President, " was that it would be considered our last *shriek*, on the retreat." (This was his *precise* expression.) " ' Now,' continued Mr. Seward, ' while I approve the measure, I suggest, sir, that you postpone its issue, until you can give it to the country supported by military success, instead of issuing it, as would be the case now, upon the greatest disasters of the war !' " Mr. Lincoln continued : " The wisdom of the view of the Secretary of State struck me with very great force. It was an aspect of the case that, in all my thought upon the subject, I had entirely overlooked. The result was that I put the draft of the proclamation aside, as you do your sketch for a picture, waiting for a victory. From time to time I added or changed a line, touching it up here and there, anxiously watching the progress of events. Well, the next news we had was of Pope's disaster, at Bull Run. Things looked darker than ever. Finally, came the week of the battle of Antietam. I determined to wait no longer The news came, I think, on Wednesday, that the advantage was on our side.   I was then staying at the Soldiers' Home, (three miles out of Washington.)   Here I finished writing the second draft of the preliminary proclamation ; came up on Saturday ; called the Cabinet together to hear it, and it was published the following Monday."

At the final meeting of September 20th, another interesting incident occurred in connection with Secretary Seward.   The President had written the important part of the proclamation in these words : —

" That, on the first day of January, in the year of our Lord one thousand eight hundred and sixty-three, all persons held as slaves within any State or designated part of a State, the people whereof shall then be in rebellion against the United States, shall be then, thenceforward, and forever FREE ; and the Executive Government of the United States, including the military and naval authority thereof, will *recognize* the freedom of such persons, and will do no act or acts to repress such persons, or any of them, in any efforts they may make for their actual freedom."   " When I finished reading this paragraph," resumed Mr. Lincoln, " Mr. Seward stopped me, and said, ' I think, Mr. President, that you should insert after the word "*recognize*," in that sentence, the words " *and maintain*." ' I replied that I had already fully considered the import of that expression in this connection, but I had not introduced it, because it was not my way to promise what I was not entirely *sure* that I could perform, and I was not prepared to say that I thought we were exactly able to ' maintain ' this."

" But," said he, " Seward insisted that we ought to take this ground ; and the words finally went in ! "

" It is a somewhat remarkable fact," he subsequently remarked, " that there were just one hundred days between the dates of the two proclamations issued upon the 22d of September and the 1st of January. I had not made the calculation at the time."

Having concluded this interesting statement, the President then proceeded to show me the various positions occupied by himself and the different members of the Cabinet, on the occasion of the first meeting. " As nearly as I remember," said he, " I sat near the head of the table ; the Secretary of the Treasury and the Secretary of War were here, at my right hand ; the others were grouped at the left."

At this point, I exhibited to him a pencil sketch of the composition as I had conceived it, with no knowledge of the facts or details. The leading idea of this I found, as I have stated on a previous page, to be entirely consistent with the account I had just heard. I saw, however, that I should have to reverse the picture, placing the President at the other end of the table, to make it accord with his description. I had resolved to discard all

applian:es and tricks of picture-making, and endeavor, as faithfully as possible, to represent the
scene as it actually transpired ; room, furniture,
accessories, all were to be painted from the actual-
ities.   It was a scene second only in historical importance and interest to that of the Declaration
of Independence; and I felt assured, that, if honestly and earnestly painted, it need borrow no interest from imaginary curtain or column, gorgeous
furniture or allegorical statue.   Assenting heartily
to what is called the " realistic" school of art,
when applied to the illustration of historic events,
I felt in this case, that I had no more right to depart from the facts, than has the historian in his
record.

When friends said to me, as they frequently did,
" Your picture will be bald and barren," my reply was, " If I cannot make the portraiture of the
scene itself sufficiently attractive without the false
glitter of tapestry hangings, velvet table-cloths, and
marble columns, then I shall at least have the satisfaction of having failed in the cause of truth."   I
reasoned in this way: The most important document submitted to a cabinet during our existence
as a nation is under discussion.   A spectator permitted to look in upon that scene would give little
thought and small heed to the mere accessories and
adjuncts of the occasion.   His mind would centre
upon the immortal document, — its anxious author,
conscious of his solemn responsibility, announcing

his matured and inflexible purpose to his assembled councillors.   He would listen with unparalleled eagerness to the momentous sentences
uttered for the first time in the ears of men, and
to the discussion upon them, impatient of mere
formalities and technicalities.   Should a thought be
sprung of important bearing, or an overlooked contingency be brought forward, how intently would
its effect be watched.   What varying emotions,
consequent upon peculiarities of temperament and
character, would be expressed in the countenances
of the different individuals composing the group.
How each in turn would be scanned.   Above all, the
issues involved: — the salvation of the Republic —
the freedom of a Race.   " Surely," I said, " such a
scene may be painted, and abiding if not absorbing
interest secured, without the aid of conventional
trappings.   The republican simplicity of the room
and furniture, with its thronging associations, will
more than counterbalance the lack of splendor, and
the artistic mania for effect.   I will depend solely
for my success upon the interest of the subject,
and its truthfulness of representation."   And this
purpose I carried with me to the end.

VIII.

The first sketch of the composition, as it was
afterward placed upon the canvas, was matured, I
believe, the same afternoon, or the following Mon-

day after the interview recorded above, upon the back of a visiting card; my pockets affording evidence of the employment of all loose material at hand in leisure moments, in the study of the work. The final arrangement of the figures was the result of much thought and many combinations, though the original conception as to the moment of time and incident of action was preserved throughout. The general arrangement of the group, as described by the President, was fortunately entirely consistent with my purpose, which was to give that prominence to the different individuals which belonged to them respectively in the Administration. There was a curious mingling of fact and allegory in my mind, as I assigned to each his place on the canvas. There were two elements in the Cabinet, the radical and the conservative. Mr. Lincoln was placed at the head of the official table, between two groups, nearest that representing the radical, but the uniting point of both. The chief powers of a government are War and Finance : the ministers of these were at his right, — the Secretary of War, symbolizing the great struggle, in the immediate foreground ; the Secretary of the Treasury, actively supporting the new policy, standing by the President's side. The Army being the right hand, the Navy may very properly be styled the left hand of the government. The place for the Secretary of the Navy seemed, therefore, very naturally to be on Mr. Lincoln's left, at the rear of the table. To the **Secretary** of State, as the great expounder of the principles **of** the Republican party, the profound and sagacious statesman, would the attention of all at such a time be given. Entitled to precedence in discussion by his position in the Cabinet, he would necessarily form one of the central figures of the group. The four chief officers of the government were thus brought, in accordance with their relations to the Administration, nearest the person of the President, who, with the manuscript proclamation in hand, which he had just read, was represented leaning forward, listening to, and intently considering the views presented by the Secretary of State. The Attorney-General, absorbed in the constitutional questions involved, with folded arms, was placed at the foot of the table opposite the President. The Secretary of the Interior and the Postmaster-General, occupying the less conspicuous positions of the Cabinet, seemed to take their proper places in the background of the picture.

When, at length, the conception as thus described was sketched upon the large canvas, and Mr. Lincoln came in to see it, his gratifying remark, often subsequently repeated, was. "It is as good as it can be made."

IX.

I have thus revealed, step by step, the mental process by which the picture of which I write came into being. Whether the story bears any analogy to that by which the works of others have been produced, or the composition conforms to established rules and precedents in art or not, is to me a matter of indifference. I was true to my intuitions, and endeavored to adhere as faithfully as practicable to the facts.

It is not my purpose to follow in detail the progress, thenceforward, of the work. As the thread upon which are strung my memories of the late President, allusions to it will be unavoidable throughout these pages ; but hereafter I intend that they shall be subordinate and incidental to matters of more general interest. It is not too much to say that the enthusiasm in which the work was conceived, flagged not to the end. The days were too short for labor upon it. Lighting at nightfall the great chandelier of the state dining-room, which was finally assigned me for a studio instead of the library, where the windows were shaded by the portico, the morning light frequently broke in upon me still standing pencil or palette in hand, before the immense canvas, unable to break the spell which bound me to it.

X.

" We will turn you in loose here," proved an " open sesame " to me during the subsequent months of my occupation at the White House. My access to the official chamber was made nearly as free as that of the private secretaries, unless special business was being transacted. Sometimes a stranger, approaching the President with a low tone, would turn an inquiring eye toward the place where I sat, absorbed frequently in a pencil sketch of some object in the room. This would be met by the hearty tones of Mr. Lincoln, — I can hear them yet ringing in my ears, — " Oh, you need not mind him; he is but a painter." There was a satisfaction to me, differing from that of any other experience, in simply sitting with him. Absorbed in his papers, he would become unconscious of my presence, while I intently studied every line and shade of expression in that furrowed face. In repose, it was the saddest face I ever knew. There were days when I could scarcely look into it without crying. During the first week of the battles of the Wilderness he scarcely slept at all. Passing through the main hall of the domestic apartment on one of these days, I met him, clad in a long morning wrapper, pacing back and forth a narrow passage leading to one of the windows, his hands behind him, great black rings under his eyes, his head bent forward upon his breast, — altogether such a picture of the effects of sorrow, care, and anxiety as would have melted the hearts of the worst of his adversaries, who so mistakenly applied to him the epithets of tyrant and usurper. With a sorrow almost divine, he, too, could have said of the rebellious States, " How often would I have gathered you together, even as a hen gathereth her chickens under her wings, *and ye would not!* " Like another Jeremiah, he wept over the desolations of the nation; " he mourned the slain of the daughter of his people."

Surely, ruler never manifested so much sympathy, and tenderness, and charity. How like the last words of the Divine one himself, " Father, forgive them, for they know not what they do," will the closing sentences of his last inaugural address resound in solemn cadence through the coming centuries. Truly and well says the London " Spectator " of that address : " We cannot read it without a renewed conviction that it is the noblest political document known to history, and should have for the nation and the statesmen he left behind him something of a sacred and almost prophetic character. Surely, none was ever written under a stronger sense of the reality of God's government. And certainly none written in a period of passionate conflict ever so completely excluded the partiality of victorious faction, and breathed so pure a strain of mingled justice and mercy."

XI.

The following Tuesday I spent with **Mr. Lin-coln** in his study. The morning was devoted to the Judge - Advocate - General, who had a large number of court-martial cases to submit to the President. Never had I realized what it was to have power, as on this occasion. As case after case was presented to Mr. Lincoln, one stroke of his pen confirmed or commuted the sentence of death. In several instances Judge Holt referred to extenuating circumstances, — extreme youth, previous good conduct, or recommendations to mercy. Every excuse of this kind, having a foun-dation in fact, was instantly seized upon by the President, who, taking the document containing the sentence, would write upon the back of it the lightest penalty consistent with any degree of jus-tice. As he added the date to one of these papers, he remarked casually, varying the subject of con-versation, " Does your mind, Judge Holt, associate events with dates ? Every time this morning that I have had occasion to write the day of the month, the thought has come up, ' This was General Har-rison's birthday.' " One of the cases brought for-ward at this time I recollect distinctly. The man's name was Burroughs ; he had been a notorious spy ; convicted and sentenced to death, a strong effort had been made in his behalf by powerful friends. It was an aggravated case, but an impression had evidently been made upon the President by the strength and pertinacity of the appeal. As Judge Holt opened the record, he stated that a short time previous Burroughs had attempted to escape from confinement, and was shot dead in the act by the sentinel on guard. With an expression of relief, Mr. Lincoln rejoined, "I ought to be obliged to him for taking his fate into his own hands ; he has saved *me* a deal of trouble."

During a brief absence of the President, Judge Holt told me that the atrocities of some of the criminals condemned, surpassed belief. "A guerilla leader in Missouri," said he, "by the name of Nichols, was in the habit of filling the ears of wounded Unionists who fell into his hands with gunpowder, setting fire to it, and blowing their heads to pieces. When captured, a number of human *ears* were found upon his person." Referring to Mr. Lincoln's disposition to pardon or commute the majority of the death sentences, he remarked, "The President is without exception the most tender-hearted man I ever knew."

Judge Holt, it will be remembered, was called into Mr. Buchanan's cabinet towards the close of his administration. Glancing around the room, — incidentally referring to my errand there, — he said, "This room was the theatre of some very exciting scenes during the last months of Mr. Buchanan's term." He spoke warmly of the courage and fearlessness of Stanton, on those occasions,

3

who did not hesitate to call *traitors* and *treason*
their right names.

When the clock struck twelve, Mr. Lincoln
drew back from the table, and with a stretch of his
long arms, remarked, " I guess we will go no far-
ther with these cases to-day ; I am a little tired,
and the Cabinet will be coming in soon." " I believe, by the by," he added, " that I have not yet
had my breakfast, — this business has been so absorbing that it has crowded everything else out of
my mind."

And so ended the work of one morning ; simple
in its detail, but pregnant with hope and joy, dark-
ness and death, to many human beings.

XII.

As the different members of the Cabinet came
in, the President introduced me, adding in several
instances, — " He has an idea of painting a picture
of us all together." This, of course, started conversation on the topic of art. Presently a reference
was made by some one to Jones, the sculptor,
whose bust of Mr. Lincoln was in the crimson
parlor below. The President, I think, was writing
at this instant. Looking up, he said, " Jones tells
a good story of General Scott, of whom he once
made a bust. Having a fine subject to start with,
he succeeded in giving great satisfaction. At the
closing sitting he attempted to define and elab-

orate the lines and markings of the face. **The**
General sat patiently; but when he came to **see**
the result, his countenance indicated decided displeasure. 'Why, Jones, what have you been doing?' he asked. 'Oh,' rejoined the sculptor, 'not
much, I confess, General; I have been working
out the details of the face a little more, this morning.' 'Details?' exclaimed the General, warmly;
'—— the details! Why, my man, you are spoil
ing the bust!'"

At three o'clock the President was to accompany
me, by appointment, to Brady's photographic gal-
leries on Pennsylvania Avenue. The carriage had
been ordered, and Mrs. Lincoln, who was to accompany us, had come down at the appointed hour,
dressed for the ride, when one of those vexations,
incident to all households, occurred. Neither carriage or coachman was to be seen. The President
and myself stood upon the threshold of the door
under the portico, awaiting the result of the inquiry for the coachman, when a letter was put
into his hand. While he was reading this, people
were passing, as is customary, up and down the
promenade, which leads through the grounds to the
War Department, crossing, of course, the portico.
My attention was attracted to an approaching party,
apparently a countryman, plainly dressed, with his
wife and two little boys, who had evidently been
straying about, looking at the places of public interest in the city. As they reached the portico, the

father, who was in advance, caught sight of the tall figure of Mr. Lincoln, absorbed in his letter. His wife and the little boys were ascending the steps. The man stopped suddenly, put out his hand with a " hush " to his family, and, after a moment's gaze, he bent down and whispered to them, — " There is the President ! " Then leaving them, he slowly made a half circuit around Mr. Lincoln, watching him intently all the while. At this point, having finished his letter, the President turned to me, and said: " Well, we will not wait any longer for the carriage ; it won't hurt you and me to walk down." The countryman here approached very diffidently, and asked if he might be allowed to take the President by the hand ; after which, " Would he extend the same privilege to his wife and little boys ? " Mr. Lincoln good-naturedly approached the latter, who had remained where they were stopped, and, reaching down, said a kind word to the bashful little fellows, who shrank close up to their mother, and did not reply. This simple act filled the father's cup full. " The Lord is with you, Mr. President," he said reverently ; and then, hesitating a moment, he added, with strong emphasis, " and the people too, sir ; and the people too ! "

The walk, of a mile or more, was made very agreeable and interesting to me by a variety of stories, of which Mr. Lincoln's mind was so prolific. Something was said soon after we started about the penalty which attached to high positions in a democratic government — the tribute those filling them were compelled to pay to the public. "Great men," said Mr. Lincoln, "have various estimates. When Daniel Webster made his tour through the West years ago, he visited Springfield among other places, where great preparations had been made to receive him. As the procession was going through the town, a barefooted little darkey boy pulled the sleeve of a man named T., and asked, — ' What the folks were all doing down the street?' 'Why, Jack,' was the reply, ' the biggest man in the world is coming.' Now, there lived in Springfield a man by the name of G., — a very corpulent man. Jack darted off down the street, but presently returned, with a very disappointed air. ' Well, did you see him ? ' inquired T. ' Yees,' returned Jack ; ' but laws — he ain't half as big as old G.' "

Shortly afterward, he spoke of Mr. Ewing, who was in both President Harrison's and President Taylor's cabinet. "Those men," said he, " were, you know, when elected, both of advanced years, — sages. Ewing had received, in some way, the nickname of ' Old Solitude.' Soon after the formation of Taylor's cabinet, Webster and Ewing happened to meet at an evening party. As they approached each other, Webster, who was in fine spirits, uttered, in his deepest bass tones, the well-known lines, —

" ' O Solitude, where are the charms
That sages have seen in thy face?' "

The evening of Tuesday I dined with **Mr.**
Chase, the Secretary of the Treasury, of whom I
painted a portrait in 1855, upon the close of his
term as United States Senator. He said during
the dinner, that, shortly after the dedication of the
cemetery at Gettysburg, the President told this
story at a cabinet meeting. "Thad. Stevens was
asked by some one, the morning of the day appointed for that ceremony, where the President
and Mr. Seward were going. 'To Gettysburg,'
was the reply. 'But where are Stanton and
Chase?' continued the questioner. 'At home,
at work,' was the surly answer; 'let the dead
bury the dead.'" This was some months previous to the Baltimore Convention, when it was
thought by some of the leaders of the party, that
Mr. Lincoln's chances for a re-nomination were
somewhat dubious.

Levee night occurring weekly, during the
regular season, was always a trying one to the
President. Whenever sympathy was expressed
for him, however, he would turn it off playfully,
asserting that the tug at his hand was much
easier to bear than that upon his heartstrings for
all manner of favors beyond his power to grant, to
which he had daily to submit. As I took his hand
at the levee, which closed my first day's experi-
ences with him, he said in his homely way,

" Well, C., you have seen one day's run;— what is your opinion of it?"

XIII.

Wednesday morning was devoted to the continued examination of the court-martial cases, to the great vexation of a score of political applicants, whom I could hear impatiently pacing the floor of the hall and waiting-room. At one o'clock, however, the doors were thrown open, and the throng admitted and dismissed, as rapidly as possible. I was much amused and interested, later in the day, in a variety of characters who presented themselves. First was an elderly lady, plainly but comfortably dressed, whose son was a prisoner in Baltimore. Her story, spun out to some length, was briefly this: Her son had been serving in the Rebel army. He heard that his sister was lying dead at home, and his mother at the supposed point of death. He determined to see them, and succeeded in getting through our lines undiscovered. He found his mother better. Before he got ready o return, he became very ill himself. She said she hid him in the house until he recovered, and on his way back to his regiment he was captured. He was now anxious to take the oath, and his mother assured the President that he should henceforth "have nothing to do with the Rebels." Mr. Lincoln sat quietly through the story,

his face in half shadow. As she finished he said,
with some impatience, — "Now this is a pretty story
to come to me with, is n't it? Your son came
home from fighting against his country; he was
sick; you secreted him, nursed him up, and when
cured, started him off again to help destroy some
more of our boys. Taken prisoner, trying to get
through our lines, you now want me to let him off
upon his oath." "Yes," said the woman, not in
the least disconcerted, "and I give you my word,
Mr. President, he shall never have anything more
to do with the Rebels — never — I was always
opposed to his joining them." "Your word," rejoined Mr. Lincoln dryly, "what do I know about
your word?" He finally took the application, and
writing something upon the back of it, returned it
to her with the words, "Now, I want you to understand that I have done this just to get rid of
you!" "Oh," said she, "Mr. President, I have
always heard that you were such a kind-hearted
man, and now I know it is true." And so, with
much apparent satisfaction, she withdrew.

The party that followed consisted of a lady and
two gentlemen. She had come to ask that her
husband, who was also a prisoner of war, might
be permitted to take the oath and be released from
confinement. To secure a degree of interest on
the part of the President, one of the gentlemen
claimed to be an acquaintance of Mrs. Lincoln;
this, however, received but little attention, and the

President proceeded to ask what position the lady's husband held in the Rebel service. "Oh," said she, "he was a captain." "*A captain!*" rejoined Mr. Lincoln, "indeed! — rather too big a fish to set free simply upon his taking the oath. If he was an officer, it is proof positive that he has been a zealous rebel; I cannot release him." Here the lady's friend reiterated the assertion of his acquaintance with Mrs. Lincoln. Instantly the President's hand was upon the bell-rope. The usher in attendance answered the summons. "Cornelius, take this man's name to Mrs. Lincoln, and ask her what she knows of him." The boy presently returned, with the reply that "*the Madam*" (as she was called by the servants) knew nothing of him whatever. The man said it was very strange. "Well, it is just as I suspected," said the President. The party made one more attempt to enlist his sympathy, but without effect. "It is of no use," was the reply; "I cannot release him;" and the trio withdrew, the lady in high displeasure.

Next came a Methodist minister by the name of "G.," claiming to be the son of the inventor of iron-clad gunboats. He had understood that the President appointed the hospital chaplains, and he greatly desired such a place. Mr. Lincoln replied rather curtly, that he could do nothing for him. "But I was told, sir, that these appointments were made by the President," said the gentleman, very respectfully. "I will just tell you how that is," was the answer; "when there are vacancies I appoint, not without." The clergyman here alluded to his having left with the private secretary a war-sermon which he had lately preached. Stepping out, he returned with the pamphlet, saying, as he handed it to the President, "I suppose, sir, you have little time to read anything of this kind; but I shall be very glad to leave it with you." Upon this he bowed himself out, and the sermon was carelessly tossed aside, never to be thought of again by Mr. Lincoln.

Subsequently the sermon fell into my hands. The only thing I remember about it was the practical application of a professional incident. The clergyman one day fell in with two soldiers fighting. One had the other down, and was severely handling him. Rebuking the men, the one underneath responded very heartily, "Plase your *riverince*, I am willing to give up this minute, solely out of respect for your *riverince*." And so the preacher thought the South should be made to say "in regard to the Constitution."

XIV.

The examples given of the observations of two days, are fair illustrations of the usual White House routine, varied of course by official or diplomatic business, and a greater or less pressure of visitors, some of whom would linger in the anteroom

day after day, waiting admission.   The incidents of
no two days could of course be alike.   I shall never
cease to regret that an additional private secretary
could not have been appointed, whose exclusive
duty it should have been to look after and keep a
record of all cases appealing to executive clemency.
It would have afforded full employment for one
man, at least; and such a volume would now be
beyond all price.

Just before leaving for Washington, I met a
brother artist, who, upon learning of my proposed
purpose, laid before me the details of an interesting case, concerning his only son, begging me to
bring the circumstances to the President's knowledge.   When the war broke out the young man
in question was living at the South.   Eventually
driven into the Rebel service, he was improving his
first opportunity to go over to the Union lines,
when he was taken prisoner.   His story was disbe-
lieved, and he had been in prison for more than a
year at Alton, Illinois.   His father had spent many
months in the endeavor to have him released, without success.   So many formalities and technicalities
were in the way that he became completely dis-
couraged, and appealed to me as his last hope.
The boy was very ill, and he feared if not speedily
released, would soon die.   Promising the father
that I would bear the case in mind, I improved an
opportunity, as soon as I felt sure of having found
favor with the President, to speak to him about it.

I believe it was on the private staircase, that, meeting him one evening, I ventured to introduce the
subject.   I assured him of the entire good faith
and loyalty of both father and son.   Of course he
had never heard of the case before.   Considering
the subject a moment, he said, " Come up-stairs
by-and-by, and I guess we can fix it up."

An hour later I entered his room, and gave him
very briefly the particulars of the case ; reading
one or two letters from the young man to his
father.   " That will do," said the President, putting on his spectacles, and taking the letter out of
my hand, he turned it over and wrote on the back
of it, " Release this man upon his taking the oath.
A. LINCOLN."   " There," said he, " you can take
that over to the War Department yourself, if you
choose.   You will find it all right."

XV.

Wednesday night, February 10th, was an exciting one at the White House, the stables belonging
to the mansion being burned to the ground.   The
loss most severely felt was of the two ponies, one
cf which had belonged to Willie Lincoln, the
President's second son, who died in 1862, and
the other to Tad, the youngest, and pet of his
father, who in his infancy nicknamed him Tad-
pole, subsequently abbreviated to Taddie, and
then Tad.   His real name is Thomas, named

for the father of Mr. Lincoln. Upon "Tad's" learning of the loss, he threw himself at full length upon the floor, and could not be comforted. The only allusion I ever heard the President make to Willie was on this occasion, in connection with the loss of his pony. John Hay, the assistant private secretary, told me that he was rarely known to speak of his lost son.

The morning following the fire, Robert Lincoln came into his father's office, and said he had a point of law which he wished to submit. It appeared that one of the coachmen had two or three hundred dollars in greenbacks in his room over the stables, which were consumed. Robert said that he and John Hay had been having an argument as to the liability of the government for its notes, where it could be shown that they had been burned, or otherwise destroyed. The President turned the matter over in his mind for a moment, and said, " The payment of a note presupposes its presentation to the maker of it. It is the sign or symbol of value received; it is not *value* itself, that is clear. At the same time the production of the note seems a necessary warrant for the demand ; and while the moral obligation is as strong without this, governments and banking institutions do not recognize any principle beyond the strictly legal. It is an established rule that the citizen cannot sue the government ; therefore, I don't see but that it is a dead loss for Jehu."

About this time a couple of Kentucky gentlemen
called.   As they rose to take leave, one of them,
who may have noticed little Tad, — as he usually spent much time in his father's office, — said to
the President: "General Crittenden told me an
interesting incident about his son, eight or nine
years old, a few days since.   A day or two after
the battle of Chickamauga, the little fellow came
into camp.   The General rode during the battle a
horse which went by the name of John Jay, a
great favorite with his son.   Manifesting his delight upon again seeing his father, by covering him
with caresses, the child at length said, 'Papa, where
is John Jay?'   'Oh,' said his father, 'your
horse behaved very badly during the fight; he
insisted, very cowardly, upon taking me to the
rear.'   The little fellow's eyes sparkled.   'Papa,'
said he, 'I know John Jay would never have
done that of his own will.   It must have been *your*
work.'"

Montgomery Blair told me that when the convention which nominated Mr. Lincoln met at Chicago, there was a hideous painting in the hall which
was brought forward subsequently as a likeness of
the nominee.   Most of the delegates having never
seen the original, the effect upon them was indescribable.   I replied to Mr. Blair that my friend Brady,
the photographer, insisted that his photograph of
Mr. Lincoln, taken the morning of the day he
made his Cooper Institute speech in New York, —

much the best portrait, by the way, in circulation of him during the campaign, — was the means of his election. That it helped largely to this end I do not doubt. The effect of such influences, though silent, is powerful. Fremont once said to me, that the villanous wood-cut published by the New York " Tribune," the next day after his nomination, lost him twenty-five votes in one township, to his certain knowledge.

On one of the last days of February, I called, with my friend W——, of New York, upon Mr. Lovejoy, who was supposed to be convalescent. He thought himself nearly well again, and was in fine spirits. Indications of an organized movement to bring forward Fremont, as an opposition candidate to Mr. Lincoln, had recently appeared. Mr. Lovejoy was very severe upon it; he said, " Any attempt to divide the party at such a time was criminal in the last degree." I remember observing that many of the extreme anti-slavery men appeared to distrust the President. This drew out his indignant condemnation. " I tell you," said he, " Mr. Lincoln is at heart as strong an anti-slavery man as any of them, but he is compelled to *feel* his way. He has a responsibility in this matter which many men do not seem to be able to comprehend. I say to you frankly, that I believe his course to be right. His mind acts slowly, but when he moves, it is *forward*. You will never find him receding from a position once taken. It is of no

use talking, or getting up conventions against **him.**
He is going to be the candidate of the Baltimore
Convention, and is sure to be reëlected. ' It was
foreordained from the foundation of the world.'
I have no sympathy or patience with those who
are trying to manufacture issues against him; but
they will not succeed; he is too strong with the
masses. For my part," he concluded, " I am not
only willing to take Mr. Lincoln for another term,
but the same cabinet, right straight through."

XVI.

Wednesday, March 2d, I had an unusually
long and interesting sitting from the President.
I invited Mr. Samuel Sinclair, of New York,
who was in Washington, to be present. The news
had recently been received of the disaster under
General Seymour in Florida. Many newspapers
openly charged the President with having sent the
expedition with primary reference to restoring the
State in season to secure its vote at the forthcom-
ing Baltimore Convention. Mr. Lincoln was deeply
wounded by these charges. He referred to them
during the sitting; and gave a simple and truthful
statement of the affair, which was planned, if I remember rightly, by General Gillmore. A few days
afterward, an editorial appeared in the New York
" Tribune," which was known not to favor Mr. Lincoln's renomination, entirely exonerating him from

all blame. I took the article to him in his study, and he expressed much gratification at its candor. It was, perhaps, in connection with the newspaper attacks, that he told, during the sitting, this story. —"A traveller on the frontier found himself out of his reckoning one night in a most inhospitable region. A terrific thunder-storm came up, to add to his trouble. He floundered along until his horse at length gave out. The lightning afforded him the only clew to his way, but the peals of thunder were frightful. One bolt, which seemed to crash the earth beneath him, brought him to his knees. By no means a praying man, his petition was snort and to the point, — " O Lord, if it is all the same to you, give us a little more light and a little less noise ! "

Presently the conversation turned upon Shakspeare, of whom it is well known Mr. Lincoln was very fond. He once remarked, " It matters not to me whether Shakspeare be well or ill acted ; with him the thought suffices." Edwin Booth was playing an engagement at this time at Grover's Theatre. He had been announced for the coming evening in his famous part of *Hamlet.* The President had never witnessed his representation of this character, and he proposed being present. The mention of this play, which I afterward learned had at all times a peculiar charm for Mr. Lincoln's mind, waked up a train of thought I was not prepared for. Said he, — and his words have often

4

returned to me with a sad interest since his own assassination, — "There is one passage of the play of "Hamlet" which is very apt to be slurred over by the actor, or omitted altogether, which seems to me the choicest part of the play. It is the soliloquy of the king, after the murder. It always struck me as one of the finest touches of nature in the world."

Then, throwing himself into the very spirit of the scene, he took up the words : —

> " O my offence is rank, it smells to heaven;
> It hath the primal eldest curse upon 't,
> A brother's murder! — Pray can I not,
> Though inclination be as sharp as will;
> My stronger guilt defeats my strong intent;
> And, like a man to double business bound,
> I stand in pause where I shall first begin,
> And both neglect. What if this cursed hand
> Were thicker than itself with brother's blood?
> Is there not rain enough in the sweet heavens
> To wash it white as snow? Whereto serves mercy
> But to confront the visage of offence;
> And what 's in prayer but this twofold force —
> To be forestalled ere we come to fall,
> Or pardoned, being down? Then I 'll look up;
> My fault is past. But O what form of prayer
> Can serve my turn? Forgive me my foul murder?
> That cannot be; since I am still possessed
> Of those effects for which I did the murder, —
> My crown, my own ambition, and my queen.
>   May one be pardoned and retain the offence?
> In the corrupted currents of this world,
> Offence's gilded hand may shove by justice,
> And oft 't is seen the wicked prize itself
> Buys out the law; but 't is not so *above*.
> There is no shuffling; there the action lies
> In its true nature; and we ourselves compelled,

> Even to the teeth and forehead of our faults,
> To give in evidence. What then? what rests?
> Try what repentance can; what can it not?
> Yet what can it when one cannot repent?
> O wretched state! O bosom black as death!
> O bruised soul that, struggling to be free,
> Art more engaged! Help, angels, make assay!
> Bow, stubborn knees! And heart with strings of steel,
> Be soft as sinews of the new-born babe;
> All may be well!"

He repeated this entire passage from memory, with a feeling and appreciation unsurpassed by anything I ever witnessed upon the stage. Remaining in thought for a few moments, he continued: —

"The opening of the play of 'King Richard the Third' seems to me often entirely misapprehended. It is quite common for an actor to come upon the stage, and, in a sophomoric style, to begin with a flourish: —

> "'Now is the winter of our discontent
> Made glorious summer by this sun of York,
> And all the clouds that lowered upon our house,
> In the deep bosom of the ocean buried!'

Now," said he, "this is all wrong. Richard, you remember, had been, and was then, plotting the destruction of his brothers, to make room for himself. Outwardly, the most loyal to the newly crowned king, secretly he could scarcely contain his impatience at the obstacles still in the way of his own elevation. He appears upon the stage, just after the crowning of Edward, burning with repressed hate and jealousy. The prologue is the utterance of the most intense bitterness and satire.'

Then, unconsciously assuming the character, Mr.
Lincoln repeated, also from memory, Richard's
soliloquy, rendering it with a degree of force and
power that made it seem like a new creation to me.
Though familiar with the passage from boyhood, I
can truly say that never till that moment had I
fully appreciated its spirit. I could not refrain
from laying down my palette and brushes, and ap-
plauding heartily, upon his conclusion, saying, at
the same time, half in earnest, that I was not
sure but that he had made a mistake in the choice
of a profession, considerably, as may be imagined,
to his amusement. Mr. Sinclair has since repeatedly said to me that he never heard these choice
passages of Shakspeare rendered with more effect
by the most famous of modern actors.

Mr. Lincoln's memory was very remarkable.
With the multitude of visitors whom he saw daily,
I was often amazed at the readiness with which he
recalled faces and events and even names. At
one of the afternoon receptions, a stranger
shook hands with him, and, as he did so, remarked, casually, that he was elected to Congress
about the time Mr. Lincoln's term as representative expired. "Yes," said the President, "you
are from ——," mentioning the State. "I remember reading of your election in a newspaper one
morning on a steamboat going down to Mount Ver-
non." At another time a gentleman addressed him,
saying, "I presume, Mr. President, that you have

forgotten me ? "   " No," was the prompt reply
" your name is Flood.   I saw you last, twelve
years ago, at ——," naming the place and the occasion.   " I am glad to see," he continued, " that
the *Flood* flows on."   Subsequent to his reëlection
a deputation of bankers from various sections were
introduced one day by the Secretary of the Treasury.   After a few moments' general conversation,
Mr. Lincoln turned to one of them, and said :
" Your district did not give me so strong a vote
at the last election as it did in 1860."   " I think,
sir, that you must be mistaken," replied the
banker.   " I have the impression that your majority was considerably increased at the last election."   " No," rejoined the President, " you fell
off about six hundred votes."   Then taking down
from the bookcase the official canvass of 1860
and 1864, he referred to the vote of the district
named, and proved to be quite right in his assertion.

During this interview, — related to me by one
of the party, Mr. P——, of Chelsea, Mass., — a
member of the delegation referred to the severity
of the tax laid by Congress upon the State Banks.
" Now," said Mr. Lincoln, " that reminds me of a
circumstance that took place in a neighborhood
where I lived when I was a boy.   In the spring of
the year the farmers were very fond of the dish
which they called greens, though the fashionable
name for it nowadays is spinach, I believe.   One day

after dinner, a large family were taken very ill,
The doctor was called in, who attributed it to the
greens, of which all had freely partaken. Living
in the family was a half-witted boy named Jake.
On a subsequent occasion, when greens had
been gathered for dinner, the head of the house
said : ' Now, boys, before running any further risk
in this thing, we will first try them on Jake. If he
stands it, we are all right.' And just so, I suppose," said Mr. Lincoln, " Congress thought of
the State Banks ! "

XVII.

While sitting one day, Secretary Stanton —
whom I usually found quite taciturn — referred
to the meeting of the Buchanan Cabinet called
upon receipt of the news that Colonel Anderson had
evacuated Moultrie, and gone into Fort Sumter.
" This little incident," said Stanton, " was the
crisis of our history, — the pivot upon which everything turned. Had he remained in Fort Moultrie,
a very different combination of circumstances would
have arisen. The attack on Sumter — commenced
by the South — united the North, and made the
success of the Confederacy impossible. I shall
never forget," he continued, "our coming together
by special summons that night. Buchanan sat in
his arm-chair in a corner of the room, white as a
sheet, with the stump of a cigar in his mouth. The

despatches were laid before us; and so much violence ensued, that he had to turn us all out-of-doors."

The day following, by special permission of Mr. Lincoln, I was present at the regular Cabinet meeting. Judge Bates came in first, and, taking a package out of his pocket, said, "You may not be aware, Mr. President, that you have a formidable rival in the field. I received this through the mail to-day." He unfolded an immense placard, on which was printed in large letters, — "I introduce for President of the United States, Mr. T. W. Smith [I think this was the name], of Philadelphia." The bill then went on to enumerate the qualifications of the candidate, which were of a stunning order; and the whole was signed "George Bates," which the Attorney-General said might be a relative of his, for aught he knew. This decidedly original document was pinned up in a conspicuous place in the council-chamber, where it hung for several days, of course attracting the attention of all visitors, and creating much amusement.

The disaster on the Red River was the subject of official consultation. The positions of the respective forces were traced on the war maps, and various suggestions and opinions offered. The Secretary of the Interior, looking over to where the Secretary of War sat, said he had a young friend whom he wished to have appointed a paymaster in the army. "How old is he?" asked Stanton, gruflly. "About twenty-one, I believe," answered the Secretary of the Interior; "he is of good family and excellent character." "Usher," was the reply, "I would not appoint the Angel Gabriel a paymaster, if he was only twenty-one."

Judge Bates, who was to have a sitting after the adjournment, here beckoned to me, signifying that he was ready for the appointment. And so ended my brief glimpse of a cabinet in session.

XVIII.

General Grant reached Washington, after his nomination to the Lieutenant-Generalship, the evening of March 8th, 1864. His reception at Willard's Hotel, unaccompanied by staff or escort, was an event never to be forgotten by those who witnessed it. Later in the evening he attended the Presidential levee, entering the reception-room unannounced. He was recognized and welcomed by the President with the utmost cordiality, and the distinguished stranger was soon nearly overwhelmed by the pressure of the crowd upon him. Secretary Seward at length mounting a sofa, pulled the modest hero up by his side, where he stood for some time, bowing his acknowledgments to the tumultucus assemblage. He subsequently remarked that this was " his warmest campaign during the war."

The next day at one o'clock he was formally

presented by the President with his commission as Lieutenant-General.   The ceremony took place in the presence of the Cabinet, the Hon. Mr. Lovejoy, and several officers of the army, and was very brief and simple, as became the character of each of the illustrious chief actors.

On the day following General Grant visited the Army of the Potomac, and upon his return to Washington he made preparations to leave immediately for the West.   At the close of a consultation with the President and Secretary of War, he was informed that Mrs. Lincoln expected his presence the same evening at a military dinner she proposed to give in his honor.   The General at once responded that it would be impossible for him to remain over, — he "must be in Tennessee at a given time."   " But we can't excuse you," returned the President.   " It would be the play of 'Hamlet' with *Hamlet* left out, over again. Twelve distinguished officers, now in the city, have been invited to meet you."   " I appreciate fully the honor Mrs. Lincoln would do me," replied the General, hesitatingly, knocking the ashes off the end of his cigar ;   " but — time is very precious just now — and — really, Mr. President, I believe I have had enough of the ' *show* ' business ! "

The dinner was given ; the twelve officers did full justice to it; but it is needless to add, the Lieutenant-General was not one of the number.

XIX.

The evening of March 25th was an intensely interesting one to me. It was passed with the President alone in his study, marked by no interruptions. Busy with pen and papers when I entered, he presently threw them aside, and commenced talking again about Shakspeare. Little Tad coming in, he sent him to the library for a copy of the plays, from which he read aloud several of his favorite passages. Relapsing into a sadder strain, he laid the book aside, and leaning back in his chair, said, " There is a poem that has been a great favorite with me for years, to which my attention was first called when a young man, by a friend, and which I afterward saw and cut from a newspaper, and carried in my pocket, till by frequent reading I had it by heart. I would give a great deal," he added, " to know who wrote it, but I never could ascertain." Then, half closing his eyes, he repeated the poem, " Oh! why should the spirit of mortal be proud ? " Surprised and delighted, I told him that I should greatly prize a copy of the lines. He replied that he had recently written them out for Mrs. Stanton, but promised that when a favorable opportunity occurred he would give them to me.

Varying the subject, he continued: " There are some quaint, queer verses, written, I think, by Oliver Wendell Holmes, entitled, ' The Last Leaf,' one of which is to me inexpressibly touching. He then repeated these also from memory. The verse he referred to occurs in about the middle of the poem, and is this :—

> "The mossy marbles rest
> On the lips that he has pressed
> In their bloom;
> And the names he loved to hear
> Have been carved for many a year
> On the tomb."

As he finished this verse, he said, in his emphatic way, "For pure pathos, in my judgment, there is nothing finer than those six lines in the English language!"

A day or two afterward, he asked me to accompany him to the temporary studio, at the Treasury Department, of Mr. Swayne, the sculptor, who was making a bust of him. While he was sitting, it occurred to me to improve the opportunity to secure the promised poem. Upon mentioning the subject, the sculptor surprised me by saying that he had at his home, in Philadelphia, a printed copy of the verses, taken from a newspaper some years previous. The President inquired if they were published in any connection with his name. Mr. Swayne said that they purported to have been *written* "by Abraham Lincoln." "I have heard of that before, and that 's why I asked," returned the President. "But there is no truth in it. The poem was first shown ,o me by a young man named 'Jason Duncan,' many years ago."

The sculptor was using for a studio the office of the Solicitor of the Treasury Department,
an irregular room, packed nearly full of law books.
Seating myself, I believe, upon a pile of these at Mr.
Lincoln's feet, he kindly repeated the lines, which I
wrote down, one by one, as they fell from his lips : —

OH! WHY SHOULD THE SPIRIT OF MORTAL BE PROUD?*

Oh! why should the spirit of mortal be proud?
Like a swift-fleeting meteor, a fast-flying cloud
A flash of the lightning, a break of the wave
He passeth from life to his rest in the grave.

The leaves of the oak and the willow shall fade,
Be scattered around, and together be laid;
And the young and the old, and the low and the high,
Shall moulder to dust, and together shall lie.

The infant a mother attended and loved;
The mother that infant's affection who proved;
The husband, that mother and infant who blest, —
Each, all, are away to their dwellings of rest.

[The maid on whose cheek, on whose brow, in whose eye,
Shone beauty and pleasure, — her triumphs are by;
And the memory of those who loved her and praised,
Are alike from the minds of the living erased.]

The hand of the king that the sceptre hath borne,
The brow of the priest that the mitre hath worn,
The eye of the sage, and the heart of the brave,
Are hidden and lost in the depths of the grave.

* The authorship of this poem has been made known since this
publication in the *Evening Post*. It was written by William Knox,
a young Scotchman, a contemporary of Sir Walter Scott. He died
in Edinburgh, in 1825, at the age of 36.

The two verses in brackets were not repeated by Mr. Lincoln,
but belong to the original poem.

The peasant, whose lot was to sow and to reap,
The herdsman, who climbed with his goats up the steep,
The beggar, who wandered in search of his bread,
Have faded away like the grass that we tread.

[The saint, who enjoyed the communion of Heaven,
The sinner, who dared to remain unforgiven,
The wise and the foolish, the guilty and just,
Have quietly mingled their bones in the dust.]

So the multitude goes — like the flower or the weed
That withers away to let others succeed;
So the multitude comes — even those we behold,
To repeat every tale that has often been told.

For we are the same our fathers have been;
We see the same sights our fathers have seen;
We drink the same stream, we view the same sun,
And run the same course our fathers have run.

The thoughts we are thinking, our fathers would think;
From the death we are shrinking, our fathers would shrink;
To the life we are clinging, they also would cling; —
But it speeds from us all like a bird on the wing.

They loved — but the story we cannot unfold;
They scorned — but the heart of the haughty is cold;
They grieved — but no wail from their slumber will come;
They joyed — but the tongue of their gladness is dumb.

They died — ay, they died; — we things that are now,
That walk on the turf that lies over their brow,
And make in their dwellings a transient abode,
Meet the things that they met on their pilgrimage road.

Yea! hope and despondency, pleasure and pain,
Are mingled together in sunshine and rain;
And the smile and the tear, the song and the dirge,
Still follow each other, like surge upon surge.

'T is the wink of an eye — 't is the draught of a breath —
From the blossom of health to the paleness of death,
From the gilded saloon to the bier and the shroud: —
Oh! why should the spirit of mortal be proud?

XX.

On the way to the sculptor's studio a conversation occurred of much significance, in view of the
terrible tragedy so soon to paralyze every loyal
heart in the nation. A late number of the New
York "Tribune" had contained an account from a
correspondent within the Rebel lines, of an elaborate conspiracy, matured in Richmond, to abduct,
or assassinate — if the first was not found practicable — the person of the President. A secret organization, composed, it was stated, of five hundred or a thousand men, had solemnly sworn to
accomplish the deed. Mr. Lincoln had not seen
or heard of this account, and at his request, I gave
him the details. Upon the conclusion, he smiled
incredulously, and said : " Well, even if true, I do
not see what the Rebels would gain by killing or
getting possession of me. I am but a single individual, and it would not help their cause or make
the least difference in the progress of the war.
Everything would go right on just the same. Soon
after I was nominated at Chicago, I began to receive letters threatening my life. The first one or
two made me a little uncomfortable, but I came at
length to look for a regular instalment of this kind
of correspondence in every week's mail, and up to
inauguration day I was in constant receipt of such
letters. It is no uncommon thing to receive them
now ; but they have ceased to give me any appre-

hension." I expressed some surprise at this, but he replied in his peculiar way, "Oh, there is nothing like getting *used* to things!"

In connection with this, Mr. Noah Brooks, — who was to have been Mr. Nicolay's successor as private secretary to the President, — and Colonel Charles G. Halpine, of New York, have referred to personal conversations of exceeding interest, which I transcribe.

In an article contributed to "Harper's Magazine," soon after the assassination, Mr. Brooks says: —

"The simple habits of Mr. Lincoln were so well known that it is a subject for surprise that watchful and malignant treason did not sooner take that precious life which he seemed to hold so lightly. He had an almost morbid dislike for an escort, or guide, and daily exposed himself to the deadly aim of an assassin. One summer morning, passing by the White House at an early hour, I saw the President standing at the gateway, looking anxiously down the street; and, in reply to a salutation, he said, ' Good morning, good morning! I am looking for a newsboy; when you get to that corner, I wish you would start one up this way.' In reply to the remonstrances of friends, who were afraid of his constant exposure to danger, he had but one answer: ' If they kill me, the next man will be just as bad for them; and in a country like this, where our habits are simple, and must be, assassi-

nation is always possible, and will come, if they are
determined upon it.' ''

A cavalry guard was once placed at the gates
of the White House for a while, and he said, privately, that " he worried until he got rid of it."
While the President's family were at their sum-
mer-house, near Washington, he rode into town
of a morning, or out at night, attended by a
mounted escort; but if he returned to town for a
while after dark, he rode in unguarded, and often
alone, in his open carriage. On more than one
occasion the writer has gone through the streets of
Washington at a late hour of the night with the
President, without escort, or even the company of
a servant, walking all of the way, going and returning.

Considering the many open and secret threats
to take his life, it is not surprising that Mr. Lincoln had many thoughts about his coming to a
sudden and violent end. He once said that he felt
the force of the expression, " To take one's life in
his hand;" but that he would not like to face death
suddenly. He said that he thought himself a great
coward physically, and was sure that he would
make a poor soldier, for, unless there was something
inspiriting in the excitement of a battle, he was
sure that he would drop his gun and run, at the
first symptom of danger. That was said sportively,
and he added, " Moral cowardice is something
which I think I never had."

Colonel Halpine, while serving as a member of General Halleck's staff, had frequently to wait upon the President, both during official hours and at other times. On one of these occasions, Mr. Lincoln concluded some interesting remarks with these words: " It would never do for a President to have guards with drawn sabres at his door, as if he fancied he were, or were trying to be, or were assuming to be, an emperor."

" This expression," writes Colonel Halpine, " called my attention afresh to what I had remarked to myself almost every time I entered the White House, and to which I had very frequently called the attention both of Major Hay and General Halleck — the utterly unprotected condition of the President's person, and the fact that any assassin or maniac, seeking his life, could enter his presence without the interference of a single armed man to hold him back. The entrance-doors, and all doors on the official side of the building, were open at all hours of the day, and very late into the evening ; and I have many times entered the mansion, and walked up to the rooms of the two private secretaries, as late as nine or ten o'clock at night, without seeing or being challenged by a single soul. There were, indeed, two attendants, — one for the outer door, and the other for the door of the official chambers ; but these — thinking, I suppose, that none would call after office hours save persons who were personally acquainted, or had the right of official en-

5

try — were, not unfrequently, somewhat remiss in their duties.

"To this fact I now ventured to call the President's attention, saying that to me — perhaps from my European education — it appeared a deliberate courting of danger, even if the country were in a state of the profoundest peace, for the person at the head of the nation to remain so unprotected.

"'There are two dangers,' I wound up by saying; 'the danger of deliberate political assassination, and the mere brute violence of insanity.'

"Mr. Lincoln heard me through with a smile, his hands locked across his knees, his body rocking back and forth, — the common indication that he was amused.

"'Now, as to political assassination,' he said, 'do you think the Richmond people would like to have Hannibal Hamlin here any better than myself? In that one alternative, I have an insurance on my life worth half the prairie land of Illinois. And beside,' — this more gravely, — 'if there were such a plot, and they wanted to get at me, no vigilance could keep them out. We are so mixed up in our affairs, that — no matter what the system established — a conspiracy to assassinate, if such there were, could easily obtain a pass to see me for any one or more of its instruments.

"'To betray fear of this, by placing guards or so forth, would only be to put the idea into their heads, and perhaps lead to the very result it was

ntended to prevent.   As to the crazy folks, **Major,**
why I must only take my chances, — the worst
crazy people at present, I fear, being some of **my**
own too zealous adherents.   That there may be such
dangers as you and many others have suggested **to**
me, is quite possible ; but I guess it would n't improve things any to publish that we were afraid of
them in advance.'

" Upon another occasion I remember his coming
over one evening after dinner, to General Halleck's
private quarters, to protest — half jocularly, half in
earnest — against a small detachment of cavalry
which had been detailed without his request, and
partly against his will, by the lamented General
Wadsworth, as a guard for his carriage in going to
and returning from the Soldiers' Home.   The burden of his complaint was that he and Mrs. Lincoln
' could n't hear themselves talk,' for the clatter of
their sabres and spurs ; and that, as many of them
appeared new hands and very awkward, he was
more afraid of being shot by the accidental discharge of one of their carbines or revolvers, than
of any attempt upon his life or for his capture **by**
the roving squads of Jeb Stuart's cavalry, then
hovering all round the exterior works of the city."

XXI.

Judge Bates, the Attorney-General, was one **day**
very severe upon the modern deal school of

art, as applied to historic characters and events. He instanced in sculpture, Greenough's "Washington," in the Capitol grounds, which, he said, was a very good illustration of the heathen idea of Jupiter Tonans, but was the farthest possible remove from any American's conception of the Father of his Country. Powell's painting in the Rotunda, "De Soto discovering the Mississippi," and Mills's equestrian statue of Jackson, in front of the President's House, shared in his sarcastic condemnation. He quoted from an old English poet — Creech, I think he said — with much unction : —

> "Whatever contradicts my sense
> 1 hate to see, and can but disbelieve."

"Genius and talent," said he, on another occasion, "are rarely found combined in one individual." I requested his definition of the distinction. "Genius," he replied, "conceives; talent executes."

Referring to Mr. Lincoln's never-failing fund of anecdote, he remarked, "The character of the President's mind is such that his thought habitually takes on this form of illustration, by which the point he wishes to enforce is invariably brought home with a strength and clearness impossible in hours of abstract argument. Mr. Lincoln," he added, "comes very near being a perfect man, according to my ideal of manhood. He lacks but one thing." Looking up from my palette, I asked,

musingly, if this was official dignity as President.
" No," replied Judge Bates, " that is of little consequence. His deficiency is in the element of *will*.
I have sometimes told him, for instance, that he was
unfit to be intrusted with the pardoning power.
Why, if a man comes to him with a touching story,
his judgment is almost certain to be affected by it.
Should the applicant be a *woman*, a wife, a mother,
or a sister, — in nine cases out of ten, her tears, if
nothing else, are sure to prevail."

XXII.

Mr. Seward, whose conversation much of the
time, while sitting, was like that of a man solil-
oquizing aloud, told me on one occasion two or
three good stories. Referring to the numerous
portraits painted of him at different times, he said,
that of all artists whom he had known, Henry Inman was most rapid in execution. For the full-
length portrait, painted while he was Governor,
for the city of New York, Inman required but two
or three sittings of an hour each, with an additional quarter of an hour for the standing figure.
This drew out something from me in relation to
Elliott's whole length of him, painted at the
same period. " My experience with Elliott," he
rejoined, " who was then in the beginning of his
career, was a very different affair. He seemed to
think me like Governor Crittenden's hen." Laugh-

ing at the recollection, he lighted a cigar, and continued: " One day the Governor was engaged with
his Council, when his little boy, of five or six years,
came into the chamber, and said, ' Father, the
black hen is *setting.*' ' Go away, my son,' re
turned the Governor; 'I am very busy.' The child
disappeared, but soon returned, and putting his head
in at the door, repeated the information. ' Well,
well,' replied the Governor, 'you must not bother
me now; let her *set.*' The door was shut,
but soon afterward again cautiously opened, in the
midst of a profound discussion, and the words
rang out, ' But father, she is setting on one
egg!' The Governor turned around, and looking
into the dilated eyes of the excited little fellow, replied dryly, ' Well, my son, I think we will let her
set. Her time is not *very* precious!'"

Another was of General R——, formerly of the
New York State Senate. At the regular session
one day, the General gave notice that the following
day he would introduce a bill providing a thermometer for every institution of learning in the
State. The next morning the clerk was in his
private office at the usual hour, reading the bills
aloud, and placing them on file for the business of
the day. A gentleman who prided himself upon
his classical attainments was present, and, as the
clerk read the notice given by Senator R——, he
was informed that a word borrowed from another
anguage should, according to the rule, always be

given its native pronunciation. The original of thermometer, the gentleman said, was a French term, which should be pronounced accordingly. By a process of reasoning the clerk was convinced; and when the bill was announced, he read it according to instructions. General R—— was observed to look up from writing, and fix his eye upon the clerk. The second reading passed, and he rose to his feet, bending forward upon his desk, listening intently, his eyebrows gradually contracting. " Third reading. Senator R—— gave notice of a bill to provide a *thermomḗtre* for every institution of learning in the State." By this time the attention of the entire house was drawn to the General. " Ther — what ? " he demanded, in a stentorian tone. " *Thermomḗtre*," quietly responded the confident clerk. " Thermometer ! thermometer ! you —— fool ; don't you know what a thermometer is ? " thundered the enraged Senator, amid roars of laughter.

Speaking once of Henry Clay and Daniel Webster, Mr. Seward remarked, that, as statesmen, they could not well be compared ; " they were no more alike than a Grecian temple and a Gothic church."

I was much interested in an opinion he once expressed of equestrian statues. He said a grand character should never be represented in this form. It was ignoring the divine in human nature to thus link man with an animal, and seemed to him a degradation of true art. "Bucephalus," in marble or bronze was well enough by itself. Place "Alexander" upon his back, and though the animal gained a degree of interest, the *man* lost immeasurably.

XXIII.

Soon after the chalk sketch of my conception had been placed upon the canvas, I attended one of the receptions given by the Secretary of the Navy and Mrs. Welles. While standing as I thought unobserved, near a corner of the room, Mr. Seward approached me, and in a manner of more than usual warmth, said, "I told the President the other day that you were painting your picture upon a false presumption." Looking at him in some surprise, I inquired his meaning. "Oh," he rejoined, "you appear to think in common with many other foolish people, that the great business of this Administration is the destruction of slavery. Now allow me to say you are much mistaken. Slavery was killed years ago. Its death knell was tolled when Abraham Lincoln was elected President. The work of this Administration is the suppression of the Rebellion and the preservation of the Union. Abolitionists, like the different religious sects, have been chasing one idea, until they have come to believe that their horizon absolutely bounds the world Slavery has been in fact but an incident in the history of the nation, inevitably bound to perish in the progress of intelligence. Future generations will scarcely credit the record that such an institution ever existed here; or existing, that it ever lived a day under such a government. But suppose, for one moment, the Republic destroyed. With it is bound up not alone the destiny of a race, but the best hopes of all mankind. With its overthrow the sun of liberty, like the Hebrew dial, would be set back indefinitely. The magnitude of such a calamity is beyond our calculation. The salvation of the nation is, then, of vastly more consequence than the destruction of slavery. Had you consulted me for a subject to paint, I should not have given you the Cabinet Council on Emancipation, but the meeting which took place when the news came of the attack upon Sumter, when the first measures were organized for the restoration of the national authority. That was the crisis in the history of this Administration — not the issue of the Emancipation Proclamation. If I am to be remembered by posterity," he concluded, with much excitement of manner, " let it not be as having loved predominantly white men or black men, but as one who loved his country."

Assenting to much that he had said, I replied, that with all deference, I could not accept his conclusions regarding slavery. Although more than a year had passed since the issue of the proclamation, the Confederacy, founded upon it, was yet powerful enough to threaten the destruction of the nation, though, for my own part, I did not question the result of the conflict. . I looked upon the Declaration of Independence as the *assertion* that all men were created free. Mr. Lincoln's Emancipation Proclamation was the *demonstration* of this great truth. Without slavery the Republic would have been in no danger. That was the canker-worm gnawing away the nation's life. Not until the Administration was ready to strike at the root and cause of the Rebellion, was there any reason to hope for the success of the national cause. Without this step, however grand or high the conception in the minds of men of the Republic, in all probability it would have perished. Therefore, in my judgment, no single act of the Administration could for one moment be compared with that of emancipation. Granting the potential view, the proclamation was necessary, as the sign and seal of the consummation.

"Well," replied Mr. Seward, "you think so, and this generation may agree with you; but posterity will hold a different opinion."

Of course this conversation could not but attract the attention of all in the immediate vicinity. A few moments later, Senator Morgan, referring to the Secretary's assertion that slavery was dead when the Rebellion broke out, told me this characteristic incident of the President, showing that he, at least, did not hold that view. Soon after the issue of the proclamation, having official business, as Gov·

ernor of New York, which called him to Washington, Mr. Lincoln remarked to him, speaking of his
action upon this subject, " We are a good deal like
whalers who have been long on a chase. At last
we have got our harpoon fairly into the monster ;
but we must now look how we steer, or with one
flop of his tail, he will yet send us all into
eternity ! "

XXIV.

Mr. George Thompson, the English anti-slavery
orator, delivered an address in the House of Representatives, to a large audience, April 6th, 1864.
Among the distinguished persons present was President Lincoln, who was greatly interested. The
following morning, Mr. Thompson and party, consisting of Rev. John Pierpont, Oliver Johnson,
formerly President of the Anti-Slavery Society of
New York, and the Hon. Lewis Clephane, of Washington, called at the White House. The President
was alone when their names were announced, with
the exception of myself. Dropping all business,
he ordered the party to be immediately admitted.
Greeting them very cordially, the gentlemen took
seats, and Mr. Thompson commenced conversation
by referring to the condition of public sentiment in
England in regard to the great conflict the nation
was passing through. He said the aristocracy and
the " money interest " were desirous of seeing the
Union broken up, but that the great heart of the

masses beat in sympathy with the North. **They** instinctively felt that the cause of liberty was **bound** up with our success in putting down the Rebellion, and the struggle was being watched with the deepest anxiety.

Mr. Lincoln thereupon said: " Mr. Thompson **the** people of Great Britain, and of other foreign governments, were in one great error in reference to this conflict. They seemed to think that, the moment I was President, I had the power to abolish slavery, forgetting that, before I could have any power whatever, I had to take the oath to support the Constitution of the United States, and execute the laws as I found them. When the Rebellion broke out, my duty did not admit of a question. That was, first, by all strictly lawful means to endeavor to maintain the integrity of the government. I did not consider that I had a *right* to touch the ' State ' institution of ' Slavery ' until all other measures for restoring the Union had failed. The paramount idea of the constitution is the preservation of the Union. It may not be specified in so many words, but that this was the idea of its founders is evident ; for, without the Union, the constitution would be worthless. It seems clear, then, that in the last extremity, if any local institution threatened the existence of the Union, the Executive could not hesitate as to his duty. In our case, the moment came when I felt that slavery must die that the nation might live ! I have sometimes used **the**

illustration in this connection of a man with a dis eased limb, and his surgeon. So long as there is a chance of the patient's restoration, the surgeon is solemnly bound to try to save both life *and* limb; but when the crisis comes, and the limb must be sacrificed as the only chance of saving the life, no honest man will hesitate.

"Many of my strongest supporters urged *Emancipation* before I thought it indispensable, and, I may say, before I thought the country ready for it. It is my conviction that, had the proclamation been issued even six months earlier than it was, public sentiment would not have sustained it. Just so, as to the subsequent action in reference to enlisting blacks in the Border States. The step, taken sooner, could not, in my judgment, have been carried out. A man watches his pear-tree day after day, impatient for the ripening of the fruit. Let him attempt to *force* the process, and he may spoil both fruit and tree. But let him patiently *wait*, and the ripe pear at length falls into his lap! We have seen this great revolution in public sentiment slowly but *surely* progressing, so that, when final action came, the opposition was not strong enough to defeat the purpose. I can now solemnly assert," he concluded, "that I have a clear conscience in regard to my action on this momentous question. I have done what no man could have helped doing, standing in my place."

Oliver Johnson, speaking, as he said, for the old

Anti-Slavery party, assured the President that they had fully appreciated the difficulties and embarrassments of his position; but when they realized the importance of the grand issue, and observed the conflicting influences that were surging around him, they were in an agony of anxiety lest he should somehow be led to take a false position. If, in the months preceding the issue of the Emancipation Proclamation, they had seemed impatient and distrustful, it was because their knowledge of his character had not been sufficient to assure them that he would be able to stand up manfully against the opposing current. He thanked God that the result had shown that we had a President who was equal to the emergency; and for *his* part he was willing to sink all minor issues in the grand consummation he believed then in sight!

A characteristic incident occurred toward the close of the interview. When the President ceased speaking, the Rev. Mr. Pierpont, impressed with his earnestness, turned to Mr. Thompson, and repeated a Latin quotation from the classics. Mr. Lincoln, leaning forward in his chair, looked from one to the other inquiringly, and then remarked, with a smile, "*Which*, I suppose you are both aware, *I* do not understand."

As the party rose to take leave, the President remarked, motioning toward me, "We have a young man here who is painting a picture down-stairs, which I should be glad to have you see." The gen-

tlemen expressed their acknowledgments of the
courtesy, and Mr. Lincoln led the way by the
private staircase to the state dining-room.   In
the passage through the hall he jocularly remarked
to Mr. Thompson, " Your folks made rather sad
work of this mansion when they came up the Potomac in 1812.   Nothing was left of it but the
bare walls."   I do not remember the reply to this
sally, save that it was given and received in good
part.   Briefly going over the portraiture and composition of the picture, then in too early a stage for
criticism, Mr. Lincoln presently excused himself,
and returned to his duties.   And thus ended an
interview doubtless indelibly stamped upon the
memory of each individual privileged in sharing it.

Upon referring to the date of the " Hodges " letter, it will be seen that it was written April 4th, only
three days before the visit of Mr. Thompson and
party.   The coincidence of thought and expression
in that statement, and the President's conversation
on this occasion, are noticeable ; and are explained by
the fact, that, with the language of that letter still
fresh in his mind, he very naturally fell into a similar
vein of illustration.

XXV.

Dr. Holland, in his " Life of Abraham Lincoln,"
I regret to observe, has thought it worth while to
notice the reports, which in one way and another
have obtained circulation, that the President habit-

ually indulged, in ordinary conversation, in a class
of objectionable stories.   The biographer, it is true,
attempts to palliate this, on the ground that it was
no innate love of impurity which prompted such
relations, but a keen relish for wit, in any form,
the lack of refining influences in early life, and
his experience as a lawyer, which necessarily induced professional familiarity with the foulest phases
of human nature.   The fault is a common one with
many men of otherwise unblemished reputation, and
cannot be too severely reprehended.   The sooner,
however, such things can be forgotten, of neighbor,
friend, or President, the better.   Weaknesses and
blemishes are inseparable from common humanity
in the present stage of its development; and though,
like the spots on the sun, they may serve to inspire
in us a feeling of kindred, — let the orb once set,
never again to rise on the world, and he who should
remember the trifling defects in the universal loss
would certainly be considered, if not captious, at
least a most inopportune critic.

Mr. Lincoln, I am convinced, has been greatly
wronged in this respect.   Every foul-mouthed man
in the country gave currency to the slime and filth
of his own imagination by attributing it to the
President.   It is but simple justice to his memory
that I should state, that during the entire period of
my stay in Washington, after witnessing his intercourse with nearly all classes of men, embracing
governors, senators, members of Congress, officers

of the army, and intimate friends, I cannot recollect to have heard him relate a circumstance to any
one of them, which would have been out of place
uttered in a ladies' drawing-room. And this testimony is not unsupported by that of others, well
entitled to consideration. Dr. Stone, his family
physician, came in one day to see my studies.
Sitting in front of that of the President, — with
whom he did not sympathize politically, — he remarked, with much feeling, "It is the province of
a physician to probe deeply the interior lives of
men; and I affirm that Mr. Lincoln is the purest
hearted man with whom I ever came in contact."
Secretary Seward, who of the Cabinet officers was
probably most intimate with the President, expressed the same sentiment in still stronger language. He once said to the Rev. Dr. Bellows:
" Mr. Lincoln is the best man I ever knew! "

XXVI.

The 25th of April, Burnside's command marched
through Washington, on the way from Annapolis,
to reinforce the army of the Potomac. The President reviewed the troops from the top of the eastern portico at Willard's Hotel, standing with un-
covered head while the entire thirty thousand men
filed through Fourteenth Street. Of course the
passage of so large a body of troops through the
city — presaging as it did the opening of the cam-
6

paign — drew out a numerous concourse of spec
tators, and the coming movement was everywhere
the absorbing topic of conversation. Early in the
evening, Governor Curtin, of Pennsylvania, with a
friend, came into the President's office. As he sat
down he referred to the fine appearance of Burnside's men; saying, with much emphasis, " Mr.
President, if there is in the world one man more
than another worthy of profound respect, it is the
volunteer citizen soldier."   To this Mr. Lincoln
assented, in a quiet way, — the peculiar dreaminess
of expression so remarkable at times, stealing over
his face as his mind reverted to the thousands whose
lives had been so freely offered upon the altar of
their country, and the myriad homes represented
by the thronging columns of the day's review, in so
many of which there was henceforth to be weary
watching and waiting for footsteps which would
return no more.

I took this opportunity to get at the truth concerning a newspaper story which went the rounds
a year or two previous, purporting to be an account of a meeting of the loyal Governors in
Washington, early in the war. It was stated that
the President laid the condition of the country before such a council, convened at the White House,
and anxiously awaited the result. An oppressive
silence followed. Curtin was represented as having been standing, looking out of one of the windows, drumming unconsciously upon a pane of glass.

Mr. Lincoln, at length addressing him personally, said: "Andy, what is Pennsylvania going to do?" Turning around, Curtin replied: "She is going to send twenty thousand men to start with, and will double it, if necessary!" "This noble response" [quoted from memory] "overwhelmed the President, and lifted the dead weight which seemed to have paralyzed all present."

I repeated this account substantially as here given; but both parties smiled and shook their heads. "It is a pity to spoil so good a story," returned the President, "but, unfortunately, there is not a word of truth in it. I believe the only convocation of Governors that has taken place during the war," he added, looking at Curtin, "was that at Altoona — was it not?"

Subsequently the two gentlemen proposed to visit my room, and Mr. Lincoln accompanied them. Sitting down under the chandelier on the edge of the long table, which ran the whole length of the apartment, swinging back and forth his long legs, passing his hand occasionally over his brow and through his rough hair (his appearance and manner come back to me most vividly, as I write), he listened abstractedly to my brief explanation of the design of the picture. When I ceased, he took up the record in his own way. "You see, Curtin," said he, "I was brought to the conclusion that there was no dodging this negro question any longer. We had reached the point where it

seemed that we must avail ourselves of this element, or in all probability go under." He then
went over the circumstances attending the step, in
much the same language he had used upon the
occasion of my first interview with him. Governor Curtin remarked that the impression pre-
vailed in some quarters that Secretary Seward
opposed the policy. "That is not true," replied
Mr. Lincoln; "he advised postponement, at the
first meeting, which seemed to me sound. It was
Seward's persistence which resulted in the insertion
of the word 'maintain,' which I feared under the
circumstances was promising more than it was quite
probable we could carry out."

The bill empowering the Secretary of the Treasury to sell the surplus gold had recently passed,
and Mr. Chase was then in New York, giving his
attention personally to the experiment. Governor
Curtin referred to this, saying, "I see by the quotations that Chase's movement has already knocked
gold down several per cent." This gave occasion
for the strongest expression I ever heard fall from
the lips of Mr. Lincoln. Knotting his face in the
ntensity of his feeling, he said, "Curtin, what do
you think of those fellows in Wall Street, who are
gambling in gold at such a time as this?" "They
are a set of sharks," returned Curtin. "For my
part," continued the President, bringing his clinched
hand down upon the table, "I wish every one of
them had his *devilish* head shot off!"

XXVII.

There was one marked element of Mr. Lincoln's character admirably expressed by the Hon. Mr. Colfax, in his oration at Chicago upon his death: " When his judgment, which acted slowly, but which was almost as immovable as the eternal hills when settled, was grasping some subject of importance, the arguments against his own desires seemed uppermost in his mind, and, in conversing upon it, he would present those arguments to see if they could be rebutted."

In illustration of this, it is only necessary to recall the fact that the interview between himself and the Chicago delegation of clergymen, appointed to urge upon him the issue of a proclamation of emancipation, took place September 13, 1862, more than a month after he had declared to the Cabinet his established purpose to take this step. He said to this committee: " I do not want to issue a document that the whole world will see must necessarily be inoperative, like the Pope's bull against the comet!" After drawing out their views upon the subject, he concluded the interview with these memorable words: —

" Do not misunderstand me, because I have mentioned these objections. They indicate the difficulties which have thus far prevented my action in some such way as you desire. I have not decided against a proclamation of liberty to the slaves, but hold the matter under advisement. And I can assure you that the subject is on my mind, by day and night, more than any other. Whatever shall appear to be God's will, I will do! I trust that, in the freedom with which I have canvassed your views, I have not in any respect injured your feelings."

In further evidence of this peculiarity of his mind, I will state that notwithstanding his apparent hesitation in the appointment of a successor to Judge Taney, it is well known to his most intimate friends, that "there had never been a time during his Presidency, when, in the event of the death of Judge Taney, he had not fully intended and expected to nominate Salmon P. Chase for Chief Justice." These were his very words uttered in connection with this subject.

XXVIII.

In Barrett's biography of Mr. Lincoln, it is stated that the first draft of the Emancipation Proclamation was written on board of the steamboat returning from his 8th of July visit to the army at Harrison's Landing. This circumstance was not included in the statement given me, and to others in my presence, at different times; but from the known relations of the author with the President, it is undoubtedly true. The original draft was written upon one side of four half sheets of official foolscap. He flung down upon the table one day for me, several sheets of the same, saying, "There, I believe, is some of the very paper which was used; — if not, it was, at any rate, just like it." The original draft is dated September 22d, 1862, and was presented to the Army Relief Bazaar, at Albany, N. Y., in 1864. It is in the proper handwriting of Mr. Lincoln, excepting two interlineations in pencil, by Secretary Seward, and the formal heading and ending, which were written by the chief clerk of the State Department.

The final Proclamation was signed on New-Year's Day, 1863. The President remarked to Mr. Colfax, the same evening, that the signature appeared somewhat tremulous and uneven. "Not," said he, " because of any uncertainty or hesitation on my part; but it was just after the public reception, and three hours' hand-shaking is not calculated to improve a man's chirography." Then changing his tone, he added: " The South had fair warning, that if they did not return to their duty, I should strike at this pillar of their strength. The promise must now be kept, and I shall never recall one word."

I remember to have asked him, on one occasion, if there was not some opposition manifested on the part of several members of the Cabinet to this policy. He replied, " Nothing more than I have stated to you. Mr. Blair thought we should lose

the fall elections, and opposed it on that ground
only." "I have understood," said I, "that Secretary Smith was not in favor of your action. Mr.
Blair told me that, when the meeting closed, he
and the Secretary of the Interior went away together, and that the latter said to him, if the President carried out that policy, he might count on
losing *Indiana,* sure!" "He never said anything
of the kind to me," returned the President. "And
what is Mr. Blair's opinion now?" I asked. "Oh,"
was the prompt reply, "he proved right in regard
to the fall elections, but he is satisfied that we have
since gained more than we lost." "I have been
told," I added, "that Judge Bates doubted the
constitutionality of the proclamation." "He never
expressed such an opinion in my hearing," replied
Mr. Lincoln. "No member of the Cabinet ever
dissented from the policy, in any conversation with
me."

XXIX.

It seems necessary at this point that an expla
nation should be given of a leading article which
appeared in the New York "Independent," upon
the withdrawal of Mr. Chase from the political canvass of 1864, widely copied by the country press,
in which it was stated that the concluding paragraph
of the proclamation was from the pen of Secretary
Chase. One of Mr. Lincoln's intimate friends, who
felt that there was an impropriety in this publication,

at that time, for which Mr. Chase was in some degree responsible, went to see the President about it. "Oh," said Mr. Lincoln, with his characteristic simplicity and freedom from all suspicion, "Mr. Chase had nothing to do with it; I think *I* mentioned the circumstance to Mr. Tilton, myself."

The facts in the case are these: While the measure was pending, Mr. Chase submitted to the President a draft of a proclamation embodying his views upon the subject, which closed with the appropriate and solemn words referred to: "And upon this act, sincerely believed to be an act of justice warranted by the Constitution, I invoke the considerate judgment of mankind and the gracious favor of Almighty God!"

Mr. Lincoln adopted this sentence intact, excepting that he inserted after the word "Constitution" the words "upon military necessity."

XXX.

Mr. Chase told me that at the Cabinet meeting, immediately after the battle of Antietam, and just prior to the issue of the September Proclamation, the President entered upon the business before them, by saying that "the time for the annunciation of the emancipation policy could be no longer delayed. Public sentiment," he thought, "would sustain it — many of his warmest friends and supporters demanded it — *and he had promised his*

God that he would do it ! "   The last part of this
was uttered in a low tone, and appeared to be
heard by no one but Secretary Chase, who was
sitting near him.   He asked the President if he
correctly understood him.   Mr. Lincoln replied :
" *I made a solemn vow before God, that if General
Lee was driven back from Pennsylvania, I would
crown the result by the declaration of freedom to the
slaves.*"

In February 1865, a few days after the passage of
the " Constitutional Amendment," I went to Washington, and was received by Mr. Lincoln with the
kindness and familiarity which had characterized our
previous intercourse.   I said to him at this time
that I was very proud to have been the artist to
have first conceived of the design of painting a
picture commemorative of the Act of Emancipation ; that subsequent occurrences had only confirmed my own first judgment of that act as the
most sublime moral event in our history.   " Yes,"
said he, — and never do I remember to have noticed in him more earnestness of expression or
manner, — " as affairs have turned, *it is the central
act of my administration, and the great event of the
nineteenth century.*"

XXXI.

The day after the review of Burnside's division, some photographers from Brady's Gallery came up to the White House to make some stereoscopic studies for me of the President's office. They requested a dark closet, in which to develop the pictures ; and without a thought that I was infringing upon anybody's rights, I took them to an unoccupied room of which little " Tad " had taken possession a few days before, and with the aid of a couple of the servants, had fitted up as a miniature theatre, with stage, curtains, orchestra, stalls, parquette, and all. Knowing that the use required would interfere with none of his arrangements, I led the way to this apartment.

Everything went on well, and one or two pictures had been taken, when suddenly there was an uproar. The operator came back to the office, and said that " Tad " had taken great offence at the occupation of his room without his consent, and had locked the door, refusing all admission. The chemicals had been taken inside, and there was no way of getting at them, he having carried off the key. In the midst of this conversation, " Tad " burst in, in a fearful passion. He laid all the blame upon me, — said that I had no right to use his room, and that the men should not go in even to get their things. He had locked the door, and they should not go there again — " they had no

business in his room!" Mr. Lincoln had been sitting
for a photograph, and was still in the chair. He
said, very mildly, "Tad, go and unlock the door."
Tad went off muttering into his mother's room,
refusing to obey. I followed him into the passage,
but no coaxing would pacify him. Upon my return
to the President, I found him still sitting patiently
in the chair, from which he had not risen. He
said: "Has not the boy opened that door?" I
replied that we could do nothing with him, — he
had gone off in a great pet. Mr. Lincoln's lips
came together firmly, and then, suddenly rising, he
strode across the passage with the air of one bent
on punishment, and disappeared in the domestic
apartments. Directly he returned with the key to
the theatre, which he unlocked himself. "There,"
said he, "go ahead, it is all right now." He then
went back to his office, followed by myself, and
resumed his seat. "Tad," said he, half apolo-
getically, "is a peculiar child. He was violently excited when I went to him. I said, 'Tad,
do you know you are making your father a great
deal of trouble?' He burst into tears, instantly
giving me up the key."

This brief glimpse of the home life of the President, though trifling in itself, is the gauge of his
entire domestic character. The Hon. W. D. Kelly,
of Philadelphia, in an address delivered in that city
soon after the assasination, said: "His intercourse
with his family was beautiful as that with his fr nds.

I think that father never loved his children more fondly than he. The President never seemed grander in my sight than when, stealing upon him in the evening, I would find him with a book open before him, as he is represented in the popular photograph, with little Tad beside him. There were of course a great many curious books sent to him, and it seemed to be one of the special delights of his life to open those books at such an hour, that his boy could stand beside him, and they could talk as he turned over the pages, the father thus giving to the son a portion of that care and attention of which he was ordinarily deprived by the duties of office pressing upon him."

No matter who was with the President, or how intently he might be absorbed, little Tad was always welcome. At the time of which I write he was eleven years old, and of course rapidly passing from childhood into youth. Suffering much from an infirmity of speech which developed in his infancy, ne seemed on this account especially dear to his father. "One touch of nature makes the whole world kin," and it was an impressive and affecting sight to me to see the burdened President lost for the time being in the affectionate parent, as he would take the little fellow in his arms upon the withdrawal of visitors, and caress him with all the fondness of a mothe: for the babe upon her bosom!

Tad, as he was universally called, almost always accompanied his father upon the various

excursions down the Potomac, which he was in the
habit of making.   Once, on the way to Fortress
Monroe, he became very troublesome.   The President was much engaged in conversation with the
party who accompanied him, and he at length said,
" Tad, if you will be a good boy, and not disturb
me any more till we get to Fortress Monroe, I will
give you a dollar."   The hope of reward was effectual for a while in securing silence, but, boy-like,
Tad soon forgot his promise, and was as noisy as
ever.   Upon reaching their destination, however, he
said very promptly, " Father, I want my dollar."
Mr. Lincoln turned to him with the inquiry: " Tad,
do you think you have earned it? "   " Yes," was
the sturdy reply.   Mr. Lincoln looked at him half
reproachfully for an instant, and then taking from
his pocket-book a dollar note, he said : " Well, my
son, at any rate, I will keep *my* part of the bargain."

While paying a visit to Commodore Porter at
Fortress Monroe, on one occasion, an incident occurred, subsequently related by Lieutenant Braine,
one of the officers on board the flag-ship, to the
Rev. Mr. Ewer, of New York.   Noticing that
the banks of the river were dotted with spring
blossoms, the President said, with the manner of
one asking a special favor: " Commodore, Tad
is very fond of flowers ; — won't you let a couple
of your men take a boat and go with him for an
hour or two along shore, and gather a few? — it
will be a great gratification to him."

There is a lesson in such simple incidents, — abounding as they did in the life of the late President, — which should not be lost upon the young men of this country. The Commander-in-Chief of the Army and Navy of the United States, — with almost unlimited power in his hands, — the meekness and simplicity with which Mr. Lincoln bore the honors of that high position, is a spectacle for all time. How paltry do conceit and vainglory appear in the majesty of such an example.

"Nothing was more marked in Mr. Lincoln's personal demeanor," writes one who knew him well,* "than his utter unconsciousness of his position. It would be difficult, if not impossible, to find another man who would not, upon a sudden transfer from the obscurity of private life in a country town to the dignities and duties of the Presidency, feel it incumbent upon him to assume something of the manner and tone befitting that position. Mr. Lincoln never seemed to be aware that his place or his business were essentially different from those in which he had always been engaged. He brought to every question — the loftiest and most imposing — the same patient inquiry into details, the same eager longing to know and to do exactly what was just and right, and the same working-day, plodding, laborious devotion, which characterized his management of a client's case at his law office in Springfield. He had duties to perform

* Hon. Henry J. Raymond.

in both places — in the one case to his country, as
to his client in the other.   But all duties were alike
to him.   All called equally upon him for the best
service of his mind and heart, and all were alike
performed with a conscientious, single-hearted devotion that knew no distinction, but was absolute
and perfect in every case."

XXXII.

In the Executive Chamber one evening, there
were present a number of gentlemen, among them
Mr. Seward.

A point in the conversation suggesting the
thought, the President said: "Seward, you never
heard, did you, how I earned my first dollar?"
"No," rejoined Mr. Seward.   "Well," continued
Mr. Lincoln, "I was about eighteen years of age.
I belonged, you know, to what they call down
South, the 'scrubs;' people who do not own
slaves are nobody there.   But we had succeeded
in raising, chiefly by my labor, sufficient produce,
as I thought, to justify me in taking it down the
river to sell.

"After much persuasion, I got the consent of
mother to go, and constructed a little flatboat, large
enough to take a barrel or two of things that we
had gathered, with myself and little bundle, down
to New Orleans.   A steamer was coming down
the river.   We have, you know, no wharves on

the Western streams ; and the custom **was, if**
passengers were at any of the landings, for them **to**
go out in a boat, the steamer stopping and **taking**
them on board.

"I was contemplating my new flatboat, and wondering whether I could make it stronger or improve
it in any particular, when two men came down to
the shore in carriages with trunks, and looking **at**
the different boats singled out mine, and asked,
' Who owns this ? ' I answered, somewhat mod-
estly, ' I do.' ' Will you,' said one of them, ' take
us and our trunks out to the steamer ? ' ' Certainly,' said I. I was very glad to have the **chance**
of earning something. I supposed that each **of**
them would give me two or three bits. The **trunks**
were put on my flatboat, the passengers seated
themselves on the trunks, and I sculled them **out to**
the steamboat.

"They got on board, and I lifted up their **heavy**
trunks, and put them on deck. The steamer **was**
about to put on steam again, when I called out **that**
they had forgotten to pay me. Each of them **took**
from his pocket a silver half-dollar, and threw it **on**
the floor of my boat. I could scarcely believe **my**
eyes as I picked up the money. Gentlemen, **you**
may think it was a very little thing, and in these
days it seems to me a trifle ; but it was a most
important incident in my life   I could scarcely
credit that I, a poor boy, had earned a dollar in **less**
than a day, — that by honest work I had **earned a**

7

dollar. The world seemed wider and fairer before me. I was a more hopeful and confident being from that time."

XXXIII.

The Hon. Robert Dale Owen was associated in a very interesting interview with Mr. Lincoln, which took place a few weeks prior to the issue of the President's Message for 1863, to which was appended the Proclamation of Amnesty. It had been understood in certain quarters that such a step was at this period in contemplation by the Executive. Being in Washington, Mr. Owen called upon the President on a Saturday morning, and said that he had a matter upon which he had expended considerable thought, which he wished to lay before him. Knowing nothing of the object, Mr. Lincoln replied: " You see how it is this morning; there are many visitors waiting; can't you come up to-morrow morning ? I shall be alone then ; and, if you have no scruples upon the subject, I can give you as much time as you wish." Mr. Owen assured him of his readiness to come at any hour most convenient, and ten o'clock was named. Punctual to the appointment, the hour found him at the house A repeated summons at the bell brought no response, and he at length pushed open the door and walked leisurely up the stairs to the reception-room Neither servant or secretary was to be seen. Presently Mr. Lincoln passed through the hall to his

office, and all was still again.   Looking vainly for a
servant to announce his name, Mr. Owen finally
went to the office-door, and knocked.

" Really," said he, " Mr. President, I owe you
an apology for coming in upon you in this unceremonious way; but I have for some time been waiting the appearance of a servant."

" Oh," was the good-natured reply, " the boys
are all out this morning.   I have been expecting
you; come in and sit down."

Proceeding directly to the subject he had in
hand, at the same time unfolding a manuscript of
large proportions, Mr. Owen said:

"I have a paper, here, Mr. President, that I
have prepared with some care, which I wish to read
to you."

Mr. Lincoln glanced at the formidable document,
(really much less voluminous than it appeared, being very coarsely written,) and then, half unconsciously relapsing into an attitude and expression
of resignation to what he evidently considered an
infliction which could not well be avoided, signified
his readiness to listen.   The article was a very
carefully prepared digest of historical precedents in
relation to the subject of amnesty, in connection
with treason and rebellion.   It analyzed English
and continental history, and reviewed elaborately
the action of President Washington in reference to
Shay's and the subsequent whiskey rebellion.

" I had read but two or three pages," said Mr.

Owen, in giving me this account, "when **Mr.** Lincoln assumed an erect posture, and, fixing his eyes intently upon me, seemed wholly absorbed in the contents of the manuscript. Frequently he would break in with: 'Was that so?' 'Please read that paragraph again,' etc. When at length I came to Washington's proclamation to those engaged in the whiskey rebellion, he interrupted me with: 'What! did Washington issue a proclamation of amnesty?' 'Here it is, sir,' was the reply. 'Well, I never knew that,' he rejoined; and so on through."

Upon the conclusion of the manuscript, Mr. Lincoln said: "Mr. Owen, is that for me?"

"Certainly, sir," said Mr. O., handing him the roll. "I understood that you were considering this subject, and thought a review of this kind might be interesting to you."

"There is a good deal of hard work in that document," continued Mr. Lincoln; "may I ask how long you were preparing it?"

"About three months; but then I have more leisure for such a work than you, Mr. President."

Mr. Lincoln took the manuscript, and, folding it up carefully, arose, and laid it away in the pigeonhole marked "O," in his desk. Returning to his chair, he said: "Mr. Owen, it is due to you that I should say that you have conferred a very essential service, both upon me and the country, by the preparation of this paper. It contains that which it was exceedingly important that I should know, but which, if left to myself, I never should have known, because I have not the time necessary for such an examination of authorities as a review of this kind involves. And I want to say, secondly, if I had *had* the time, I could not have done the work so well as you have done it."

This frank and generous avowal — so unlike what might be expected, under similar circumstances, from most public men — was exceedingly characteristic of Mr. Lincoln.

XXXIV.

The morning of the last day of April, Mr. Wilkeson, the head of the New York "Tribune" bureau of correspondence in Washington at that period, called upon me with his sister-in-law, Mrs. Elizabeth Cady Stanton, well known for her radical views on political and social questions, who wished an introduction to the President. Later in the day, after the accustomed pressure of visitors had subsided, I knocked at the door of the President's study, and asked if I might bring up two or three New York friends. Mr. Lincoln fortunately was alone, and at once accorded the desired permission. Laying aside his papers, as we entered, he turned around in his chair for a leisurely conversation. One of the party took occasion shortly to endorse very decidedly the Amnesty Proclamation, which had been severely censured by many friends of the Administration. This approval appeared to touch Mr. Lincoln deeply. He said, with a great deal of emphasis, and with an expression of countenance I shall never forget, " When a man is sincerely *penitent* for his misdeeds, and gives satisfactory evidence of the same, he can safely be pardoned, and there is no exception to the rule."

Soon afterward he mentioned having received a visit the night before from Colonel Moody, " the fighting Methodist parson," as he was called in Tennessee, who had come on to attend the Philadelphia Conference. " He told me," said he, " this story of Andy Johnson and General Buel, which interested me intensely. The Colonel happened to be in Nashville the day it was reported that Buel had decided to evacuate the city. The Rebels, strongly reënforced, were said to be within two days' march of the capital. Of course, the city was greatly excited. Moody said he went in search of Johnson, at the edge of the evening, and found him at his office, closeted with two gentlemen, who were walking the floor with him, one on each side. As he entered, they retired, leaving him alone with Johnson, who came up to him, manifesting intense feeling, and said, ' Moody, we are sold out! Buel is a traitor! He is going to evacuate the city, and in forty-eight hours we shall all be in the hands of the Rebels!' Then he commenced pacing the floor again, twisting his hands,

and chafing like a caged tiger, utterly insensible to
his friend's entreaties to become calm. Suddenly
he turned and said, 'Moody, can you pray?'
'That is my business, sir, as a minister of the Gospel,' returned the Colonel. 'Well, Moody, I
wish you would pray,' said Johnson; and instantly
both went down upon their knees, at opposite sides
of the room. As the prayer waxed fervent, Johnson began to respond in true Methodist style.
Presently he crawled over on his hands and knees
to Moody's side, and put his arm over him, manifesting the deepest emotion. Closing the prayer
with a hearty 'Amen' from each, they arose.
Johnson took a long breath, and said, with emphasis, 'Moody, I feel better!' Shortly afterwards he asked, 'Will you stand by me?' 'Certainly I will,' was the answer. 'Well, Moody, I
can depend upon you; you are one in a hundred
thousand!' He then commenced pacing the floor
again. Suddenly he wheeled, the current of his
thought having changed, and said, 'Oh! Moody,
I don't want you to think I have become a religious
man because I asked you to pray. I am sorry to
say it, but I am not, and have never pretended to
be, religious. No one knows this better than you;
but, Moody, there is one thing about it — I DO believe in ALMIGHTY GOD! And I believe also in
the BIBLE, and I say "d——n" me, if Nashville
shall be surrendered!'"

And Nashville was not surrendered.

XXXV.

I have elsewhere intimated that Mr. Lincoln was capable of much dramatic power. It is true this was never exhibited in his public life, or addresses, but it was shown in his keen appreciation of Shakspeare, and unrivalled faculty of story-telling. The incident just related, for example, was given with a thrilling effect which mentally placed Johnson, for the time being, alongside of Luther and Cromwell. Profanity or irreverence was lost sight of in the fervid utterance of a highly wrought and great-souled determination, united with a rare exhibition of pathos and self-abnegation.

A narrative of quite a different character followed closely upon this, suggested by a remark made by myself. It was an account of how the President and Secretary of War received the news of the capture of Norfolk, early in the war. "Chase and Stanton," said Mr. Lincoln, "had accompanied me to Fortress Monroe. While we were there, an expedition was fitted out for an attack on Norfolk. Chase and General Wool disappeared about the time we began to look for tidings of the result, and after vainly waiting their return till late in the evening, Stanton and I concluded to retire. My room was on the second floor of the Commandant's house, and Stanton's was below. The night was very warm, — the moon shining brightly, — and, 'oo restless to sleep, I threw off my clothes and sat for some time by the table, reading. Suddenly hearing footsteps, I looked out of the window, and saw two persons approaching, whom I knew by their relative size to be the missing men. They came into the passage and I heard them rap at Stanton's door and tell him to get up, and come up-stairs. A moment afterward they entered my room. 'No time for ceremony, Mr. President,' said General Wool; 'Norfolk is ours!' Stanton here burst in, just out of bed, clad in a long night-gown, which nearly swept the floor, his ear catching, as he crossed the threshold, Wool's last words. Perfectly overjoyed, he rushed at the General, whom he hugged most affectionately, fairly lifting him from the floor in his delight. The scene altogether must have been a comical one, though at the time we were all too greatly excited to take much note of mere appearances."

XXXVI.

A great deal has been said of the uniform meekness and kindness of heart of Mr. Lincoln, but there would sometimes be afforded evidence that one grain of sand too much would break even *this* camel's back. Among the callers at the White House one day, was an officer who had been cashiered from the service. He had prepared an elaborate defence of himself, which he consumed much time in reading to the President. When he had finished, Mr. Lincoln replied, that even upon his own statement of the case, the facts would not warrant executive interference. Disappointed, and considerably crestfallen, the man withdrew. A few days afterward he made a second attempt to alter the President's convictions, going over substantially the same ground, and occupying about the same space of time, but without accomplishing his end. The *third* time he succeeded in forcing himself into Mr. Lincoln's presence, who with great forbearance listened to another repetition of the case to its conclusion, but made no reply. Waiting for a moment, the man gathered from the expression of his countenance that his mind was unconvinced. Turning very abruptly, he said: "Well, Mr. President, I see you are fully determined not to do me justice!" This was too aggravating, even for Mr. Lincoln. Manifesting, however, no more feeling than that indicated by a slight compression of the lips, he very quietly arose, laid down a package of papers he held in his hand, and then suddenly seizing the defunct officer by the coat-collar, he marched him forcibly to the door, saying, as he ejected him into the passage: "Sir, I give you fair warning never to show yourself in this room again. I can bear censure, but not insult!" In a whining tone the man begged for his papers, which he had dropped. "Begone, sir," said the President, "your papers will be sent to you. I never wish to see your face again!"

Upon another occasion, as I was going through the passage, the door of the President's office suddenly opened, and two ladies, one of whom seemed in a towering passion, were unceremoniously ushered out by one of the attendants. As they passed me on their way down the stairs, I overheard the elder remonstrating with her companion upon the violence of her expressions. I afterward asked old Daniel what had happened? "Oh," he replied, "the younger woman was very saucy to the President. She went one step too far; and he told me to show them out of the house?"

Of a similar character is an incident given by "N. C. J.," in a letter to the New York "Times": —

"Among the various applicants, a well-dressed lady came forward, without apparent embarrassment in her air or manner, and addressed the President. Giving her a very close and scrutinizing look, he said, 'Well, madam, what can I do for you?' She proceeded to tell him that she lived in Alexandria; that the church where she worshipped had been taken for a hospital. 'What church, madam?' Mr. Lincoln asked, in a quick, nervous manner. 'The —— church,' she replied; 'and as there are only two or three wounded soldiers in it, I came to see if you would not let us have it, as we want it very much to worship God in.' 'Madam, have you been to see the Post Surgeon at Alexandria about this matter?' 'Yes, sir; but we could do nothing with him.' 'Well, we put him there to attend to just such business, and it is reasonable to suppose that he knows better what should be done under the circumstances than I do. See here: you say you live in Alexandria; probably you own property there. How much will you give to assist in building a hospital?'

" 'You know, Mr. Lincoln, our property is very much embarrassed by the war; — so, really, I could hardly afford to give much for such a purpose.'

" 'Well, madam, I expect we shall have another fight soon; and my candid opinion is, God wants that church for poor wounded Union soldiers, as much as he does for secesh people to worship in.' Turning to his table, he said, quite abruptly, 'You will excuse me; I can do nothing for you. Good day, madam.'

" I had noticed two other women who stood just back of me. I was fully convinced that I had rightly guessed their errand from their appearance; for one of them, whose wicked eyes shot fire, said to her companion in a spiteful under-tone, 'Oh! the old brute, — there is no use asking for our passes; come, let's go.' And they did go, in evident wrath; leaving the President to perform more pleasant duties."

The same correspondent witnessed also the following scene —

" A couple of aged, plain country people, poorly clad, but with frank open countenances, now came

forward. 'Now is your time, dear,' said the husband, as the President dismissed the one preceding
them. The lady stepped forward, made a low
courtesy, and said, 'Mr. President.'

"Mr. Lincoln, looking over his spectacles, fixed
those gray, piercing, yet mild eyes upon her, then
lifting his head and extending his hand, he said, in
the kindest tones: 'Well, good lady, what can I
do for you?'

"'Mr. President,' she resumed, 'I feel so embarrassed I can hardly speak. I never spoke to a
President before; but I am a good Union woman
down in Maryland, and my son is wounded badly,
and in the hospital, and I have been trying to get
him out, but somehow could n't, and they said I had
better come right to you. When the war first
broke out I gave my son first to God, and then told
him he might go fight the Rebels; and now if you
will let me take him home I will nurse him up,
and just as soon as he gets well enough he shall go
right back and help put down the rebellion. He is
a good boy, and don't want to shirk the service.'

"I was looking full in Mr. Lincoln's face. I saw
the tears gathering in his eyes, and his lips quiv-
ered as he replied:

"'Yes, yes, God bless you! you shall have your
son. What hospital did you say?' It seemed a
relief to him to turn aside and write a few words,
which he handed to the woman, saying: 'There,
give that to —— ; and you will get your son, if he
is able to go home with you.'

"'God bless you, Mr. President!' said the
father, the only words he had uttered; and the
mother, making a low courtesy, fairly sobbed:
'O sir, we are so much obliged to you.' 'Yes,
yes; all right; and you will find that *that* will
bring him,' was spoken in tones so kindly and
tender, that they have often since thrilled my
memory."

XXXVII.

In the year 1855 or '56, George B. Lincoln,
Esq., of Brooklyn, was travelling through the West
in connection with a large New York dry-goods
establishment. He found himself one night in an
insignificant town on the Illinois River, by the name
of Naples. The only tavern of the place had evidently been constructed with reference to business
on the smallest possible scale. Poor as the prospect
seemed, Mr. Lincoln had no alternative but to
put up at the place. The supper-room was also
used as a lodging-room. After a tolerable supper
and a comfortable hour before the fire, Mr. L.
told his host that he thought he would "go to
bed." "Bed!" echoed the landlord; "there is
no bed for you in this house, unless you sleep with
that man yonder. He has the only one we have
to spare." "Well," returned Mr. Lincoln, "the
gentleman has possession, and perhaps would not
ike a bedfellow." Upon this, a grizzly head ap-

peared out of the pillows, and said, " What is your name?" " They call me Lincoln at home," was the reply. " Lincoln!" repeated the stranger; "any connection of our Illinois Abraham?" "No," replied Mr. L., "I fear not." " Well," said the old man, "I will let any man by the name of 'Lincoln' sleep with me, just for the sake of the name. You have heard of Abe?" he inquired. " Oh yes, very often," replied Mr. Lincoln. " No man could travel far in this State without hearing of *him*, and I would be very glad to claim connection, if I could do so honestly." " Well," said the old gentleman, " my name is Simmons. 'Abe' and I used to live and work together when we were young men. Many a job of wood-cutting and rail-splitting have I done up with him. Abe Lincoln," said he with emphasis, " was the *likeliest* boy in God's world. He would work all day as hard as any of us — and study by firelight in the log-house half the night; and in this way he made himself a thorough practical surveyor. Once, during those days, I was in the upper part of the State, and I met General Ewing, whom President Jackson had sent to the Northwest to make surveys. I told him about Abe Lincoln, what a student he was, and that I wanted he should give him a job. He looked over his memoranda, and, pulling out a paper, said: 'There is —— county must be surveyed; if your friend can do the work properly, I shall be glad to have him undertake it — the com·

pensation will be six hundred dollars!' Pleased
as I could be, I hastened to Abe, after I got
home, with an account of what I had secured for
him. He was sitting before the fire in the log-
cabin when I told him ; and what do you think was
his answer? When I finished, he looked up very
quietly, and said, ' Mr. Simmons, I thank you very
sincerely for your kindness, but I don't think I will
undertake the job.' ' In the name of wonder,' said
I, ' why? Six hundred dollars does not grow upon
every bush out here in Illinois.' ' I know that,'
said Abe, ' and I need the money bad enough,
Simmons, as you know ; but I never have been
under obligation to a Democratic administration,
and I never intend to be so long as I can get my
living another way. General Ewing must find
another man to do his work.' "

I related this story to the President one day, and
asked him if it was true. " Pollard Simmons !"
said he : " well do I remember him. It is correct
about our working together ; but the old man must
have stretched the facts somewhat about the survey
of the county. I think I should have been very
glad of the job at that time, no matter what administration was in power." Notwithstanding this, however, I am inclined to believe Mr. Simmons
was not far out of the way. His statement seems
very characteristic of what Abraham Lincoln may
be supposed to have been at twenty-three or
twenty-five years of age.

Mr. G. B. Lincoln also told me of an amusing circumstance which took place at Springfield soon after Mr. Lincoln's nomination in 1860. A hatter in Brooklyn secretly obtained the size of the future President's head, and made for him a very elegant hat, which he sent by his townsman, Lincoln, to Springfield. About the time it was presented, various other testimonials of a similar character had come in from different sections. Mr. Lincoln took the hat, and after admiring its texture and workmanship, put it on his head and walked up to a looking-glass. Glancing from the reflection to Mrs. Lincoln, he said, with his peculiar twinkle of the eye, "Well, wife, there is one thing likely to come out of this scrape, any how. We are going to have some *new clothes!*"

One afternoon during the summer of 1862, the President accompanied several gentlemen to the Washington Navy-yard, to witness some experiments with a newly-invented gun. Subsequently the party went aboard of one of the steamers lying at the wharf. A discussion was going on as to the merits of the invention, in the midst of which Mr. Lincoln caught sight of some *axes* hanging up outside of the cabin. Leaving the group, he quietly went forward, and taking one down, returned with it, and said: "Gentlemen, you may talk about your 'Raphael repeaters' and 'eleven-inch Dahlgrens;' but *here* is an institution which I guess I understand better than either of you." With that

8

he held the axe out at arm's length by the end of
the handle, or "helve," as the wood-cutters cal.
it — a feat not another person of the party could
perform, though all made the attempt.   In such
acts as this, showing that he neither forgot nor was
ashamed of his humble origin, the late President
exhibited his true nobility of character.   He was a
perfect illustration of his favorite poet's words : —

> " The rank is but the guinea's stamp,
> The man's the gold, for a' that ! "

XXXVIII.

In March, 1864, Edwin Forrest came to Washington to fulfil an engagement at Ford's Theatre.
It was announced one day that he was to appear
that evening in "Richelieu."   I was with the
President, when Senator Harris of New York came
in.   After he had finished his business, which was
to secure the remittance of the sentence of one of
his constituents, who had been imprisoned on what
seemed insufficient grounds, I told the President
that Forrest was to play *Richelieu* that evening,
and, knowing his tastes, I said it was a play
which I thought he would enjoy, for Forrest's representation of it was the most life-like of anything
I had ever seen upon the stage.   "Who wrote the
play?" said he.   "Bulwer," I replied.   "Ah!"
he rejoined; "well, I knew Bulwer wrote novels,
but I did not know he was a play-writer also.   It

may seem somewhat strange to say," he continued, "but I never read an entire novel in my life!" Said Judge Harris, "Is it possible?" "Yes," returned the President, "it is a fact. I once commenced 'Ivanhoe,' but never finished it." This statement, in this age, of the world, seems almost incredible — but I give the circumstance as it occurred.

However it may have been with regard to novels, it is very certain — as I have already illustrated — that he found time to read Shakspeare; and that he was also fond of certain kinds of poetry. N. P. Willis once told me, that he was taken quite by surprise, on a certain occasion when he was riding with the President and Mrs. Lincoln, by Mr. Lincoln, of his own accord, referring to, and quoting several lines from his poem entitled "Parrhasius."

In the spring of 1862, the President spent several days at Fortress Monroe, awaiting military operations upon the Peninsula. As a portion of the Cabinet were with him, that was temporarily the seat of government, and he bore with him constantly the burden of public affairs. His favorite diversion was reading Shakspeare. One day (it chanced to be the day before the capture of Norfolk) as he sat reading alone, he called to his aide * in the adjoining room, — "You have been writing long enough, Colonel; come in here; I

* Colonel Le Grand B. Cannon, of General Wool's staff.

want to read you a passage in ' Hamlet.' " He read
the discussion on ambition between Hamlet and his
courtiers, and the soliloquy, in which conscience
debates of a future state.   This was followed by
passages from " Macbeth."   Then opening to " King
John," he read from the third act the passage in
which Constance bewails her imprisoned, lost boy.

Closing the book, and recalling the words, —

> " And, father cardinal, I have heard you say
>   That we shall see and know our friends in heaven:
>   If that be true, I shall see my boy again," —

Mr. Lincoln said : " Colonel, did you ever dream
of a lost friend, and feel that you were holding
sweet communion with that friend, and yet have a
sad consciousness that it was not a reality ? — just
so I dream of my boy Willie."   Overcome with
emotion, he dropped his head on the table, and
sobbed aloud.

XXXIX.

William Wallace Lincoln, I never knew.   He
died Thursday, February 20th, 1862, nearly two
years before my intercourse with the President
commenced.   He had just entered upon his twelfth
year, and has been described to me as of an unusually serious and thoughtful disposition.   His
death was the most crushing affliction Mr. Lincoln
had ever been called upon to pass through.

After the funeral, the President resumed his

official duties, but mechanically, and with a terrible weight at his heart. The following Thursday he gave way to his feelings, and shut himself from all society. The second Thursday it was the same; he would see no one, and seemed a prey to the deepest melancholy. About this time the Rev. Francis Vinton, of Trinity Church, New York, had occasion to spend a few days in Washington. An acquaintance of Mrs. Lincoln and of her sister, Mrs. Edwards, of Springfield, he was requested by them to come up and see the President. The setting apart of Thursday for the indulgence of his grief had gone on for several weeks, and Mrs. Lincoln began to be seriously alarmed for the health of her husband, of which fact Dr. Vinton was apprised. Mr. Lincoln received him in the parlor, and an opportunity was soon embraced by the clergyman to chide him for showing so rebellious a disposition to the decrees of Providence. He told him plainly that the indulgence of such feelings, though natural, was sinful. It was unworthy one who believed in the Christian religion. He had duties to the living, greater than those of any other man, as the chosen father, and leader of the people, and he was unfitting himself for his responsibilities by thus giving way to his grief. To mourn the departed as *lost* belonged to heathenism — not to Christianity. "Your son," said Dr. Vinton, "is *alive*, in Paradise. Do you remember that passage in the Gospels: 'God is not the God of the *dead*

but of the living, for *all* live unto him'?" The
President had listened as one in a stupor, until his
ear caught the words, "Your son is alive." Starting from the sofa, he exclaimed, "Alive! *alive!*
Surely you mock me." "No, sir, believe me," replied Dr. Vinton; "it is a most comforting doctrine
of the church, founded upon the words of Christ
himself." Mr. Lincoln looked at him a moment,
and then, stepping forward, he threw his arm
around the clergyman's neck, and, laying his head
upon his breast, sobbed aloud. "*Alive? alive?*"
he repeated. "My dear sir," said Dr. Vinton,
greatly moved, as he twined his own arm around
the weeping father, "believe this, for it is God's
most precious truth. Seek not your son among the
dead; he is not there; he lives to-day in Paradise!
Think of the full import of the words I have
quoted. The Sadducees, when they questioned
Jesus, had no other conception than that Abraham, Isaac, and Jacob were dead and buried.
Mark the reply: 'Now that the dead *are* raised,
even Moses showed at the bush when he called the
Lord the God of Abraham, the God of Isaac, and
the God of Jacob. For he is not the God of the
dead, but of the living, *for all live unto him!*' Did
not the aged patriarch mourn his sons as dead? —
'Joseph is not, and Simeon is not, and ye will take
Benjamin also.' But Joseph and Simeon were
both living, though he believed it not. Indeed,
Joseph being taken from him, was the eventual

means of the preservation of the whole family. And so God has called your son into his upper kingdom — a kingdom and an existence as real, more real, than your own.   It may be that he too, like Joseph, has gone, in God's good providence, to be the salvation of *his* father's household.   It is a part of the Lord's plan for the ultimate happiness of you and yours.   Doubt it not.   I have a sermon," continued Dr. Vinton, " upon this subject, which I think might interest you."   Mr. Lincoln begged him to send it at an early day — thanking him repeatedly for his cheering and hopeful words. The sermon was sent, and read over and over by the President, who caused a copy to be made for his own private use before it was returned. Through a member of the family, I have been informed that Mr. Lincoln's views in relation to spiritual things seemed changed from that hour.   Certain it is, that thenceforth he ceased the observance of the day of the week upon which his son died, and gradually resumed his accustomed cheerfulness

XL.

Among my visitors in the early part of May was the Hon. Mr. Alley, of Massachusetts, who gave me a deeply interesting inside glimpse of the Chicago Republican Convention in 1860.   The popular current had, at first, set very strongly in favor of Mr. Seward, who, many supposed, would be

nominated almost by acclamation.   The evening
before the balloting the excitement was at the
highest pitch.   Mr. Lincoln was telegraphed at
Springfield, that his chances with the Convention
depended upon obtaining the votes of two delegations which were named in the despatch; and that,
to secure this support, he must pledge himself, if
elected, to give places in his Cabinet to the respective heads of those delegations.   A reply was immediately returned over the wires, characteristic of
the man.   It was to this effect: —

" *I authorize no bargains, and will be bound by*
none.   A. LINCOLN."

It is unqestionable that the country was not prepared for the final action of this Convention.   In
various sections of the Eastern and Middle States,
the antecedents and even the name of Mr. Lincoln
were entirely unknown.   The newspapers announced
the nominee as the " Illinois Rail-splitter ; " and
however popular this title may have been with the
masses, it is not to be denied that it seemed to
many people a very extraordinary qualification for
the Presidency.   An acquaintance of mine, who
happened to be in Boston on the evening of the
day the Convention adjourned, formed one of a
large group at his hotel, eagerly discussing the
result.   Only one or two of the party knew anything whatever of the first name on the " ticket,"
and what they knew was soon told.   Considerable

disappointment could be seen in the faces of those composing the circle. One rough-looking sovereign, from Cape Cod, or Nantucket, had listened attentively, but taken no part in the conversation. Turning away at length, with an expression of deep disgust, he muttered: " A set of consummate fools! Nominate a man for the Presidency who has never smelt salt water!"

Some of Mr. Lincoln's immediate neighbors were taken as completely by surprise as those in distant States. An old resident of Springfield told me that there lived within a block or two of his house, in that city, an Englishman, who of course still cherished to some extent the ideas and prejudices of his native land. Upon hearing of the choice at Chicago he could not contain his astonishment.

" What!" said he, " *Abe Lincoln* nominated for President of the United States? Can it be possible! A man that buys a ten-cent beefsteak for his breakfast, and carries it home himself. "

A correspondent of the " Portland Press " has given to the public the following account of Mr. Lincoln's reception of the nomination : —

" In June, 1860, a Massachusetts gentleman was induced to take the opportunity, in company with several delegates and others interested in the objects of the Convention, to go to Chicago and spend a few days in visiting that section of our country. In a very few minutes after the final balloting, when Mr. Lincoln was nominated, it happened that a train of cars started upon the Central Railroad, passing through Springfield, and Mr. R. took passage in the same. Arriving at Springfield, he put up at a public house, and, loitering upon the front door-steps, had the curiosity to inquire of the landlord where Mr. Lincoln lived. While giving the necessary directions, the landlord suddenly remarked, ' There is Mr. Lincoln now, coming down the sidewalk; that tall, crooked man, loosely walking this way. If you wish to see him, you will have an opportunity by putting yourself in his track.'

" In a few moments the object of his curiosity reached the point the gentleman occupied, who, advancing, ventured to accost him thus : ' Is this Mr. Lincoln ? ' ' That, sir, is my name,' was the courteous reply. ' My name is R., from Plymouth County, Massachusetts,' returned the gentleman, and learning that you have to lay been made the public property of the United States, I have ventured to introduce myself, with a view to a brief acquaintance, hoping you will pardon such a patriotic curiosity in a stranger.' Mr. Lincoln received his salutations with cordiality, told him no apology was necessary for his introduction, and asked him to accompany him to his residence. He had just come from the telegraph office, where he had learned the fact of his nomination ; and was on his return home, when Mr. R. met and accompanied him thither.

" Arriving at Mr. Lincoln's residence, he was

introduced to Mrs. Lincoln and the two boys, and entered into conversation in relation to the Lincoln family of the Old Colony, — the Hingham General Lincoln of the Revolutionary army, and the two Worcester Lincolns, brothers, who were governors of Massachusetts and Maine at one and the same time.   In reply to Mr. R.'s inquiry, whether he could trace his ancestry to either of those early families of his own name, Mr. Lincoln, with characteristic facetiousness, replied that he could not say that he ever had an ancestor older than his father; and therefore had it not in his power to trace his genealogy to so patriotic a source as old General Lincoln of the Revolution; though he wished he could.   After some further pleasant conversation, chiefly relating to the early history of the Pilgrim Fathers, with which he seemed familiar, Mr. R. desired the privilege of writing a letter to be despatched by the next mail.   He was very promptly and kindly provided with the necessary means.   As he began to write, Mr. Lincoln approached, and tapping him on the shoulder, expressed the hope that he was not a spy who had come thus early to report his faults to the public.   'By no means, sir,' protested Mr. R.; 'I am writing home to my wife, who, I dare say, will hardly credit the fact that I am writing in your house.'   'O, sir,' rejoined Mr. Lincoln, 'if your wife doubts your word, I will cheerfully indorse it, if you will give me permission;' and taking the pen from Mr. R., he wrote the following words in a clear hand upon the blank page of the letter: —

" ' I am happy to say that your husband is at the present time a guest in my house, and in due time I trust you will greet his safe return to the bosom of his family.   A. LINCOLN.'

" This gave Mr. R. an excellent autograph of Mr. Lincoln, besides bearing witness to his hospitable and cheerful spirit.

" Whilst thus engaged in pleasant conversation, the cars arrived that brought from Chicago the committee of the Convention appointed to notify Mr. Lincoln of his nomination. He received them at the door, and conducted them to seats in his parlor. On the reception of this committee, Mr. Lincoln appeared somewhat embarrassed, but soon resumed his wonted tranquillity and cheerfulness. At the proper time, Governor Morgan, of New York, chairman of the committee, arose, and, with becoming dignity, informed Mr. Lincoln that he and his fellows appeared in behalf of the Convention in session at Chicago, to inform him that he had that day been unanimously nominated to the office of President of the United States ; and asked his permission to report to that body his acceptance of the nomination. Mr. Lincoln, with becoming modesty, but very handsomely, replied that he felt his insufficiency for the vast responsibilities which must devolve upon that office under the impending circum stances of the times ; but if God and his country called for his services in that direction, he should shrink from no duty that might be imposed upon him, and therefore he should not decline the nomination.

" After this ceremony had passed, Mr. Lincoln remarked to the company, that as an appropriate conclusion to an interview so important and interesting as that which had just transpired, he supposed good manners would require that he should treat the committee with something to drink ; and opening a door that led into a room in the rear, he called out ' Mary! Mary!' A girl responded to the call, to whom Mr. Lincoln spoke a few words in an under-tone, and, closing the door, returned again to converse with his guests. In a few minutes the maiden entered, bearing a large waiter, containing several glass tumblers, and a large pitcher in the midst, and placed it upon the centre-table. Mr. Lincoln arose, and gravely addressing the company, said: ' Gentlemen, we must pledge our mutual healths in the most healthy beverage which God has given to man — it is the only beverage I have ever used or allowed in my family, and I cannot conscientiously depart from it on the present occasion — it is pure Adam's ale from the spring;' and, taking a tumbler, he touched it to his lips, and pledged them his highest respects in a cup of cold water. Of course, all his guests were constrained o admire his consistency, and to join in his ex ample.

" Mr. R., when he went to Chicago, had **but** little political sympathy with the Republican **Convention** which nominated Mr. Lincoln; but when he saw, as he did see for himself, his sturdy adherence to a high moral principle, he returned an admirer of the man, and a zealous advocate of his election."

XLI.

In the July following Mr. Lincoln's inauguration, an extra session of Congress was called. In the message then sent in, speaking of secession, and the measures taken by the Southern leaders to bring it about, there occurs the following sentence: " With rebellion thus *sugar-coated*, they have been drugging the public mind of their section for more than thirty years; until, at length, they have brought many good men to a willingness to take up arms against the government," etc. Mr. Defrees, the government printer, told me that, when the message was being printed, he was a good deal disturbed by the use of the term " sugar-coated," **and** finally went to the President about it. Their **relations** to each other being of the most intimate **character**, he told Mr. Lincoln frankly, that he **ought** to remember that a message to Congress **was** a different affair from a speech at a mass-neeting in Illinois; that the messages became **a** part of history, and should be written accordingly.

" What is the matter now? " inquired the Presi-dent.

" Why," said Mr. Defrees, " you have used an undignified expression in the message ; " and then, reading the paragraph aloud, he added, " I would alter the structure of that, if I were you."

" Defrees," replied Mr. Lincoln, " that word expresses precisely my idea, and I am not going to change it. The time will never come in this coun- try when the people won't know exactly what *su- gar-coated* means ! "

On a subsequent occasion, Mr. Defrees told me, a certain sentence of another message was very awkwardly constructed. Calling the President's attention to it in the proof-copy, the latter acknowl- edged the force of the objection raised, and said, " Go home, Defrees, and see if you can better it." The next day Mr. Defrees took in to him his amendment. Mr. Lincoln met him by saying: " Seward found the same fault that you did, and he has been rewriting the paragraph also." Then, reading Mr. Defrees's version, he said, " I believe you have beaten Seward ; but, ' I jings,' I think I can beat you both." Then, taking up his pen, he wrote the sentence as it was finally printed."

Mr. George E. Baker, Mr. Seward's private secretary, informed me that he was much amused and interested in a phase of Mr. Lincoln's char- acter which came under his own observation. It was Mr. Baker's province to take to the Presi- dent all public documents from the State Depart- ment requiring his signature. During the first few

months, Mr. Lincoln would read each paper care
fully through, always remarking, " I never sign a
document I have not first read." As his cares
increased, he at length departed from his habit so
far as to say to the messenger, " Won't you read
these papers to me ? " This went on for a few
months, and he then modified this practice by re-
questing " a synopsis of the contents." His time
became more and more curtailed, and for the last
year his only expression was, " Show me where
you want my name ? "

It is not generally known that the speech always
made by the President, upon the presentation of a
foreign minister, is carefully written for him by the
Secretary of State. A clerk in the department,
ignorant of this custom, was one day sent to the
White House by Mr. Seward, with the speech to
be delivered upon such an occasion. Mr. Lincoln
was writing at his desk, as the clerk entered — a
half-dozen senators and representatives occupying
the sofa and chairs. Unable to disguise a feeling
of delicacy, in the discharge of such an errand, the
young man approached, and in a low voice said to
the President : " The Secretary has sent the speech
you are to make to-day to the Swiss minister."
Mr. Lincoln laid down his pen, and, taking the
manuscript, said in a loud tone : " Oh, this is a
speech Mr. Seward has written for me, is it ? I
guess I will try it before these gentlemen, and see
how it goes." Thereupon he proceeded to read it,

in a waggish manner, remarking, as he concluded,
with sly humor : " There, I like that. It has the
merit of *originality*."

" Within a month after Mr. Lincoln's first accession to office," says the Hon. Mr. Raymond, " when
the South was threatening civil war, and armies
of office-seekers were besieging him in the Executive Mansion, he said to a friend that he wished
he could get time to attend to the Southern question ; he thought he knew what was wanted, and
believed he could do something towards quieting
the rising discontent; but the office - seekers demanded all his time. ' I am,' said he, ' like a
man so busy in letting rooms in one end of his
house, that he can't stop to put out the fire that is
burning the other.' Two or three years later,
when the people had made him a candidate for
reëlection, the same friend spoke to him of a member of his Cabinet who was a candidate also. Mr.
Lincoln said he did not concern himself much
about that. It was important to the country that
the department over which his rival presided should
be administered with vigor and energy, and whatever would stimulate the Secretary to such action
would do good. ' R——,' said he, ' you were
brought up on a farm, were you not ? Then you
know what a *chin fly* is. My brother and I,' he
added, ' were once ploughing corn on a Kentucky
farm, I driving the horse, and he holding the
plough. The horse was lazy ; but on one occasion

9

rushed across the field so that I, with my long legs, could scarcely keep pace with him. On reaching the end of the furrow, I found an enormous *chin fly* fastened upon him, and knocked him off. My brother asked me what I did that for. I told him I didn't want the old horse bitten in that way "Why," said my brother, "*that's all that made him go!*" Now,' said Mr. Lincoln, 'if Mr. —— has a presidential *chin fly* biting him, I'm not going to knock him off, if it will only make his department *go.*'

" On another occasion the President said he was in great distress; he had been to General McClellan's house, and the General did not ask to see him ; and as he must talk to somebody, he had sent for General Franklin and myself, to obtain our opinion as to the possibility of soon commencing active operations with the Army of the Potomac. To use his own expression, if something was not soon done, the bottom would fall out of the whole affair ; and if General McClellan did not want to use the army, he would like to *borrow it,* provided he could see how it could be made to do something." *

XLII.

One bright morning in May, the Sunday-school children of the city of Washington, marching in procession on anniversary day, passed in review

* **Raymond's** *Life of Lincoln.*

through the portico on the north side of the White
House. The President stood at the open window
above the door, responding with a smile and a bow
to the lusty cheers of the little folks as they passed.
Hon. Mr. Odell, of Brooklyn, with one or two
other gentlemen, stood by his side as I joined the
group. It was a beautiful sight; the rosy-cheeked
boys and girls, in their "Sunday's best," with
banners and flowers, all intent upon seeing the
President, and, as they caught sight of his tall
figure, cheering as if their very lives depended
upon it. After enjoying the scene for some time,
making pleasant remarks about a face that now
and then struck him, Mr. Lincoln said: "Mrs.
Ann S. Stephens told me a story last night about
Daniel Webster, when a lad, which was new to me,
and it has been running in my head all the morning. When quite young, at school, Daniel was one
day guilty of a gross violation of the rules. He
was detected in the act, and called up by the
teacher for punishment. This was to be the old-
fashioned 'feruling' of the hand. His hands happened to be very dirty. Knowing this, on his way
to the teacher's desk, he *spit* upon the palm of
his *right* hand, wiping it off upon the side of his
pantaloons. 'Give me your hand, sir,' said the
teacher, very sternly. Out went the right hand,
partly cleansed. The teacher looked at it a moment, and said, 'Daniel, if you will find another
hand in this school-room as filthy as that, I will let

you off this time!' Instantly from behind his
back came the *left* hand. 'Here it is, sir,' was the
ready reply. 'That will do,' said the teacher,
'for this time; you can take your seat, sir.'"

Mr. Lincoln's heart was always open to children.
I shall never forget his coming into the "studio"
one day, and finding my own little boy of two sum-
mers playing on the floor. A member of the Cabinet was with him, but laying aside all restraint, he
took the little fellow at once in his arms, and they
were soon on the best of terms.

Old Daniel — alluded to on a previous page
— gave me a touching illustration of this element
in his character. A poor woman from Philadelphia had been waiting with a baby in her arms for
several days to see the President. It appeared by
her story, that her husband had furnished a sub-
stitute for the army, but sometime afterward, in
a state of intoxication, was induced to enlist. Upon
reaching the post assigned his regiment, he deserted, thinking the government was not entitled
to his services. Returning home, he was arrested,
tried, convicted, and sentenced to be shot. The
sentence was to be executed on a Saturday. On
Monday his wife left her home with her baby, to
endeavor to see the President. Said Daniel, "She
had been waiting here three days, and there was
no chance for her to get in. Late in the afternoon of the third day, the President was going
through the passage to his private room to get a

cup of tea.   On the way he heard the baby cry.
He instantly went back to his office and rang the
bell.   'Daniel,' said he, 'is there a woman with a
baby in the anteroom?'   I said there was, and if
he would allow me to say it, it was a case he ought
to see; for it was a matter of life and death.   Said
he, 'Send her to me at once.'   She went in, told
her story, and the President pardoned her husband.
As the woman came out from his presence, her
eyes were lifted and her lips moving in prayer, the
tears streaming down her cheeks."   Said Daniel,
"I went up to her, and pulling her shawl, said,
Madam, it was the baby that did it.'"

When Mr. Lincoln visited New York in 1860,
he felt a great interest in many of the institutions
for reforming criminals and saving the young from
a life of crime.   Among others, he visited, unat-
tended, the Five Points' House of Industry, and
the Superintendent of the Sabbath-school there
gave the following account of the event: —

" One Sunday morning, I saw a tall, remarkable-
looking man enter the room and take a seat among
us.   He listened with fixed attention to our exercises, and his countenance expressed such genuine
interest that I approached him and suggested that
he might be willing to say something to the children.   He accepted the invitation with evident
pleasure; and, coming forward, began a simple
address, which at once fascinated every little hearer
and hushed the room into silence.   His language

was strikingly beautiful, and his tones musical with intense feeling. The little faces would droop into sad conviction as he uttered sentences of warning, and would brighten into sunshine as he spoke cheerful words of promise. Once or twice he attempted to close his remarks, but the imperative shout of ' Go on ! Oh, do go on ! ' would compel him to resume. As I looked upon the gaunt and sinewy frame of the stranger, and marked his powerful head and determined features, now touched into softness by the impressions of the moment, I felt an irrepressible curiosity to learn something more about him, and while he was quietly leaving the room I begged to know his name. He courteously replied, ' It is Abraham Lincoln, from Illinois.' "

Mr. Nelson Sizer, one of the gallery ushers of Henry Ward Beecher's church in Brooklyn, told me that about the time of the Cooper Institute speech, Mr. Lincoln was twice present at the morning services of that church. On the first occasion, he was accompanied by his friend, George B. Lincoln, Esq., and occupied a prominent seat in the centre of the house. On a subsequent Sunday morning, not long afterwards, the church was *packed*, as usual, and the services had proceeded to the announcement of the text, when the gallery door at the right of the organ-loft opened, and the tall figure of Mr. Lincoln entered, alone. Again in the city over Sunday, he started out by himself to find the church, which he reached considerably

behind time. Every seat was occupied; but the
gentlemanly usher at once surrendered his own, and,
stepping back, became much interested in watching
the effect of the sermon upon the western orator.
As Mr. Beecher developed his line of argument,
Mr. Lincoln's body swayed forward, his lips parted,
and he seemed at length entirely unconscious of his
surroundings, — frequently giving vent to his satisfaction, at a well-put point or illustration, with a
kind of involuntary Indian exclamation, — "*ugh!*"
— not audible beyond his immediate presence, but
very expressive! Mr. Lincoln henceforward had a
profound admiration for the talents of the famous
pastor of Plymouth Church. He once remarked
to the Rev. Henry M. Field, of New York, in my
presence, that "he thought there was not upon
record, in ancient or modern biography, so *produc-
tive* a mind, as had been exhibited in the career of
Henry Ward Beecher!"

XLIII.

One of Mr. Lincoln's biographers, speaking of
the relations which existed between the President
and his Cabinet, says : —

"He always maintained that the proper duty of each
Secretary was to direct the details of everything done
within his own department, and to tender such suggestions, information, and advice to the President, as he
might solicit at his hands. But the duty and responsi-

bility of deciding what line of policy should be pursued, or what steps should be taken in any specific case, in his judgment, belonged exclusively to the President; and he was always willing and ready to assume it." *

The suppression of a portion of Secretary Cameron's official report for 1861, is a case in point. A number of printed copies of the report had left Washington before the " incendiary " passage was observed by Mr. Lincoln. The New York " Tribune " published it as originally written. Late in the evening of the day that these were sent, the government printer took a copy to the President, saying he thought he ought to look it over and see if it was satisfactory. He stated, also, that a number of copies of the report had been already ordered from the printing-office. Mr. Lincoln glanced over the copy placed in his hands, and his eye rested upon the passage in question, which had reference to arming the slaves. Instantly he was aroused. " This will never do ! " said he. " Gen. Cameron must take no such responsibility. That is a question which belongs exclusively to me ! " Then, with a pencil, he struck out the objectionable clause, and ordered measures to be taken at once to suppress the copies already issued. This decided action created considerable excitement at the time, as the President's policy in reference to slavery had not then been indicated. In the light of subsequent history, it will be regarded as striking evidence of

* Hon. H. J. Raymond.

the caution with which he felt his way on this intri-
cate and momentous question. In his own language,
in the letter to Col. Hodges, he objected, because
the indispensable necessity had not then arrived.
To Simon Cameron, however, the honor will ever
belong of being the first man connected with the
Administration to strike an official blow at the great
cause of the war.

Some time after the first battle of Bull Run, General Patterson, who had been severely censured for
his action, or want of action, on that occasion, called
upon Secretary Cameron, and demanded an investigation of the causes of the failure of the campaign.
After listening to his statement, the Secretary said
that he would like the President to see the orders
and correspondence, and an interview was accordingly arranged for the same evening. The result
is given in General Patterson's own words : —

"I called at the hour named, was most kindly
received, and read the papers, to which the President attentively listened. When I had finished, Mr.
Lincoln said, in substance, ' General, I have never
found fault with you nor censured you ; I have
never been able to see that you could have done
anything else than you did do. You obeyed orders,
and I am satisfied with your conduct.' This was
said with a manner so frank, candid, and manly as
to secure my respect, confidence, and good-will. I
expressed my gratification with and sincere thanks
for his fairness toward me, and his courtesy in

hearing my case, — giving me some five hours of
his time.   I said that so far as he and the War De
partment were concerned I was satisfied ; but that
I must have a trial by my peers, to have a public
approval, and to stop the abuse daily lavished upon
me.   The President replied that he would cheerfully accede to any practicable measure to do me
justice, but that I need not expect to escape abuse
as long as I was of any importance or value to the
community ; adding that he received infinitely more
abuse than I did, but that he had ceased to regard
it, and I must learn to do the same."

Although the friendly relations which existed
between the President and Secretary Cameron
were not interrupted by the retirement of the latter from the War Office, so important a change in
the Administration could not of course take place
without the irrepressible "story" from Mr. Lincoln.
Shortly after this event some gentlemen called
upon the President, and expressing much satisfaction at the change, intimated that in their judgment the interests of the country required an entire
reconstruction of the Cabinet.   Mr. Lincoln heard
them through, and then shaking his head dubiously,
replied, with his peculiar smile : "Gentlemen, when
I was a young man I used to know very well one
Joe Wilson, who built himself a log-cabin not
far from where I lived.   Joe was very fond of
eggs and chickens, and he took a good deal of pains
.n fitting up a poultry shed.   Having at length got

together a choice lot of young fowls, — of which he was very proud, — he began to be much annoyed by the depredations of those little black and white spotted animals, which it is not necessary to name. One night Joe was awakened by an unusual cackling and fluttering among his chickens. Getting up, he crept out to see what was going on. It was a bright moonlight night, and he soon caught sight of half a dozen of the little pests, which with their dam were running in and out of the shadow of the shed. Very wrathy, Joe put a double charge into his old musket, and thought he would ' clean ' out the whole tribe at one shot. Somehow he only killed *one*, and the balance scampered off across the field. In telling the story, Joe would always pause here, and hold his nose. ' Why did n't you follow them up, and kill the rest ? ' inquired the neighbors. ' Blast it,' said Joe, ' why, it was eleven weeks before I got over killin' *one*. If you want any more skirmishing in that line you can just do it yourselves ! ' "

XLIV.

The battle of Fair Oaks was fought **May 31, 1862 ;** or rather this is the date of the first of the series of battles before Richmond, when, as is now abundantly established, even by Rebel testimony, it would have been an easy matter for McClellan to have captured what proved to be the

Sebastopol of the Rebellion.   During these terri
ble battles, many of our wounded men were sent
on steamboats and transports to White House
landing, upon the estate of Mrs. Fitz Hugh Lee,
wife of the Rebel General.   Prosper M. Wetmore,
of New York city, was, at this juncture, on a visit
to the army.   Very ill himself while on the Peninsula, his sympathies were greatly excited for the
wounded soldiers, confined, during the broiling
weather, to the boats, compelled to quench the
burning thirst created by their wounds with the
muddy water of the Pamunkey, which caused and
aggravated disease in a fearful manner.   As a ci-
vilian, he was permitted to go on shore, and there
found the magnificent lawns and grounds, including
one of the finest springs of water in the world, all
under a protective guard, set over the property by
order of the commanding general ; and, while civil-
ians like himself were permitted freely to drink at
the spring, the suffering soldiers were prohibited
from approaching it !   Mr. W.'s indignation was so
greatly aroused that, upon reaching Baltimore, on
his return home, he, with two other gentlemen,
cognizant of the facts, determined to go to Washington and lay the case before the War Department.   Upon hearing their statement, the Secretary of War referred them to Surgeon-General
Hammond, saying that a requisition from him, to
the effect that the grounds of the estate were
needed for the wounded, would be instantly re-

sponded to by the War Department in the issue of the necessary order, taking possession. They immediately waited upon the Surgeon-General, and procured the document required, upon which Secretary Stanton made out the order, saying, as he signed it : "Now, gentlemen, you had better see the President also about this matter, and get his indorsement of the order." Proceeding to the Executive Mansion, they found, as usual, the waiting-rooms thronged with visitors ; but, representing to the usher in attendance that their business was extremely urgent, and concerned the wounded of the army, they were at once shown into Mr. Lincoln's presence. It was late in what had perhaps been a trying or vexatious day. Very briefly, but unceremoniously, the object of their visit was stated. In the language of Mr. W——, " The President listened to the account half impatiently, saying, as the speaker concluded, with an expression of countenance very like a sneer, 'This is another *raid* upon McClellan, I take it!' 'Mr. President,' was the reply, ' we came here to lay these facts before you solely from a sense of duty. Had I the power, sir, I would take possession of the lawns in front of *this* mansion for the benefit of our wounded men, so many of whom are now dying on the Pamunkey, for want of pure air and water. After the sights witnessed upon those seven steamboats now lying at White House, I covet every spot of greensward my eyes rest upon. What I have

told you of the actual condition of things at that
landing is below the truth, as the gentlemen who
accompany me will confirm to your satisfaction.
For myself, allow me to say, sir, that I belong to
that political organization which opposed your election to the Presidency — the same organization to
which General McClellan is presumed to belong.
This is no raid upon him or upon you. It is
simple justice to the wounded and suffering soldiers
that we ask of you.' Entirely convinced by the
candor of this reply, Mr. Lincoln then proceeded to
a minute questioning in regard to the scenes they
had witnessed; and when subsequently told that
they had called at Secretary Stanton's request, to
secure his approval of the order issued, which embraced only the grounds and spring, ' Not only
these,' said he, with emphasis, ' but the order must
include the house, and everything else which can in
any way contribute to the comfort of the poor
boys!' And so the order was made to read before
it left Washington."

There is scarcely a parallel in history to the forbearance exhibited by the President toward General McClellan. The incident given above is but
one illustration of his impatience with those who
preferred charges against the " Commanding General." During the last year of his life, however,
in friendly conversation, he could not refrain sometimes from an impromptu sarcasm, nevertheless so
blended with wit that it must, one would think,
effectually disarm all resentment.

About two weeks after the Chicago Convention, the Rev. J. P. Thompson, of New York, called upon the President, in company with the Assistant Secretary of War, Mr. Dana. In the course of conversation, Dr. T. said : " What do you think, Mr. President, is the reason General McClellan does not reply to the letter from the Chicago Convention ? " " Oh ! " replied Mr. Lincoln, with a characteristic twinkle of the eye, " *he is intrenching.*"

XLV.

One Saturday afternoon, when the lawn in front of the White House was crowded with people listening to the weekly concert of the Marine Band, the President appeared upon the portico. Instantly there was a clapping of hands and clamor for a speech. Bowing his thanks, and excusing himself, he stepped back into the retirement of the circular parlor, remarking to me, with a disappointed air, as he reclined upon the sofa, " I wish they would let me sit out there quietly, and enjoy the music." I stated to him on this occasion, that I believed no President, since the days of Washington, ever secured the hearts of the people, and carried them with him as he had done. To this he replied that, in such a crisis as the country was then passing through, it was natural that the people should look more earnestly to their leaders than at other periods. He thought their regard for any man in his position who should sincerely have done his best to save the government from destruction, would have been equally as marked and expressive ; to which I did not by any means assent.

I do not recall an instance of Mr. Lincoln's ever referring to any act of his administration with an appearance of complacency or self-satisfaction. I watched him closely during the political excitement previous to the Baltimore Convention, to see if I could discover signs of personal ambition, and I am free to say that, apart from the welfare of the country, there was no evidence to show to my mind that he ever thought of himself. And yet he was very sensitive to the opinions of his friends. A governor of a western State, true and loyal as the best, at a certain juncture conceived himself for some reason aggrieved by Executive action. Having occasion to send in the names of two officers for promotion, he said, in his note to the President, that he hoped whatever feeling he might have against him personally would not prevent his doing justice to the merits of the officers in question. Mr. Lincoln had been utterly unconscious of having given offence, either by lack of appreciation or otherwise, and he seemed greatly touched at the aspersion. He said that, if he had been asked to say which of all the loyal governors had been most active and efficient in raising and equipping troops, if he had made any distinction, where all had done so well, it would have been in favor of the gov-

ernor in question. At another time, when several
conflicting delegations were pressing the claims of
different candidates for a position of importance,
he said that he had been so troubled about the
matter that he had that day refused to see one of
the candidates, an old and dear personal friend, lest
his judgment should be warped. "If I was less
thin-skinned about such things," he added, "I
should get along much better."

When he had thought profoundly, however, upon
certain measures, and felt sure of his ground, criticism, either public or private, did not disturb him.
Upon the appearance of what was known as the
"Wade and Davis manifesto," subsequent to his
renomination, an intimate friend and supporter,
who was very indignant that such a document
should have been put forth just previous to the
presidential election, took occasion to animadvert
very severely upon the course that prompted it.
"It is not worth fretting about," said the President ; "it reminds me of an old acquaintance, who,
having a son of a scientific turn, bought him a
microscope. The boy went around, experimenting
with his glass upon everything that came in his
way. One day, at the dinner-table, his father took
up a piece of cheese. ' Don't eat that, father,'
said the boy ; ' it is full of *wrigglers*.' ' My son,'
replied the old gentleman, taking, at the same time,
a huge bite, ' let 'em *wriggle;* I can stand it if they
can.' "

10

No President ever manifested such a willingness to receive and act upon advice and suggestions from all sources, as Mr. Lincoln. On a certain occasion a leading officer of the government, and the governor of the State he represented, had each a candidate for a high State position. The claims of both were urged with great strength. The President was "in a strait betwixt the two." A personal friend from the same State, to whom he mentioned the difficulty of deciding the question without giving offence to one or the other of the parties, suggested that he appoint neither of the candidates, but bestow the office upon a certain officer of the army from that State, who had distinguished himself, losing an arm or a leg in the service, but who had not solicited in any way the position. Mr. Lincoln instantly fell in with the idea, saying that it seemed to him "just the right thing to do;" and he immediately made out the nomination.

XLVI.

Among the numerous visitors on one of the President's reception days, were a party of Congressmen, among whom was the Hon. Thomas Shannon, of California. Soon after the customary greeting, Mr. Shannon said : —

" Mr. President, I met an old friend of yours in California last summer, Thompson Campbell, who had a good deal to say of your Springfield life."

"Ah!" returned Mr. Lincoln, "I am glad to hear of him. Campbell used to be a dry fellow," he continued. "For a time he was Secretary of State. One day, during the legislative vacation, a meek, cadaverous-looking man, with a white neck-cloth, introduced himself to him at his office, and, stating that he had been informed that Mr. C. had the letting of the Assembly Chamber, said that he wished to secure it, if possible, for a course of lectures he desired to deliver in Springfield. 'May I ask,' said the Secretary, 'what is to be the subject of your lectures?' 'Certainly,' was the reply, with a very solemn expression of countenance. 'The course I wish to deliver, is on the Second Coming of our Lord.' 'It is of no use,' said C. 'If you will take my advice, you will not waste your time in this city. It is my private opinion that if the Lord has been in Springfield *once*, He will not come the second time!'"

Representative Shannon, previous to the war, had been an "Old Hunker" Democrat. Converted by the Rebellion, he had gone to the other extreme, and was one of the radical Abolitionists of the Thirty-Eighth Congress. The last Sunday in May, the Rev. Dr. Cheever, of New York, delivered one of his most pungent, denunciatory anti-slavery discourses, in the Hall of the House of Representatives. Among the numerous auditors attracted by the name of the preacher, I noticed Mr Shannon, whose face was not often seen in church

On the way to my hotel, we fell in together.
"Well, S.," said I, "what think you of that style
of preaching?"   "It was the first '*Gospel*' sermon I ever heard in my life!" was the emphatic
rejoinder.

One of Mr. Shannon's California colleagues, the
Hon. Mr. Higby, told me that having special business one evening, which called him to the White
House, the President came into the office, dressed
for a state dinner.   In the conversation which
followed, holding up his hands, encased in white
gloves, he remarked, with a laugh, that one of his
Illinois friends never could see his hands in that
"predicament," without being reminded of "*canvassed hams!*"

Mr. Lincoln was always ready to join in a laugh
at the expense of his person, concerning which he
was very indifferent.   Many of his friends will
recognize the following story, — the incident having
actually occurred, — which he used to tell with
great glee : —

"In the days when I used to be ' on the circuit,'
I was once accosted in the cars by a stranger, who
said, ' Excuse me, sir, but I have an article in my
possession which belongs to you.'   ' How is that?'
I asked, considerably astonished.   The stranger
took a jack-knife from his pocket.   ' This knife,'
said he, ' was placed in my hands some years ago,
with the injunction that I was to keep it until I
found a man *uglier* than myself.   I have carried it

from that time to this. Allow me *now* to say,
sir, that I think *you* are fairly entitled to the property.'"

XLVII.

I had been engaged in the official chamber until
quite late one evening, upon some pencil studies
of accessories, necessary to introduce in my picture.   The President, Mrs. Lincoln, and the Private Secretaries had gone to the opera, and for the
time being I had undisturbed possession.   Towards
twelve o'clock I heard some persons enter the
sleeping apartment occupied by Mr. Nicolay and
Major Hay, which was directly opposite the room
where I was sitting; and shortly afterward the
hearty laugh of Mr. Lincoln broke the stillness,
proceeding from the same quarter.   Throwing aside
my work, I went across the hall to see what had
occasioned this outbreak of merriment.   The Secretaries had come in and Hay had retired; Mr.
Nicolay sat by the table with his boots off, and the
President was leaning over the "footboard" of
the bed, laughing and talking with the hilarity of a
schoolboy.   It seemed that Hay, or "John," as
the President called him, had met with a singular
adventure, which was the subject of the amusement.   Glancing through the half-open door, Mr
Lincoln caught sight of me, and the story had to
be repeated for my benefit.   The incident was

trifling in itself, but the President's enjoyment of it was very exhilarating. I never saw him in so frolicsome a mood as on this occasion.

It has been well said by a critic of Shakspeare, that "the spirit which held the woe of 'Lear,' and the tragedy of 'Hamlet,' would have broken, had it not also had the humor of the 'Merry Wives of Windsor,' and the merriment of 'Midsummer Night's Dream.'" With equal justice can this profound truth be applied to the late President. The world has had no better illustration of it since the immortal plays were written.

Mr. Lincoln's "laugh" stood by itself. The "neigh" of a wild horse on his native prairie is not more undisguised and hearty. A group of gentlemen, among whom was his old Springfield friend and associate, Hon. Isaac N. Arnold, were one day conversing in the passage near his office, while waiting admission. A congressional delegation had preceded them, and presently an unmistakable voice was heard through the partition, in a burst of mirth. Mr. Arnold remarked, as the sound died away: "That laugh has been the President's life-preserver!"

In a corner of his desk he kept a copy of the latest humorous work; and it was his habit when greatly fatigued, annoyed, or depressed, to take this up and read a chapter, frequently with great relief.

Among the callers in the course of an evening

which I well remember, was a party composed of
two senators, a representative, an ex-lieutenant-gov-
ernor of a western State, and several private citizens.
They had business of great importance, involving the
necessity of the President's examination of voluminous documents.   He was at this time, from an unusual pressure of office-seekers, in addition to his
other cares, literally worn out.   Pushing everything
aside, he said to one of the party : " Have you seen
the ' Nasby Papers'? "   " No, I have not," was the
answer ; " who is ' Nasby?' "   " There is a chap
out in Ohio," returned the President, " who has
been writing a series of letters in the newspapers
over the signature of ' Petroleum V. Nasby.'
Some one sent me a pamphlet collection of them
the other day.   I am going to write to ' Petroleum ' to come down here, and I intend to tell him
if he will communicate his talent to me, I will
' *swap* ' places with him."   Thereupon he arose,
went to a drawer in his desk, and, taking out the
" Letters," sat down and read one to the company
finding in their enjoyment of it the temporary excitement and relief which another man would have
found in a glass of wine.   The instant he ceased,
the book was thrown aside, his countenance relapsed
into its habitual serious expression, and the business
before him was entered upon with the utmost earnestness.

During the dark days of '62, the Hon. Mr.
Ashley, of Ohio, had occasion to call at the White

House early one morning, just after news of a disaster.   Mr. Lincoln commenced some trifling nar-
ration, to which the impulsive congressman was in
no mood to listen.   He rose to his feet and said:
" Mr. President, I did not come here this morning
to hear stories ; it is too serious a time."   Instantly
the smile faded from Mr. Lincoln's face.   " Ashley," said he, " sit down !   I respect you as an
earnest, sincere man.   You cannot be more anxious
than I have been constantly since the beginning of
the war ; and I say to you now, that were it not
for this occasional *vent*, I should die."

XLVIII.

About the first of June I received a call from
the Hon. Horace Greeley, who was temporarily in
Washington.   Very near-sighted, his comments
upon my work, then about half completed, were not
particularly gratifying.   He thought the steel like-
nesses in his book, " The American Conflict," were
much better.   I called his attention, among other
points, to a newspaper introduced in the foreground
of the picture, " symbolizing," I said, " the agency
of the ' Press ' in bringing about *Emancipation ;* "
—stating, at the same time, that this accessory was
studied from a copy of the " Tribune."   Upon this
nis face relaxed ; — " I would not object," said he,
' to your putting in my letter to the President on
that subject."

Knowing that he had not been friendly to the renomination of Mr. Lincoln, it occurred to me, in my simplicity, that if I could bring them together, an interview might result in clearing up what was, perhaps, a mutual misunderstanding of relative positions, — though I had never known Mr. Lincoln to mention the name of the editor of the " Tribune," otherwise than with profound respect. Leaving my visitor in front of the picture, I went to the President's office to inform him of the presence of Mr. G. in the house, thinking that he might deem it best, under the circumstances, to receive him below stairs. In this, however, I " reckoned without my host." He looked up quickly, as I mentioned the name, but recovering himself, said, with unusual blandness: " Please say to Mr. Greeley that I shall be *very* happy to see him, *at his leisure.*"

I have been repeatedly asked to what extent Mr. Lincoln read the newspapers. It might have damp‧ened the patriotic ardor of many ambitious editors, could they have known that their elaborate disquisitions, sent in such numbers to the White House, were usually appropriated by the servants, and rarely, or never, reached the one they were preëminently intended to enlighten as to his duty and policy. I recollect of but a single instance of newspaper reading on the part of the President, during the entire period of my intercourse with him. One evening, having occasion to go to the Private Secretary's office, supposing the rooms to be vacant, I came upon Mr. Lincoln, seated quietly by himself, for once engaged in looking over the contents of a journal, which he had casually taken up.

The Washington dailies, — the "Chronicle," "Republican," and "Star," — were usually laid upon his table, and I think he was in the habit of glancing at the telegraphic reports of these; but rarely beyond this. All war news of importance, of course, reached him previous to its publication. He had, therefore, little occasion to consult newspapers on this account. The Private Secretaries, however, usually kept him informed of the principal subjects discussed editorially in the leading organs of the country.

The journals I became most familiar with, in the Secretaries' quarters, besides those mentioned, were the Philadelphia "Press" and "North American;" the Baltimore "American" and "Sun;" the New York "Tribune," "Evening Post," "Independent," "Times," "Herald," and "World;" the Albany "Evening Journal;" the Boston "Advertiser," "Journal," and "Transcript;" the Chicago "Tribune" and "Journal," (the latter valued chiefly for the letters of its war correspondent, B. F. Taylor); the St. Louis "Republican" and "Democrat;" and the Cincinnati "Gazette" and "Commercial."

Violent criticism, attacks, and denunciations, coming either from radicals or conservatives, rarely ruffled the President, if they reached his ears. It must have been in connection with something of this kind, that he once told me this story. "Some years ago," said he, "a couple of 'emigrants,' fresh from the 'Emerald Isle,' seeking labor, were making their way toward the West. Coming suddenly, one evening, upon a pond of water, they were greeted with a grand chorus of bull-frogs, — a kind of music they had never before heard. 'B–a–u–m!' — 'B–a–u–m!' Overcome with terror, they clutched their 'shillelahs,' and crept cautiously forward, straining their eyes in every direction, to catch a glimpse of the enemy; but he was not to be found! At last a happy idea seized the foremost one, — he sprang to his companion and exclaimed, 'And sure, Jamie! it is my opinion it's nothing but a "*noise!*"'"

On a certain occasion, the President was induced by a committee of gentlemen to examine a newly invented "repeating" gun; the peculiarity of which was, that it prevented the escape of gas. After due inspection, he said: "Well, I believe this really does what it is represented to do. Now have any of you heard of any machine, or invention, for preventing the escape of 'gas' from newspaper establishments?"

One afternoon he came into the studio, while Mrs. Secretary Welles and a party of friends were viewing the picture. Mrs. Welles said that she "understood from the newspapers that the work was nearly completed; which appeared to be far

from the truth." In reply, I made the common
place remark, that the "papers" were not always
"*reliable*." "That is to say, Mrs. Welles," broke
in the President, "they '*lie*,' and then they '*re-
lie!*'"

At one of the "levees," in the winter of 1864,
during a lull in the hand-shaking, Mr. Lincoln was
addressed by two lady friends, one of whom is the
wife of a gentleman subsequently called into the
Cabinet. Turning to them with a weary air, he
remarked that it was a relief to have now and then
those to talk to who had no favors to ask. The
lady referred to is a radical, — a New Yorker by
birth, but for many years a resident of the West.
She replied, playfully, "Mr. President, I *have* one
request to make." "Ah!" said he, at once looking
grave. "Well, what is it?" "That you suppress
the infamous 'Chicago Times,'" was the rejoinder.
After a brief pause, Mr. Lincoln asked her if she
had ever tried to imagine how she would have felt,
in some former administration to which she was
opposed, if her favorite newspaper had been seized
by the government, and suppressed. The lady
replied that it was not a parallel case; that in
circumstances like those then existing, when the
nation was struggling for its very life, such utterances as were daily put forth in that journal should
be suppressed by the strong hand of authority; that
the cause of loyalty and good government demanded
it. "I fear you do not fully comprehend," returned

the President, "the danger of abridging the *liber-*
ties of the people. Nothing but the very sternest
necessity can ever justify it. A government had
better go to the very extreme of toleration, than
to do aught that could be construed into an interference with, or to jeopardize in any degree, the
common rights of its citizens."

XLIX.

A morning or two after the visit of Mr. Greeley,
I was called upon by a gentleman, who requested
my assistance in securing a brief interview with
the President, for the purpose of presenting him
with an elaborate pen-and-ink " allegorical, sym-
bolic " representation of the " Emancipation Proclamation ; " which, in a massive carved frame, had
been purchased at a recent "Sanitary Fair," in
one of the large cities, by a committee of gentlemen, expressly for this object. The composition
contained a tree, representing Liberty ; a portrait
of Mr. Lincoln ; soldiers, monitors, broken fetters,
etc. ; together with the text of the proclamation,
all executed with a pen. Artistically speaking,
such works have no value, — they are simply
interesting, as curiosities. Mr. Lincoln kindly
accorded the desired opportunity to make the
presentation, which occupied but a few moments,
and was in the usual form. He accepted the
testimonial, he said, not for himself, but in be-

half of " the cause in which all were engaged."
When the group dispersed, I remained with the
President. He returned to his desk ; while I examined curiously the pen work, which was
exceedingly minute in detail. " This is quite wonderful ! " I said, at length. Mr. Lincoln looked up
from his papers ; " Yes," he rejoined ; " it is
what I call *ingenious nonsense !* "

The evening following this affair, on entering the
President's office, about eleven o'clock, I found
him alone, seated at the long table, with a large
pile of military commissions before him, which he
was signing one by one. As I sat down beside him,
he presently remarked, " I do not, as you see,
pretend to read over these documents. I see that
Stanton has signed them, so I conclude they are
all right." Pausing here, he read a portion of one,
beginning with the name of the individual, " ——
—— is hereby appointed adjutant-general, with the
rank of captain, etc. E. M. Stanton, Secretary of
War." " There," said he, appending his own signature in the opposite corner : " that fixes *him*
out." Thus he went on chatting and writing,
until he had finished the lot ; then, rising from his
chair, he stretched himself, and said, " Well, I
have got that job *husked out ;* now I guess I
will go over to the War Department before I go
to bed, and see if there is any news. Walking
over with him at his request, — to divert his mind
I repeated a story told me the night previous con-

cerning a 'contraband' who had fallen into the
hands of some good pious people, and was being
taught by them to read and pray. Going off by
himself one day, he was overheard to commence a
prayer by the introduction of himself as " Jim
Williams — a berry good nigga' to wash windows ;
'spec's you know me now ? ' "

An amusing illustration of the fact that whatever
the nature of an incident related to the President,
it never failed to remind him of something
similar, followed.   After a hearty laugh at what
he called this " direct way of putting the case,"
he said : " The story that suggests to me, has no
resemblance to it save in the ' washing windows '
part. A lady in Philadelphia had a pet poodle dog,
which mysteriously disappeared. Rewards were
offered for him, and a great ado made without
effect. Some weeks passed, and all hope of the
favorite's return had been given up, when a servant
brought him in one day, in the filthiest condition
imaginable. The lady was overjoyed to see her pet
again, but horrified at his appearance. ' Where
did you find him ? ' she exclaimed. ' Oh,' replied
the man, very unconcernedly, ' a negro down the
street had him tied to the end of a pole, *swab-
bing* windows.' "

L.

A day or two previous to the meeting of the Republican Convention, the President read me his letter to the "Owen Lovejoy Monument Association,"— lately written, and not then published, — in which he expressed his appreciation of Mr. Lovejoy in nearly the same language I had heard him use on a former occasion. "Throughout my heavy and perplexing responsibilities here," ran the letter, "to the day of his death, it would scarcely wrong any other to say he was my most generous friend. Let him have the marble monument, along with the well assured and more enduring one in the hearts of those who love liberty unselfishly for all men." A noble tribute, in fitly chosen words!

The evening following the reading of this letter, he said that Mrs. Lincoln and he had promised half an hour to a sort of "artist" who wished to "exhibit" before them in the red-room below. "What kind of an artist?" I inquired. "Oh, not in your line," he answered; "I think he is a sort of mountebank, or comic lecturer, or something of the kind." On my way to my own room, I met in the passage the well-known "Jeems Pipes of Pipesville," — otherwise Stephen Massett, — whom I at once conjectured to be the individual the President had referred to. The two rooms communicating by double doors, I could not well avoid overhearing a portion of the performance, or more properly lecture, which I think was announced by the title of "Drifting About." Comic imitations of various characters were given, among others that of a stammering man, which appeared greatly to amuse Mr. Lincoln. I could only now and then catch a word of the burlesque, but the voice and ringing laugh of the President were perfectly distinguishable. When the "lecture" ceased, Mr. Lincoln said, "I want to offer a suggestion. I once knew a man who invariably '*whistled*' with his stammering," and he then gave an imitation. "Now," he continued, "if you could get in a touch of nature like that it would be irresistibly ludicrous." "Pipes" applauded the amendment, rehearsing it several times, until he had mastered it to the President's satisfaction ; and I dare say the innovation became a part of all subsequent performances.

About this period numerous delegations from various religious bodies and associations thronged the White House. Among the number none met so cordial a reception as that of the "Christian Commission," composed of volunteer clergymen who had just returned from the Wilderness battleground. In the brief address by the chairman of the occasion, he stated that the group before the President embraced those who had been first on the field to offer aid and refreshments to the wounded of that terrible series of battles. In reply Mr. Lincoln expressed his appreciation of the

11

self-denying services rendered by the Commission, in feeling terms. He concluded his response
in these words : " And I desire also to add to what
I have said, that there is one association whose
object and motives I have never heard in any degree impugned or questioned ; and that is the
' Christian Commission.' And in ' these days of
villany,' as Shakspeare says, that is a record,
gentlemen, of which you may justly be proud ! "
Upon the conclusion of the " ceremony," he added,
in a conversational tone, " I believe, however, it is
old ' Jack Falstaff ' who talks about ' villany,'
though of course Shakspeare is responsible."

After the customary hand-shaking, which followed, several gentlemen came forward and asked
the President for his autograph. One of them gave
his name as " Cruikshank." " That reminds me,"
said Mr. Lincoln, " of what I used to be called
when a young man — ' long-shanks.' " Hereupon
the rest of the party, emboldened by the success
of the few, crowded around the desk, and the President good naturedly wrote his name for each ; the
scene suggesting forcibly to my mind a country
schoolmaster's weekly distribution of " tickets "
among his pupils.

LI.

The " Baltimore Convention," which renomi-
nated Mr. Lincoln, was convened June 7, 1864

It created comparatively little excitement in Washington or elsewhere, as the action of the various State legislatures and local mass meetings had prepared the public mind for the result.

Toward evening of the 8th, — the day the nominations were made, — Major Hay and myself were alone with the President in his office. He did not seem in any degree exhilarated by the action of the convention ; on the contrary, his manner was subdued, if not sad. Upon the lighting of the gas, he told us how he had that afternoon received the news of the nomination for Vice-President before he heard of his own. It appeared that the despatch announcing his renomination had been sent to his office from the War Department while he was at lunch. Afterward, without going back to the official chamber, he proceeded to the War Department. While there, the telegram came in announcing the nomination of Johnson. " What ! " said he to the operator, " do they nominate a Vice-President before they do a President ? " " Why ! " rejoined the astonished official, " have you not heard of your own nomination ? It was sent to the White House two hours ago." " It is all right," was the reply ; " I shall probably find it on my return."

Laughing pleasantly over this incident, he said, soon afterward, — "A very singular occurrence took place the day I was nominated at Chicago, four years ago, of which I am reminded to-night. In

the afternoon of the day, returning home from
down town, I went up-stairs to Mrs. Lincoln's
sitting-room.   Feeling somewhat tired, I lay down
upon a couch in the room, directly opposite a bureau
upon which was a looking-glass.   As I reclined,
my eye fell upon the glass, and I saw distinctly *two*
images of myself, exactly alike, except that one was
a little paler than the other.   I arose, and lay down
again, with the same result.   It made me quite
uncomfortable for a few moments, but some friends
coming in, the matter passed out of my mind.   The
next day, while walking in the street, I was suddenly reminded of the circumstance, and the disa-
greeable sensation produced by it returned.   I had
never seen anything of the kind before, and did not
know what to make of it.   I determined to go
home and place myself in the same position, and if
the same effect was produced, I would make up my
mind that it was the natural result of some principle
of refraction or optics which I did not understand,
and dismiss it.   I tried the experiment, with a like
result ; and, as I had said to myself, accounting for
it on some principle unknown to me, it ceased to
trouble me.   But," said he, " some time ago, I
tried to produce the same effect *here*, by arranging
a glass and couch in the same position, without
success."   He did not say, at this time, that either
he or Mrs. Lincoln attached any omen to the phe-
nomenon ; neither did he say that the double
reflection was seen while he was walking about the

room.   On the contrary, it was only visible in a
certain position and at a certain angle ; and therefore, he thought, could be accounted for upon scientific principles.*

A little later in the evening, the Hon. Mr. Kelley, of Philadelphia, came in.   As he sat down, he
took a letter out of his pocket, saying : " Mr. President, while on a visit home, a week or two ago, I
took up a number of the " Anti-Slavery Standard,"
in which there happened to be a communication
from Mrs. Caroline H. Dall, of Boston, giving
her views of the Fremont movement, and the
situation generally ; so admirable in its tone and
spirit, that I could not resist the inclination to write
to the author, expressing the interest with which I
had read the article.   The result was a reply, which
I hold in my hand, which seems to me so just and
able a statement of your position, from the stand-
point of a true woman, that I have brought it up to
read to you."   Mr. Lincoln nodded assent, and lis-

---

* Mr. Lincoln's friend Brooks, of the *Sacramento Union*, has given
to the public a somewhat different version of this story, placing its
occurrence on the day of the election in 1860.   The account, as I
have given it, was written before I had seen that by Mr. Brooks, and
is very nearly as Hay and myself heard it, — the incident making a
powerful impression upon my mind.   I am quite confident that Mr.
Lincoln said it occurred the day he was first nominated; for he
related it to us a few hours after having received intelligence of his
renomination, saying, " I am reminded of it to-night."   It is possible,
however, that I am mistaken in the date.   Mr. Brooks's statement
that " Mrs. Lincoln " was " troubled " about it, regarding it as a " sign
that Mr. Lincoln would be reëlected, but would not live through his
second term," is undoubtedly correct.

tened pensively to the eloquent tones of the Congressman's voice, who entered into the spirit of the
letter with his whole heart, — affirming, as it did,
unwavering confidence in the President; the sincerity of his anti-slavery convictions and purposes;
and appreciation of the difficulties which had en-
vironed him, — presenting, in this respect, a marked
contrast to the letters and speeches of many of the
so-called radicals.   Mr. Lincoln said but little,
as Judge Kelley concluded; but one or two expressions, and the manner accompanying them,
showed that the sentiments of the writer of the
letter were gratefully appreciated.

The day following the adjournment at Baltimore,
various political organizations called to pay their
respects to the President.   First came the Convention Committee, embracing one from each State represented,— appointed to announce to him, formally,
the nomination.   Next came the Ohio delegation,
with Menter's Band, of Cincinnati.   Following
these were the representatives of the National
Union League, to whom he said, in concluding his
brief response : —

"I do not allow myself to suppose that either
the Convention, or the League, have concluded to
decide that I am either the greatest or the best man
in America ; but, rather, they have concluded that
it is not best to *swap* horses while crossing the
river, and have further concluded that I am not so
poor a horse, but that they might make a *botch*
of it in trying to *swap!* "

Another incident, which occurred in the course of the day, created considerable amusement. When the Philadelphia delegation was being presented, the chairman of that body, in introducing one of the members, said : " Mr. President, this is Mr. S———, of the Second District of our State,— a most active and earnest friend of yours and the cause. He has, among other things, been good enough to paint, and present to our League rooms, a most beautiful portrait of yourself." Mr. Lincoln took the gentleman's hand in his, and shaking it cordially, said with a merry voice, — " I presume, sir, in painting your beautiful portrait, you took your idea of me from my principles, and not from my person."

Among the visitors, the same afternoon, were William Lloyd Garrison and Theodore Tilton. In the " Editorial Notes," concerning the convention and nominations, in his newspaper, the New York " Independent," the following week, Mr. Tilton wrote : —

" On his reception day, the President's face wore an expression of satisfaction rather than elation. His reception of Mr. Garrison was an equal honor to host and guest. In alluding to our failure to find the old jail, he said, — ' Well, Mr. Garrison, when you first went to Baltimore you could n't get *out ;* but the second time you could n't get *in !* ' When one of us mentioned the great enthusiasm at the convention, after Senator Morgan s proposition

to amend the Constitution, abolishing slavery, Mr.
Lincoln instantly said, — ' It was I who suggested
to Mr. Morgan that he should put that idea into his
opening speech.' This was the very best word he
has said since the proclamation of freedom."

LII.

I have alluded, on a previous page, to the public
concerts of the Marine Band, — from the Washington Navy-yard, — given every Saturday afternoon, during the summer, on the grounds in front
of the White House; which, on such occasions,
were thronged with visitors. The Saturday following the nominations I invited my friend Cropsey,
the landscape-painter, from New York, — who, with
his wife, was spending a few days in the city, — to
come up with Mrs. C. to the studio, which overlooked the pleasure-grounds, and presented a fine
opportunity of enjoying both spectacle and music.
The invitation was accepted, and the afternoon was
devoted to my guests.

Towards the close of the concert the door suddenly opened, and the President came in, as he
was in the habit of doing, alone. Mr. and Mrs.
Cropsey had been presented to him in the course
of the morning; and as he came forward, half
uesitatingly, Mrs. C., who held a bunch of beautiful flowers in her hand, tripped forward playfully,
and said: " Allow me, Mr. President, to present

you with a bouquet!" The situation was momentarily embarrassing; and I was puzzled to know how " His Excellency " would get out of it. With no appearance of discomposure, he stooped down, took the flowers, and, looking from them into the sparkling eyes and radiant face of the lady, said, with a gallantry I was unprepared for, — " Really, madam, if you give them to *me*, and they are *mine*, I think I cannot possibly make so good a *use* of them as to present them to *you*, in return!" Chesterfield could not have extricated himself from the dilemma with more tact and address; and the incident, trifling in itself, may serve to illustrate that there existed in the *ci-devant* " rail-splitter" and " flat-boatman " — uncouth and half-civilized as many supposed him — the essential elements of the true gentleman.

I was always touched by the President's manner of receiving the salute of the guard at the White House. Whenever he appeared in the portico, on his way to or from the War or Treasury Department, or on any excursion down the avenue, the first glimpse of him was, of course, the signal for the sentinel on duty to " present arms." This was always acknowledged by Mr. Lincoln with a peculiar bow and touch of the hat, no matter how many times it might occur in the course of a day; and it always seemed to me as much a compliment to the devotion of the soldiers, on his part, as it was the sign of duty and deference on the part of the guard.

The Hon. Mr. Odell gave me a deeply interesting incident, which occurred in the winter of 1864, at one of the most crowded of the Presidential levees, illustrating very perfectly Mr. Lincoln's true politeness and delicacy of feeling.

On the occasion referred to, the pressure became so great that the usual ceremony of hand-shaking was, for once, discontinued. The President had been standing for some time, bowing his acknowledgments to the thronging multitude, when his eye fell upon a couple who had entered unobserved, — a wounded soldier, and his plainly dressed mother. Before they could pass out, he made his way to where they stood, and, taking each of them by the hand, with a delicacy and cordiality which brought tears to many eyes, he assured them of his interest and welcome. Governors, senators, diplomats, passed with simply a nod ; but that pale young face he might never see again. To him, and to others like him, did the nation owe its life ; and Abraham Lincoln was not the man to forget this, even in the crowded and brilliant assembly of the distinguished of the land.

LIII.

The opinion of the Attorney-General, Judge Bates, as to the safety of Mr. Lincoln's being intrusted with the pardoning power, was founded upon an intimate knowledge of the man. A nature of such tenderness and humanity would have been in danger of erring on what many would call the weak side, had it not been balanced by an un usual degree of strong practical good sense and judgment.

The Secretary of War, and generals in command, were frequently much annoyed at being overruled, — the discipline and efficiency of the service being thereby, as they considered, greatly endangered. But there was no going back of the simple signature, " A. LINCOLN," attached to proclamation or reprieve.

The Hon. Mr. Kellogg, representative from Essex County, New York, received a despatch one evening from the army, to the effect that a young townsman, who had been induced to enlist through his instrumentality, had, for a serious misdemeanor, been convicted by a court-martial, and was to be shot the next day. Greatly agitated, Mr. Kellogg went to the Secretary of War, and urged, in the strongest manner, a reprieve. Stanton was inexorable. " Too many cases of the kind had been let off," he said; "and it was time an example was made." Exhausting his eloquence in vain, Mr. Kellogg said, — " Well, Mr. Secretary, the boy is not going to be *shot*, — of that I give you fair warning! " Leaving the War Department, he went directly to the White House, although the hour was late. The sentinel on duty told him that special orders had been issued to admit no one whatever that night. After a long parley, by pledging himself to assume the responsibility of the act, the congressman passed in. The President had retired; but, indifferent to etiquette or ceremony, Judge Kellogg pressed his way through all obstacles to his sleeping apartment. In an excited manner he stated that the despatch announcing the hour of execution had but just reached him. "This man must not be shot, Mr. President," said he. "I can't help what he may have done. Why, he is an old neighbor of mine; I can't allow him to be shot!" Mr. Lincoln had remained in bed, quietly listening to the vehement protestations of his old friend, (they were in Congress together.) He at length said: "Well, I don't believe *shooting* him will do him any good. Give me that pen." And, so saying, "red tape" was unceremoniously cut, and another poor fellow's lease of life was indefinitely extended.

One night Speaker Colfax left all other business to ask the President to respite the son of a constituent, who was sentenced to be shot, at Davenport, for desertion. He heard the story with his usual patience, though he was wearied out with incessant calls, and anxious for rest, and then replied: "Some of our generals complain that I impair discipline and subordination in the army by my pardons and respites, but it makes me rested, after a hard day's work, if I can find some good excuse for saving a man's life, and I go to bed happy as I think how joyous the signing of my name will make him and his family and his friends."

Mr. Van Alen, of New York, in an account furnished the "Evening Post," wrote: "I well remember the case of a poor woman who sought,
with the persistent affection of a mother, for the
pardon of her son condemned to death. She was
successful in her petition. When she had left the
room, Mr. Lincoln turned to me and said: 'Perhaps I have done wrong, but at all events I have
made that poor woman happy.'"

The Hon. Thaddeus Stevens told me that on one
occasion he called at the White House with an
elderly lady, in great trouble, whose son had been
in the army, but for some offence had been court-
martialled, and sentenced either to death, or impris-
onment at hard labor for a long term. There were
some extenuating circumstances; and after a full
hearing, the President turned to the representative,
and said: "Mr. Stevens, do you think this is a case
which will warrant my interference?" "With my
knowledge of the facts and the parties," was the
reply, "I should have no hesitation in granting a
pardon." "Then," returned Mr. Lincoln, "I
will pardon him," and he proceeded forthwith to
execute the paper. The gratitude of the mother
was too deep for expression, and not a word was
said between her and Mr. Stevens until they were
half way down the stairs on their passage out, when
she suddenly broke forth in an excited manner with
the words, "I knew it was a copperhead lie!"
"What do you refer to, madam?" asked Mr. Ste-

vens. " Why, they told me he was an ugly looking man," she replied, with vehemence. " He is
the handsomest man I ever saw in my life ! " And
surely for that mother, and for many another
throughout the land, no carved statue of ancient or
modern art, in all its symmetry, can have the
charm which will for evermore encircle that careworn but gentle face, expressing as lineaments of
ruler never expressed before, " Malice towards none
— Charity for all."

Though kind-hearted almost to a fault, nevertheless Mr. Lincoln always endeavored to be *just*.
The Hon. S. F. Miller, of New York, called upon
him one day with the brother of a deserter who
had been arrested. The excuse was that the soldier
had been home on a sick-furlough, and that he
afterwards became partially insane, and had consequently failed to return and report in proper time.
He was on his way to his regiment at the front to
be tried. The President at once ordered him to be
stopped at Alexandria and sent before a board of sur-
geons for examination as to the question of insanity.
" This seemed to me so proper," said the representative, " that I expressed myself satisfied. But on
going out, the brother, who was anxious for an immediate discharge, said to me, ' The trouble with
your President is, that he is so afraid of doing
something wrong.' "

A young man, connected with a New York regiment, had become to all appearance a hardened

criminal. He had deserted two or three times, and, when at last detected and imprisoned, had attempted to poison his guards, one of whom subsequently died from the effects of the poison unconsciously taken. Of course, there seemed no defence possible in such a case. But the fact came out that the boy had been of unsound mind. Some friends of his mother took up the matter, and an appeal was made to the Secretary of War. He declined, positively, to listen to it, — the case was too aggravating. The prisoner (scarcely more than a boy) was confined at Elmira, New York. The day for the execution of his sentence had nearly arrived, when his mother made her way to the President. He listened to her story, examined the record, and said that his opinion accorded with that of the Secretary of War; he could do nothing for her. Heart-broken, she was compelled to relinquish her last hope. One of the friends who had become interested, upon learning the result of the application, waited upon Senator Harris. That gentleman said that his engagements utterly precluded his going to see the President upon the subject, until twelve o'clock of the second night following. This brought the time to Wednesday night, and the sentence was to be executed on Thursday. Judge Harris, true to his word, called at the White House at twelve o'clock Wednesday night. The President had retired, but the interview was granted. The point made was that the boy was insane, — thus irresponsible, and his execution would be murder. Pardon was not asked, but a reprieve, until a proper medical examination could be made. This was so reasonable that Mr. Lincoln acquiesced in its justice. He immediately ordered a telegram sent to Elmira, delaying the execution of the sentence. Early the next morning he sent another, by a different line, and, before the hour of execution arrived, he had sent no less than *four* different reprieves, by different lines, to different individuals in Elmira, so fearful was he that the message would fail, or be too late.

This incident suggests another, similar only, however, in the fact that both boys were alleged to be irresponsible. A washerwoman in Troy had a son nearly imbecile as to intellect, yet of good physical proportions. The boy was kidnapped, or inveigled away by some scoundrels, who "enlisted" him, dividing his bounty among themselves. For some time his mother could learn nothing of him. At length she was told that he was in the army. Alone and unfriended she went to Washington to see, in her simplicity, if she could not get his discharge. The gentleman who related the circumstance to me said that she did not even know to which of the New York regiments her son belonged. She could get no chance to speak to the President. At length she watched her opportunity, and intercepted him on his way from the War Department. The result was, that taking down the lad's name

at. 1 place of residence, this message was written **on**
the back of the card, and sent to the War Department : —

*"This poor boy is said to be idiotic.   Find him, if
possible, and return him to his mother.*

A. LINCOLN."

" Calling," says Mr. Colfax, " upon the President
one morning in the winter of 1863, I found him
looking more than usually pale and careworn, and
inquired the reason.   He replied, with the bad
news he had received at a late hour the previous
night, which had not yet been communicated to the
press, — he had not closed his eyes or breakfasted ;
and, with an expression I shall never forget, he
exclaimed, ' How willingly would I exchange places
to-day with the soldier who sleeps on the ground in
the Army of the Potomac.' "

And yet, in the face of such evidence, showing
how the great sympathy and sorrow of the late
President took hold upon the very roots and springs
of his nature, there are not found wanting assertions
that he showed a criminal indifference to the sufferings of our prisoners at Libby, Andersonville, and
other places ; and, in proof of this, it is stated that
there is no record of his ever alluding to the subject
in any of his public addresses or messages.   The
questions involved in the suspension of the exchange
of prisoners are difficult of decision.   Whoever
was the cause of this, certainly has a fearful respon

12

sibility.   That it was the President's fault, I do not
believe.   When the reports, in an authentic form,
first reached Washington of the sufferings of the
Union prisoners, I know he was greatly excited
and overcome by them.   He was told that justice demanded a stern retaliation.   He said to his
friend Mr. Odell, with the deepest emotion : "*I
can never, never starve men like that!*"   "*Whatever others may say or do, I never can, and I
never will, be accessory to such treatment of human
beings!*"   And although he spoke with the deepest feeling at the Baltimore Fair of the Fort Pillow
massacre, and pledged retaliation, yet that pledge
was never carried into execution.   It was simply
impossible for Mr. Lincoln to be cruel or vindictive,
no matter what the occasion.   In the serene light
of history, when party strife and bitterness shall
have passed away, it will be seen that, if he erred
at all, it was always on the side of mercy and magnanimity.

LIV.

At a private dinner-party at Willard's Hotel,
given by Charles Gould, Esq., of New York, I
met for the first time the Hon. Hugh McCulloch,
then Comptroller of the Currency.   An acquaintance commenced, under circumstances calculated to inspire in me a sentiment of profound
respect for this gentleman's character and talents.
I was much interested, a few days afterward, in an

incident in the career of Mr. McCulloch, given me by the Rev. John Pierpont, who was an occasional visitor at the studio, and who, in his hale old age, was occupying one of the subordinate positions in the Department.

The desk at which Dr. Pierpont was occupied was in a room with those of a large number of other clerks, among whom the tall figure and silvery beard of the poet-preacher were very conspicuous. One day, just after Mr. McCulloch had entered upon his duties in Washington, it was announced at the entrance of this room, that the new Comptroller had called to see "Dr. Pierpont." The clerks looked up from their books, and at one another, inquiringly, as Mr. McCulloch took a seat by the poet's desk. "I perceive, Dr. Pierpont," said he, "that you do not remember me?" The venerable preacher looked at him a moment, and replied that he did not think he ever had seen him before. "Oh yes, you have," returned the Comptroller; "I was a member of —— Class, in Cambridge, in 1833 and '34, and used to hear you preach. Upon leaving the Law School, purposing to take up my residence at the West, I called upon you and requested one or two letters of introduction to parties in Cincinnati. You gave me two letters, one to a Mr. S——, and the other to a Mr. G——, of that city. Those letters, my dear sir, were the stepping-stones to my fortune. I have not seen you since; but learning that you were in

Washington, I told my wife, upon leaving home to take the position offered me here, that the first call I made in Washington should be upon the Rev. John Pierpont." As the Comptroller concluded, Dr. Pierpont put on his spectacles, and looked at him a moment in silence. He at length said: — " Why, Mr. McCulloch, you are the most extraordinary man I ever saw in my life ! " " How so ? " was the reply. " Why, you have remembered a favor for thirty years."

Dr. Pierpont told me, on another occasion, that in the prosecution of a duty once assigned him in the Department, he had to review a letter-book, containing correspondence with the different officers of the government. Among the letters was a private note, written by Secretary Chase to the Secretary of War, calling his attention to a complaint, made by the colored people of Cincinnati, against certain orders, or officers of the War Department. The letter closed with these words: —

" We cannot afford to lose the support of any part of our people. One poor man, colored though he be, with God on his side, is stronger *against us* than the hosts of the rebellion."

LV.

On the 30th of June, Washington was thrown into a ferment, by the resignation of Mr. Chase as Secretary of the Treasury. The publication, some

weeks before, of the "'Pomeroy' secret circular," in
the interest of Mr. Chase, as a presidential candidate, had created much talk, and considerable bad
feeling in the party.   The President, however,
took no part in the discussion, or criticism, which
followed ; — on the contrary, he manifested a sincere desire to preserve pleasant relations, and har-
monize existing differences in the Cabinet.   In
proof of this, I remember his sending one day
for Judge Lewis, the Commissioner of Internal
Revenue, and entering into a minute explanation
of a misapprehension, which he conceived the Secretary of the Treasury to be laboring under ; expressing the wish that the Commissioner would
mediate, on his behalf, with Mr. Chase.

Many sincere friends of Secretary Chase considered his resignation, at this juncture, unfortunate
and ill-timed.   The financial situation was more
threatening than at any period during the war.   Mr.
Chase's administration of the Treasury Department,
amid unparalleled difficulties, had been such as to
secure the confidence and satisfaction of the masses ;
and his withdrawal at such a time was regarded as
a public calamity, giving rise to the suspicion that
he apprehended national insolvency.   The resignation, however had been twice tendered before,
— the *third* time it was accepted.

I never saw the President under so much excitement as on the day following this event.   Without
consultation or advice, so far as I ever could learn,

he sent to the Senate, the previous afternoon, the name of Ex-Governor Todd, of Ohio, for the successorship. This nomination was not popular, and great relief was experienced the next morning, when it was announced that Governor Todd had declined the position. Mr. Lincoln passed an anxious night. He received the telegram from Governor Todd, declining the nomination, in the evening. Retiring, he laid awake some hours, canvassing in his mind the merits of various public men. At length he settled upon the Hon. William P. Fessenden, of Maine; and soon afterward fell asleep. The next morning he went to his office and wrote the nomination. John Hay, the assistant private secretary, had taken it from the President on his way to the Capitol, when he encountered Senator Fessenden upon the threshold of the room. As chairman of the Finance Committee, he also had passed an anxious night, and called thus early to consult with the President, and offer some suggestions. After a few moments' conversation, Mr. Lincoln turned to him with a smile, and said : " I am obliged to you, Fessenden, but the fact is, I have just sent your own name to the Senate for Secretary of the Treasury. Hay had just received the nomination from my hand as you entered." Mr. Fessenden was taken completely by surprise, and, very much agitated, protested his inability to accept the position. The state of his health, he said, if no other consideration, made it impossible. Mr. Lincoln would

not accept the refusal as final.   He very justly felt
that with Mr. Fessenden's experience and known
ability at the head of the Finance Committee, his
acceptance would go far toward reëstablishing a
feeling of security.   He said to him, very earnestly,
" Fessenden, *the* LORD *has not deserted me thus far,
and He is not going to now,* — you must accept ! "
They separated, the Senator in great anxiety of
mind.   Throughout the day, Mr. Lincoln urged
almost all who called to go and see Mr. Fessenden,
and press upon him the duty of accepting.   Among
these was a delegation of New York bankers, who,
in the name of the banking community, expressed
their satisfaction at the nomination.   This was
especially gratifying to the President; and, in the
strongest manner, he entreated them to " see Mr.
Fessenden and assure him of their support."

I am tempted, just here, to introduce a circumstance which occurred in the course of the day, in
which the President and myself were the only
actors.   In the solitude of the state dining-room,
I resumed my work, as usual, that morning; but
my mind had been too distracted over night for
success.   Participating in the general solicitude, I
also had been intently revolving the question of a
successor to Mr. Chase.   Unaccustomed to political
currents, and rejecting all considerations of *this*
character in a candidate, my thought fastened upon
Comptroller McCulloch, as the man for the crisis.
His name, at that time, singular as it may seem.

had not been suggested by any one, so far as 1 knew, — certainly no newspaper had advocated his merits or claims. I was at length impelled, by the force of the convictions which engaged my mind, to lay down my palette and brushes, and go up-stairs and state them to the President.

Improving the first opportunity when we were left alone, I said, half playfully, — " Mr. President, would you like the opinion of a painter as to who would make a good Secretary of the Treasury?" He looked at me a moment, and said : " Yes, I think I would. What is your advice ?" Said I, " Nominate Hugh McCulloch." " Why," said he, " what do you know of McCulloch ?" " Mr. President," I rejoined, " you know painters are thought generally to have very little knowledge of financial matters. I admit that this is true, so far as *I* am concerned ; but I do claim to know some-thing of *men*, from the study of character as ex-pressed in *faces*. Now, in my humble judgment, McCulloch is the most suitable man in the com-munity for the position. First ; his ability and in-tegrity are unquestionable. Second ; as Comptroller of the Currency, he is fully acquainted with the past, present, and proposed future policy of Secre-tary Chase, and the entire ' machinery ' of the Department. Third ; he is a practical financier. Having made finance the study of his life, it is obvious he is already educated to the position ; whereas, a man taken from the political arena would have everything to learn, and then even, his judgment would be distrusted." Upon this Mr. Lincoln said, with emphasis, — " I believe McCulloch is a very good man!" I think he repeated this once or twice. My errand accomplished, I returned to my labor, satisfied that the instincts of the President could be safely trusted with this, as with other matters; and that, though he might temporarily err, he would ultimately solve the question satisfactorily.

LVI.

Much has been said and written, since Mr. Lincoln's death, in regard to his religious experience and character. Two or three stories have been published, bearing upon this point, which I have never been able to trace to a reliable source; and I feel impelled to state my belief that the facts in the case — if there were such — have received in some way an unwarranted embellishment. Of all men in the world, the late President was the most unaffected and truthful. He rarely or never used language loosely or carelessly, or for the sake of compliment. He was the most indifferent to the effect he was producing, either upon official representatives or the common people, of any man ever in public position.

In the ordinary acceptation of the term, I would scarcely have called Mr. Lincoln a *religious* man, — and yet I believe him to have been a sincere *Christian*. A constitutional tendency to dwell upon sacred things, an emotional nature which finds ready expression in religious conversation and revival meetings, the culture and development of the devotional element till the expression of such thought and experience becomes habitual, were not among his characteristics. Doubtless he felt as deeply upon the great questions of the soul and eternity as any other thoughtful man ; but the very tenderness and humility of his nature would not permit the exposure of his inmost convictions, except upon the rarest occasions, and to his most intimate friends. And yet, aside from emotional expression, I believe no man had a more abiding sense of his dependence upon God, or faith in the Divine government, and in the power and ultimate triumph of Truth and Right in the world. The Rev. J. P. Thompson, of New York, in an admirable discourse upon the life and character of the departed President, very justly observed: "It is not necessary to appeal to apocryphal stories — which illustrate as much the assurance of his visitors as the simplicity of his faith — for proof of Mr. Lincoln's Christian character." If his daily life and various public addresses and writings do not show this, surely nothing can demonstrate it.

Fortunately there is sufficient material before the public, upon which to form a judgment in this respect, without resorting to apocryphal resources.

The Rev. Mr. Willets, of Brooklyn, gave me
an account of a conversation with Mr. Lincoln, on
the part of a lady of his acquaintance, connected
with the " Christian Commission," who in the prosecution of her duties had several interviews with
him. The President, it seemed, had been much
impressed with the devotion and earnestness of
purpose manifested by the lady, and on one occasion, after she had discharged the object of her
visit, he said to her : " Mrs. ——, I have formed a
high opinion of your Christian character, and now,
as we are alone, I have a mind to ask you to give
me, in brief, your idea of what constitutes a true
religious experience." The lady replied at some
length, stating that, in her judgment, it consisted
of a conviction of one's own sinfulness and weak-
ness, and personal need of the Saviour for strength
and support; that views of mere doctrine might
and would differ, but when one was really brought
to feel his need of Divine help, and to seek the aid
of the Holy Spirit for strength and guidance, it
was satisfactory evidence of his having been born
again. This was the substance of her reply. When
she had concluded, Mr. Lincoln was very thoughtful for a few moments. He at length said, very
earnestly, " If what you have told me is really a
correct view of this great subject, I think I can say
with sincerity, that I hope I am a Christian. I
had lived," he continued, " until my boy Willie
died, without realizing fully these things. That

blow overwhelmed me. It showed me my weak ness as I had never felt it before, and if I can take what you have stated as a *test*, I think I can safely say that I know something of that *change* of which you speak ; and I will further add, that it has been my intention for some time, at a suitable opportunity, to make a public religious profession."

Mr. Noah Brooks, in some " reminiscences," already quoted from in these pages, gives the following upon this subject : —

" Just after the last Presidential election he said, ' Being only mortal, after all, I should have been a little mortified if I had been beaten in this canvass ; but that sting would have been more than compensated by the thought that the people had notified me that all my official responsibilities were soon to be lifted off my back.' In reply to the remark that he might remember that in all these cares he was daily remembered by those who prayed, not to be heard of men, as no man had ever before been remembered, he caught at the homely phrase, and said, ' Yes, I like that phrase, " not to be heard of men," and guess it is generally true, as you say ; at least, I have been told so, and I have been a good deal helped by just that thought.' Then he solemn.y and slowly added : ' I should be the most presumptuous blockhead upon this footstool, if I for one day thought that I could discharge the duties which have come upon me since I came into this place, without the aid and enlighten ment of One who is stronger and wiser than all others.' "

" At another time he said cheerfully, ' I am very sure that if I do not go away from here a wiser man, I shall go away a better man, for having learned here what a very poor sort of a man I am.' Afterwards, referring to what he called a change of heart, he said he did not remember any precise time when he passed through any special change of purpose, or of heart ; but he would say, that his own election to office, and the crisis immediately following, influentially determined him in what he called ' a process of crystallization,' then going on in his mind.   Reticent as he was, and shy of discoursing much of his own mental exercises, these few utterances now have a value with those who knew him, which his dying words would scarcely have possessed."

" On Thursday of a certain week, two ladies, from Tennessee, came before the President, asking the release of their husbands, held as prisoners of war at Johnson's Island.   They were put off until Friday, when they came again, and were again put off until Saturday.   At each of the interviews one of the ladies urged that her husband was a religious man.   On Saturday, when the President ordered the release of the prisoner, he said to this lady, —

You say your husband is a religious man ; tell him, when you meet him, that I say I am not much of a judge of religion, but that in my opinion the religion which sets men to rebel and fight against their government, because, as they think, that government does not sufficiently help *some* men to eat their bread in the sweat of *other* men's faces, is not the sort of religion upon which people can get to heaven.' "

" On an occasion I shall never forget," says the Hon. H. C. Deming, of Connecticut, " the conversation turned upon religious subjects, and Mr. Lincoln made this impressive remark : ' I have never united myself to any church, because I have found difficulty in giving my assent, without mental reservation, to the long, complicated statements of Christian doctrine which characterize their Articles of Belief and Confessions of Faith. When any church will inscribe over its altar, as its sole qualification for membership,' he continued, ' the Saviour's condensed statement of the substance of both Law and Gospel, " Thou shalt love the Lord thy God with all thy heart, and with all thy soul, and with all thy mind, and thy neighbor as thyself," that church will I join with all my heart and all my soul.' "

At a dinner - party in Washington, composed mainly of opponents of the war and the administration, Mr. Lincoln's course and policy was, as usual with this class, the subject of vehement denunciation. This had gone on for some time, when one of the company, who had taken no part in the discussion, asked the privilege of saying a few words.

"Gentlemen," said he, "you may talk as you please about Mr. Lincoln's capacity; I don't believe him to be the ablest statesman in America, by any means, and I voted against him on both occasions of his candidacy. But I happened to see, or, rather, to hear something, the other day, that convinced me that, however deficient he may be in the head, he is all right in the heart. I was up at the White House, having called to see the President on business. I was shown into the office of his private secretary, and told that Mr. Lincoln was busy just then, but would be disengaged in a short time. While waiting, I heard a very earnest prayer being uttered in a loud female voice in the adjoining room. I inquired what it meant, and was told that an old Quaker lady, a friend of the President's, had called that afternoon and taken tea at the White House, and that she was then praying with Mr. Lincoln. After the lapse of a few minutes the prayer ceased, and the President, accompanied by a Quakeress not less than eighty years old, entered the room where I was sitting. I made up my mind then, gentlemen, that Mr. Lincoln was not a bad man; and I don't think it will be easy to efface the impression that the scene I witnessed and the voice I heard made on my mind!"

Nothing has been given to the public since Mr. Lincoln's death, more interesting and valuable than the following, from the pen of Dr. Holland: — *

* Holland's *Life of Abraham Lincoln.*

" At the time of the nominations at Chicago, Mr. Newton Bateman, Superintendent of Public Instruction for the State of Illinois, occupied a room adjoining and opening into the Executive Chamber at Springfield. Frequently this door was open during Mr. Lincoln's receptions, and throughout the seven months or more of his occupation, he saw him nearly every day. Often when Mr. Lincoln was tired, he closed the door against all intruders, and called Mr. Bateman into his room for a quiet talk. On one of these occasions Mr. Lincoln took up a book containing a careful canvass of the city of Springfield in which he lived, showing the candidate for whom each citizen had declared it his intention to vote in the approaching election. Mr. Lincoln's friends had, doubtless at his own request, placed the result of the canvass in his hands. This was towards the close of October, and only a few days before election. Calling Mr. Bateman to a seat by his side, having previously locked all the doors, he said : ' Let us look over this book ; I wish particularly to see how the ministers of Springfield are going to vote.' The leaves were turned, one by one, and as the names were examined Mr. Lincoln frequently asked if this one and that were not a minister, or an elder, or a member of such or such church, and sadly expressed his surprise on receiving an affirmative answer. In that manner they went through the book, and then he closed it and sat silently for some minutes, regarding a memorandum in pencil which lay before him.   At length he turned to Mr. Bateman, with a face full of sadness, and said : ' Here are twenty-three ministers, of different denominations, and all of them are against me but three ; and here are a great many prominent members of the churches, a very large majority are against me.   Mr. Bateman, I am not a Christian, — God knows I would be one, — but I have carefully read the Bible, and I do not so understand this book ; ' and he drew forth a pocket New Testament.   ' These men well know,' he continued, ' that I am for freedom in the Territories, freedom everywhere as free as the Constitution and the laws will permit, and that my opponents are for slavery.   They *know* this, and yet, with this book in their hands, in the light of which human bondage cannot live a moment, they are going to vote against me ; I do not understand it at all.'

" Here Mr. Lincoln paused, — paused for long minutes, — his features surcharged with emotion. Then he rose and walked up and down the reception-room in the effort to retain or regain his self-possession.   Stopping at last, he said, with a trembling voice and his cheeks wet with tears : ' I know there is a God, and that He hates injustice and slavery.   I see the storm coming, and I know that his hand is in it.   If He has a place and work for me — and I think He has — I believe I am ready. I am nothing, but Truth is everything.   I know I am right, because I know that liberty is right, for

13

Christ teaches it, and Christ is God. I have told them that a house divided against itself cannot stand; and Christ and Reason say the same; and they will find it so.'

" ' Douglas don't care whether slavery is voted up or down, but God cares, and humanity cares, and I care; and with God's help I shall not fail. I may not see the end; but it will come, and I shall be vindicated; and these men will find that they have not read their Bibles right.'

" Much of this was uttered as if he was speaking to himself, and with a sad, earnest solemnity of manner impossible to be described. After a pause, he resumed: ' Does n't it appear strange that men can ignore the moral aspect of this contest ? A revelation could not make it plainer to me that slavery or the Government must be destroyed. The future would be something awful, as I look at it, but for this rock on which I stand,' (alluding to the Testament which he still held in his hand,) ' especially with the knowledge of how these ministers are going to vote. It seems as if God had borne with this thing [slavery] until the very teachers of religion had come to defend it from the Bible, and to claim for it a divine character and sanction ; and now the cup of iniquity is full, and the vials of wrath will be poured out.' After this the conversation was continued for a long time. Everything he said was of a peculiarly deep, tender, and religious tone, and all was tinged with a touching melancholy. He repeatedly referred to his conviction that the day of wrath was at hand, and that he was to be an actor in the terrible struggle which would issue in the overthrow of slavery, though he might not live to see the end.

" After further reference to a belief in Divine Providence, and the fact of God in history, the conversation turned upon prayer. He freely stated his belief in the duty, privilege, and efficacy of prayer, and intimated, in no unmistakable terms, that he had sought in that way the Divine guidance and favor. The effect of this conversation upon the mind of Mr. Bateman, a Christian gentleman whom Mr. Lincoln profoundly respected, was to convince him that Mr. Lincoln had, in his quiet way, found a path to the Christian standpoint — that he had found God, and rested on the eternal truth of God. As the two men were about to separate, Mr. Bateman remarked : ' I have not supposed that you were accustomed to think so much upon this class of subjects ; certainly your friends generally are igno-rant of the sentiments you have expressed to me.' He replied quickly : ' I know they are, but I think more on these subjects than upon all others, and I have done so for years ; and I am willing you should know it.' "

Schuyler Colfax once said to me that " Mr. Lincoln had two ruling ideas, or principles, which governed his life. The first was hatred of slavery, which he inherited in part from his parents ; the

other was sympathy with the lowly born and hum‑
ble, and the desire to lift them up." I know of no
better epitaph for his tombstone than this, save
that suggested by Theodore Tilton, the editor of
the New York " Independent," — " He bound the
nation, and unbound the slave."

LVII.

On the Fourth of July an unprecedented event
was witnessed in Washington. By special consent
of the President, the White House grounds were
granted to the colored people of the city for a grand
Sunday-school festival, and never did they present
a busier or more jubilant scene. Inside the grounds
a platform was erected, upon which accommoda-
tions were placed for speakers. Around this were
rows of benches, which, during the greater part
of the day, were not only well filled but crowded.
Meanwhile groups reposed under every tree or
walked to and fro along the shaded paths. From
the thick-leaved branches of the trees were sus-
pended swings, of which all, both old and young,
made abundant use. Every contrivance which could
add to the pleasure of the time was brought into
energetic requisition, and altogether no celebration
of the day presented a greater appearance of enjoyment and success.

By the Act of Emancipation, Mr. Lincoln built
for himself the first place in the affections of the

African race on this continent. The love and reverence manifested for his name and person on all occasions during the last two years of his life, by this down-trodden people, were always remarkable, and sometimes of a thrilling character. In the language of one of the poor creatures who stood weeping and moaning at the gateway of the avenue in front of the White House, while the beloved remains were lying in state in the East Room, " *they* had him."

No public testimonial of regard, it is safe to say, gave Mr. Lincoln more sincere pleasure during his entire public life, than that presented by the colored people of the city of Baltimore, in the summer of 1864, consisting of an elegant copy of the Holy Bible. The volume was of the usual pulpit size, bound in violet-colored velvet. The corners were bands of solid gold, and carved upon a plate also of gold, not less than one fourth of an inch thick. Upon the left-hand cover, was a design representing the President in a cotton-field knocking the shackles off the wrists of a slave, who held one hand aloft as if invoking blessings upon the head of his benefactor, — at whose feet was a scroll upon which was written " Emancipation " ; upon the other cover was a similar plate bearing the inscription : —

"To ABRAHAM LINCOLN, President of the United States, the friend of Universal Freedom. From the loyal colored people of Baltimore, as a token of respect and gratitude. Baltimore, July 4th, 1864."

The presentation was made by a committee of colored people, consisting of three clergymen and two laymen, who were received by the President in the most cordial manner, after which the Rev. S. W. Chase, on the part of the committee, said: —

"MR. PRESIDENT: The loyal colored people of Baltimore have delegated to us the authority to present this Bible, as a token of their appreciation of your humane part towards the people of our race. While all the nation are offering their tributes of respect, we cannot let the occasion pass by without tendering ours. Since we have been incorporated in the American family we have been true and loyal, and we now stand by, ready to defend the country. We are ready to be armed and trained in military matters, in order to protect and defend the Star-spangled Banner.

" Our hearts will ever feel the most unbounded gratitude towards you. We come forward to present a copy of the Holy Scriptures as a token of respect to you for your active part in the cause of emancipation. This great event will be a matter of history. In future, when our sons shall ask what mean these tokens, they will be told of your mighty acts, and rise up and call you blessed.

" The loyal colored people will remember your Excellency at the throne of Divine Grace. May the King Eternal, an all-wise Providence, protect and keep you, and when you pass from this world, may you be borne to the bosom of your Saviour and God."

The President, in reply, said: —

" It would be a very fitting occasion to make a response at length to the very appropriate address which you have just made. I would do so if I were prepared. I would promise you to make a response in writing, had not experience taught me that business will not allow me to do so. I can only say now, as I have often said before, it has always been a sentiment with me that all mankind should be free.

"So far as I have been able, so far as came within my sphere, I have always acted as I believed was right and just, and done all I could for the good of mankind. I have, in letters and documents sent forth from this office, expressed myself better than I can now. In regard to the great book, I have only to say, it is the best gift which God has ever given man.

"All the good from the Saviour of the World is communicated to us through this book. But for that book we could not know right from wrong. All those things desirable to man are contained in it. I return you my sincere thanks for this very elegant copy of the great book of God which you present."

After some time spent in the examination of the gift, which drew out many expressions of admiration from the President, the party withdrew, Mr. Lincoln taking each of them by the hand as they passed out.

Caroline Johnson, an estimable colored woman of Philadelphia, an active nurse in the hospitals during the war, who had once been a slave, as an expression of reverence and affection for President Lincoln, prepared, with much taste and ingenuity, a superb collection of wax fruits, together with a stem-table, appropriately ornamented, which

she desired to present to the President. Through a
friend an opportunity was secured, and she went to
Washington, with her minister, to attend personally
to the setting up of the stand and fruit.

The result is given by a correspondent of the
" Anti-Slavery Standard," in her own words : —

" The Commissioner, Mr. Newton, received us
kindly, and sent the box to the White House, with
directions that it should not be opened until I came.
The next day was reception day, but the President
sent me word that he would receive me at one
o'clock. I went and arranged the table, placing it
in the centre of the room. Then I was introduced
to the President and his wife. He stood next to
me ; then Mrs. Lincoln, Mr. Newton, and the minister; the others outside. Mr. Hamilton (the minister) made an appropriate speech, and at the conclusion said: ' Perhaps Mrs. Johnson would like to
say a few words ? ' I looked down to the floor, and
felt that I had not a word to say, but after a moment or two, the fire began to burn, (laying her
hand on her breast,) and it burned and burned till
it went all over me. I think it was the Spirit,
and I looked up to him and said : ' Mr. President, I
believe God has hewn you out of a rock, for this
great and mighty purpose. Many have been led
away by bribes of gold, of silver, of presents ; but
you have stood firm, because God was with you,
and if you are faithful to the end, he will be with
you.' With his eyes full of tears, he walked round

and examined the present, pronounced it beautiful, thanked me kindly, but said: 'You must not give me the praise — it belongs to God.' "

LVIII.

" Sojourner Truth," the slave preacher whom Mrs. Stowe has described as embodying all the elements of an African prophetess or sibyl, when over eighty years old, left her home, at Battlecreek, Michigan, with the unalterable purpose of seeing the Emancipator of her race before her death. Provided for throughout her journey, she reached Washington the last of October, 1864, and subsequently, at her dictation, the following account of her interview with Mr. Lincoln was written out by a friend : —

" It was about eight o'clock, A. M., when I called on the President. Upon entering his reception-room we found about a dozen persons in waiting, among them two colored women. I had quite a pleasant time waiting until he was disengaged, and enjoyed his conversation with others ; he showed as much kindness and consideration to the colored persons as to the whites, — if there was any difference, more. One case was that of a colored woman, who was sick and likely to be turned out of her house on account of her inability to pay her rent. The President listened to her with much attention, and spoke to her with kindness and tenderness. He said he had

given so much he could give no more, but told her
where to go and get the money, and asked Mrs.
C——, who accompanied me, to assist her, which
she did.

" The President was seated at his desk. Mrs. C.
said to him: ' This is Sojourner Truth, who has
come all the way from Michigan to see you.' He
then arose, gave me his hand, made a bow, and
said: ' I am pleased to see you.'

" I said to him : ' Mr. President, when you first
took your seat I feared you would be torn to pieces,
for I likened you unto Daniel, who was thrown into
the lions' den ; and if the lions did not tear you into
pieces, I knew that it would be God that had saved
you; and I said if He spared me I would see you
before the four years expired, and He has done so,
and now I am here to see you for myself.'

" He then congratulated me on my having been
spared. Then I said: ' I appreciate you, for you
are the best President who has ever taken the seat.'
He replied thus : ' I expect you have reference to
my having emancipated the slaves in my proclamation. But,' said he, mentioning the names of several of his predecessors, (and among them emphatically that of Washington,) ' they were all just as
good, and would have done just as I have done if
the time had come. If the people over the river
(pointing across the Potomac) had behaved themselves, I could not have done what I have ; but they
did not, and I was compelled to do these things.' I

then said : ' I thank God that you were the **instru-**ment selected by Him and the people to do it.'

" He then showed me the Bible presented to him by the colored people of Baltimore, of which you have heard. I have seen it for myself, and it is beautful beyond description. After I had looked it over, I said to him : ' This is beautiful indeed ; the colored people have given this to the Head of the Government, and that Government once sanctioned laws that would not permit its people to learn enough to enable them to read this Book. And for what ? Let them answer who can.'

" I must say, and I am proud to say, that I never was treated by any one with more kindness and cordiality than was shown me by that great and good man, Abraham Lincoln, by the grace of God President of the United States for four years more. He took my little book, and with the same hand that signed the death-warrant of slavery, he wrote as follows : —

' For Aunty Sojourner Truth,
'Oct. 29, 1864.   A. LINCOLN.'

" As I was taking my leave, he arose and took my hand, and said he would be pleased to have me call again. I felt that I was in the presence of a friend, and I now thank God from the bottom of my heart that I always have advocated his cause, and have done it openly and boldly. I shall feel still more in duty bound to do so in time to come. May God assist me."

Mr. Lincoln's cordial reception of Frederick Douglass, the distinguished anti-slavery orator, also once a slave, was widely made known through that gentleman's own account of it in one his public lectures.

In August or September, 1864, Mr. Douglass again visited Washington. The President heard of his being in the city, and greatly desiring a second conversation upon points on which he considered the opinion and advice of a man of Mr. Douglass's antecedents valuable, he sent his carriage to the boarding-house where he was staying, with a request that Mr. D. would " come up and take a cup of tea " with him. The invitation was accepted ; and probably never before, in our history, was the executive carriage employed to convey *such* a guest to the White House. Mr. Douglass subsequently remarked that " Mr. Lincoln was one of the few white men he ever passed an hour with, who failed to remind him in some way, before the interview terminated, that he was a ' negro.' "

A memorial, on a certain occasion, was presented to the President from the children and young people of Concord, Mass., petitioning for the freedom of all slave children. In reply, he wrote the following : —

" Tell those little people I am very glad their young hearts are so full of just and generous sympathy, and that while I have not the power to grant

all they ask, I trust they will remember that GOD
has ; and that as it seems He *wills* to do it.

A. LINCOLN. '

LIX.

" On New Year's day, 1865," wrote a correspondent of the New York " Independent," " a
memorable incident occurred, of which the like
was never before seen at the White House. I had
noticed, at sundry times during the summer, the
wild fervor and strange enthusiasm which our colored friends always manifest over the name of
Abraham Lincoln. His name with them seems
to be associated with that of his namesake, the Father
of the Faithful. In the great crowds which gather
from time to time in front of the White House, in
honor of the President, none shout so loudly or so
wildly, and swing their hats with such utter *abandon*, while their eyes are beaming with the intensest
joy, as do these simple-minded and grateful people.
I have often laughed heartily at these exhibitions.
But the scene yesterday excited far other emotions.
As I entered the door of the President's House, I
noticed groups of colored people gathered here and
there, who seemed to be watching earnestly the in-
pouring throng.   For nearly two hours they hung
around, until the crowd of white visitors began sen-
sibly to diminish.   Then they summoned up courage, and began timidly to approach the door. Some

of them were richly and gayly dressed; some were in tattered garments, and others in the most fanciful and grotesque costume. All pressed eagerly forward. When they came into the presence of the President, doubting as to their reception, the feelings of the poor creatures overcame them, and here the scene baffles my powers of description.

"For two long hours Mr. Lincoln had been shaking the hands of the 'sovereigns,' and had become excessively weary, and his grasp languid; but here his nerves rallied at the unwonted sight, and he welcomed this motley crowd with a heartiness that made them wild with exceeding joy. They laughed and wept, and wept and laughed, — exclaiming, through their blinding tears: 'God bless you!' 'God bless Abraham Lincoln!' 'God bress Massa Linkum!' Those who witnessed this scene will not soon forget it. For a long distance down the Avenue, on my way home, I heard fast young men cursing the President for this act; but all the way the refrain rang in my ears, — 'God bless Abraham Lincoln!'"

Miss Betsey Canedy, of Fall River, Massachusetts, while engaged in teaching a school among the colored people of Norfolk, Virginia, had in her school-room a plaster bust of the President. One day she called some colored carpenters who were at work on the building, and showed it to them, writing down their remarks, some of which were as follows: —

" He's brought us safe through the Red Sea.'
" He looks as deep as the sea himself." " He's king of the United States." " He ought to be king of all the world." " We must all pray to the Lord to carry him safe through, for it 'pears like he's got everything hitched to him." " There has been a right smart praying for him, and it must n't stop now."

A southern correspondent of the New York " Tribune," in Charleston, South Carolina, the week following the assassination, wrote : —

" I never saw such sad faces, or heard such heavy hearts beatings, as here in Charleston the day the dreadful news came ! The colored people — the native loyalists — were like children bereaved of an only and loved parent. I saw one old woman going up the street wringing her hands and saying aloud, as she walked looking straight before her, so absorbed in her grief that she noticed no one, —

" ' O Lord ! O Lord ! O Lord ! Massa Sam's dead ! Massa Sam's dead ! O Lord ! Massa Sam's dead ! '

" ' Who's dead, Aunty ? ' I asked her.

" ' Massa Sam ! ' she said, not looking at me, — renewing her lamentations : ' O Lord ! O Lord ! Lord ! Massa Sam's dead ! '

" ' Who's Massa Sam ? ' I asked.

" ' Uncle Sam ! ' she said. ' O Lord ! Lord ! '

" I was not quite sure that she meant the President, and I spoke again : —

" ' Who's Massa Sam, Aunty?'

" ' Mr. Lincum!' she said, and resumed wringing her hands and moaning in utter hopelessness of sorrow. The poor creature was too ignorant to comprehend any difference between the very unreal Uncle Sam and the actual President; but her heart told her that he whom Heaven had sent in answer to her prayers was lying in a bloody grave, and she and her race were left — *fatherless*."

In 1863, Colonel McKaye, of New York, with Robert Dale Owen and one or two other gentlemen, were associated as a committee to investigate the condition of the freedmen on the coast of North Carolina. Upon their return from Hilton Head they reported to the President; and in the course of the interview Colonel McKaye related the following incident.

He had been speaking of the ideas of power entertained by these people. He said they had an idea of God, as the Almighty, and they had realized in their former condition the power of their masters. Up to the time of the arrival among them of the Union forces, they had no knowledge of any other power. Their masters fled upon the approach of our soldiers, and this gave the slaves a conception of a power greater than that exercised by them. This power they called " Massa Linkum."

Colonel McKaye said that their place of worship was a large building which they called " the praise nouse ; " and the leader of the meeting, a venerable black man, was known as " the praise man." On a certain day, when there was quite a large gathering of the people, considerable confusion was created by different persons attempting to tell who and what " Massa Linkum " was.   In the midst of the excitement the white-headed leader commanded silence.   " Brederin," said he, " you don't know nosen' what you'se talkin' 'bout.   Now, you just listen to me.   Massa Linkum, he eberywhar.   He know eberyting."   Then, solemnly looking up, he added, — "*He walk de earf like de Lord!* "

Colonel McKaye told me that Mr. Lincoln seemed much affected by this account.   He did not smile, as another man might have done, but got up from his chair, and walked in silence two or three times across the floor.   As he resumed his seat, he said, very impressively : " It is a momentous thing to be the instrument, under Providence, of the liberation of a race."

LX.

The famous " peace " conference, on board the *River Queen*, in Hampton Roads, between President Lincoln and Secretary Seward, and the Rebel commissioners Stephens, Hunter, and Campbell, took place the 3d of February, 1865.   A few days afterward * I asked the President if it was true,

* My " six months " proper, at the White House, terminated, as will be seen, the last week in July, 1864.   February and a part of March

14

as reported by the New York "Herald," that he told a "little story" on that occasion? — "Why," said he, "has it leaked out? I was in hopes nothing would be said about *that*, lest some over-sensitive people should imagine there was a degree of levity in the intercourse between us." He then went on to relate the circumstances which called it out. "You see," said he, "we had reached and were discussing the *slavery* question. Mr. Hunter said, substantially, that the slaves, always accustomed to an overseer, and to work upon compulsion, suddenly freed, as they would be if the South should consent to peace on the basis of the 'Emancipation Proclamation,' would precipitate not only themselves but the entire Southern society into irremediable ruin. No work would be done, nothing would be cultivated, and both blacks and whites would *starve!*" Said the President, "I waited for Seward to answer that argument, but as he was silent, I at length said: 'Mr. Hunter, *you* ought to know a great deal better about this matter than *I*, for you have always lived under the slave system. I can only say, in reply to your statement of the case, that it reminds me of a man out in Illinois, by the name of Case, who undertook, a few years ago, to raise a very large herd of hogs. It was a great trouble to *feed* them, and how to get around this was a puzzle to him. At length he hit on the plan

bllowing I passed in Washington, and was privileged with a renewal of my previous intercourse with Mr. Lincoln.

of planting an immense field of potatoes, and, when they were sufficiently grown, he turned the whole herd into the field, and let them have full swing, thus saving not only the labor of feeding the hogs, but also that of digging the potatoes. Charmed with his sagacity, he stood one day leaning against the fence, counting his hogs, when a neighbor came along. ' Well, well,' said he, ' Mr. Case, this is all very fine. Your hogs are doing very well just now, but you know out here in Illinois the frost comes early, and the ground freezes a foot deep. Then what are they going to do ? ' This was a view of the matter Mr. Case had not taken into account. Butchering-time for hogs was 'way on in December or January. He scratched his head, and at length stammered, ' Well, it may come pretty hard on their *snouts*, but I don't see but that it will be " root, hog, or die ! " ' "

" Shortly afterward," he continued, " a reference was casually made to Colonel Hardin, who was killed in the Mexican War, — who at one time was a representative in Congress from Illinois ; and this drew out a story from Stephens. ' On a certain occasion,' he said, ' when the House was in session, a dispute arose between Hardin and others of the Illinois delegation as to the proper pronunciation of the name of their State. Some insisted it was ' *Illinoy*," others as stoutly that it was " *Illinois*." Hardin at length appealed to the venerable John Quincy Adams. " If one were to judge from the character of the representatives in this Congress from that State," said the o_d man, with a malicious smile, " I should decide unhesitatingly that the proper pronunciation was ' *All noise!* ' " ' "

In the Augusta (Ga.) " Chronicle," of the 17th of June, 1865, there appeared a report of this conference, purporting to have been written out from the lips of Mr. Stephens, so characteristic of Mr. Lincoln, that I subjoin the following extracts : —

" The three Southern gentlemen met Mr. Lincoln and Mr. Seward, and after some preliminary remarks, the subject of peace was opened.   Mr. Stephens, well aware that one who asks much may get more than he who confesses to humble wishes at the outset, urged the claims of his section with that skill and address for which the Northern papers have given him credit.   Mr. Lincoln, holding the vantage-ground of conscious power, was, however, perfectly frank, and submitted his views almost in the form of an argument.

. . . . . " Davis had on this occasion, as on that of Mr. Stephens's visit to Washington, made it a condition that no conference should be had unless his rank as commander or President should first be recognized.   Mr. Lincoln declared that the only ground on which he could rest the justice of the war — either with his own people or with foreign powers — was that it was not a war for conquest, °or that the States had never been separated from the Union.   Consequently, he could not recognize another government inside of the one of which he alone was President, nor admit the separate independence of States that were yet a part of the Union. 'That,' said he, 'would be doing what you have so long asked Europe to do in vain, and be resigning the only thing the armies of the Union are fighting for.'

"Mr. Hunter made a long reply to this, insisting that the recognition of Davis's power to make a treaty was the first and indispensable step to peace, and referred to the correspondence between King Charles I. and his Parliament, as a trustworthy precedent of a constitutional ruler treating with rebels.

"Mr. Lincoln's face then wore that indescribable expression which generally preceded his hardest hits, and he remarked: 'Upon questions of history I must refer you to Mr. Seward, for he is posted in such things, and I don't pretend to be bright. My only distinct recollection of the matter is, that Charles lost his head.' That settled Mr. Hunter for a while."

.   .   .   .

"During the interview it appears that Hunter declared that he had never entertained any fears for his person or life from so mild a government as that of the United States. To which Mr. Lincoln retorted that he, also, had felt easy as to the Rebels, but not always so easy about the lamp-posts around Washington City, — a hint that he had already done more favors for the Rebels than was exactly popular with the radical men of his own party.

" Mr. Lincoln's manner had now grown more positive. He suggested that it would be better for the Rebel States to return at once than to risk the chances of continuing the war, and the increasing bitterness of feeling in Congress. The time might come, he said, when they would not be considered as an erring people invited back to citizenship, but would be looked upon as enemies to be exterminated or ruined.

" During the conference, the amendment to the Federal Constitution, which has just been adopted by Congress, was read, providing that neither slavery nor involuntary servitude, except for crime, should exist within the United States, or any place within its jurisdiction, and Congress should have power to enforce the amendment by appropriate legislation." The report says, " Mr. Seward then remarked : Mr President, it is as well to inform these gentlemen that yesterday Congress acted upon the amendment of the Constitution abolishing slavery."

" Mr. Lincoln stated this to be true, and suggested that there was a question as to the right of the in-surgent States to return at once and claim a right to vote upon the amendment, to which the concur-rence of two thirds of the States was required. He stated that it would be desirable to have the insti-tution of slavery abolished by the consent of the people as soon as possible, — he hoped within six

years. He also stated that four hundred millions
of dollars might be offered as compensation to the
owners, and remarked, ' You would be surprised
were I to give you the names of those who favor
that.' "

   . . . .

" Mr. Stephens came home with a new cause of
sorrow, and those who said he talked of coming
home to make war speeches and denounce the terms
offered, simply lied. Before Mr. Lincoln's death,
he thought he was doing a favor to him not to include that offer of four hundred millions in gold for
the Southern slaves in the published report, for it
would be used to the injury of Mr. Lincoln by those
of his enemies who talk about taxation and the
debt.

" Mr. Stephens has frequently expressed no apprehensions should the fortunes of war throw him
into the hands of Mr. Lincoln, and said he would
not get out of the way of a raid were it not for
appearances, on account of the office he held. He
spoke of Mr. Lincoln as an old friend who had
generally voted with him in Congress, and who had
a good heart and fine mind, and was undoubtedly
honest."

LXI.

Visitors to the Executive Chamber, during the
administration of Mr. Lincoln, will remember the
lithographic map, showing the slave population of

the Southern States in graduated light and shade, which usually leaned against a leg of his desk or table, and bore the marks of much service. The States and counties most abounding in slaves were indicated on this map by degrees of blackness, so that by a glance the proportion of whites and blacks in the different States at the commencement of the Rebellion could be easily comprehended.

Wishing to introduce this map into my picture, I carried it off one day, without the President's knowledge, and as the copying of it was a tedious affair, it remained in the studio for some time. This chanced to be during the week of Kilpatrick's great cavalry raid in Virginia. One afternoon the President came in alone, as was his wont, — the observation of the daily progress of the picture appearing to afford him a species of recreation. Presently his eye fell upon the map, leaning against a chair, as I had left it after making the study. "Ah!" said he, "*you* have appropriated my map, have you? I have been looking all around for it." And with that he put on his spectacles, and, taking it up, walked to the window; and sitting down upon a trunk began to pore over it very earnestly. He pointed out Kilpatrick's position, when last heard from, and said : —

"It is just as I thought it was. He is close upon —— County, where the slaves are thickest. Now we ought to get a 'heap' of them, when he returns."

This conversation occurred, I recollect, just after his solitary lunch, — the family being away at the time. It was often a matter of surprise to me how the President sustained life; for it seemed, some weeks, as though he neither ate nor slept. His habits continued as simple as when he was a practising lawyer in Springfield, but they came to be very irregular. During the months of my intercourse with him he rarely entertained company at dinner. Almost daily, at this hour, I met a servant carrying a simple meal upon a tray up-stairs, where it was received, perhaps two hours later, in the most unceremonious manner. I knew this irregularity of life was his own fault; but the wonder as to how his system endured the strain brought to bear upon it was not lessened by this knowledge.

All familiar with him will remember the weary air which became habitual during his last years. This was more of the mind than the body, and no rest and recreation which he allowed himself could relieve it. As he sometimes expressed it, the remedy " seemed never to reach the *tired* spot."

Mr. Lincoln's height was six feet three and three-quarter inches " in his stocking-feet." He stood up, one day, at the right of my large canvas, while I marked his exact height upon it.

His frame was gaunt but sinewy, and inclined to stoop when he walked. His head was of full medium size, with a broad brow, surmounted by rough, unmanageable hair, which, he once said, had " a

way of getting up as far as possible in the world."
Lines of care ploughed his face, — the hollows in
his cheeks and under his eyes being very marked.
The mouth was his plainest feature, varying widely
from classical models, — nevertheless expressive of
much firmness and gentleness of character.

His complexion was inclined to sallowness, though
I judged this to be the result, in part, of his anxious
life in Washington.   His eyes were blueish-gray in
color, — always in deep shadow, however, from the
upper lids, which were unusually heavy, (remind-
ing me, in this respect, of Stuart's portrait of Washington,) — and the expression was remarkably pen-
sive and tender, often inexpressibly sad, as if the
reservoir of tears lay very near the surface, — a
fact proved not only by the response which accounts
of suffering and sorrow invariably drew forth, but
by circumstances which would ordinarily affect few
men in his position.

The Hon. Mr. Frank, of New York, told me
that just after the nomination of Mr. Chase as
Chief Justice, a deeply interesting conversation
upon this subject took place one evening between
himself and the President, in Mrs. Lincoln's private
sitting-room.   Mr. Lincoln reviewed Mr. Chase's
political course and aspirations at some length, alluding to what he had felt to be an estrangement
from him personally, and to various sarcastic and
bitter expressions reported to him as having been
indulged in by the ex-Secretary, both before and

after his resignation.   The Congressman replied
that such reports were always exaggerated, and
spoke very warmly of Mr. Chase's great services in
the hour of the country's extremity, his patriotism,
and integrity to principle.   The tears instantly
sprang into Mr. Lincoln's eyes.   " Yes," said he,
" that is true.   We have stood together in the time
of trial, and I should despise myself if I allowed
personal differences to affect my judgment of his
fitness for the office of Chief Justice."

LXII.

The President's friend, the Hon. H. C. Deming
of Connecticut, once ventured to ask him " if he
had ever despaired of the country?"   "When the
Peninsula campaign terminated suddenly at Harrison's Landing," rejoined Mr. Lincoln, " I was
as nearly inconsolable as I could be and live."   In
the same connection Colonel Deming inquired if
there had ever been a period in which he thought
that better management upon the part of the
commanding general might have terminated the
war?   " Yes," answered the President, " there were
three: at ' Malvern Hill,' when McClellan failed to
command an immediate advance upon Richmond;
at ' Chancellorville,' when Hooker failed to reën-
force Sedgwick, after hearing his cannon upon the
extreme right; and at ' Gettysburg,' when Meade
failed to attack Lee in his retreat at the bend of the

Potomac." After this commentary, the Congress·
man waited for an outburst of denunciation — for a
criticism, at least — upon the delinquent officers ; but
he waited in vain. So far from a word of censure
escaping Mr. Lincoln's lips, he soon added, that his
first remark might not appear uncharitable : " I do
not know that I could have given any different
orders had I been with them myself. I have not
fully made up my mind how I should behave when
minie-balls were whistling, and those great oblong
shells shrieking in my ear. I might run away."

The interview at which this conversation took
place, occurred just after General Fremont had declined to run against him for the presidency. The
magnificent Bible which the negroes of Baltimore
had just presented to him lay upon the table, and
while examining it, Colonel Deming recited the
somewhat remarkable passage from the Chronicles :
" Eastward were six Levites, northward four a day,
southward four a day, and toward Assuppim, two
and two. At Parbar westward, four at the cause-
way, and two at Parbar." The President immediately challenged his friend to find any such pas·
sage in *his* Bible. After it was pointed out to him,
and he was satisfied of its genuineness, he asked the
Congressman if he remembered the text which his
friends had recently applied to Fremont, and in·
stantly turned to a verse in the first of Samuel, put
on his spectacles, and read in his slow, peculiar, and
waggish tone : " And every one that was in distress,

and every one that was in debt, and every one that was discontented, gathered themselves unto him, and he became a captain over them, and there were with him about four hundred men."

LXIII.

The letter of General Fremont withdrawing from the presidential canvass of 1864, after having accepted the nomination of the Cleveland Convention, was an unfortunate one for his political reputation, whatever may have been thought of the military career of that once popular leader. Without attempting any discussion of the merits of the controversy between him and the Government, I think it cannot be denied that Mr. Lincoln ever bore toward General Fremont the sincerest good will, though for reasons perhaps not yet fairly estimated, as a commander he had failed to realize the public expectation.

Some months subsequent to Fremont's removal from the Western Department, one of his personal friends, Mr. Henry C. Bowen, of Brooklyn, happened to be in Washington. Passing the Executive Chamber, on his way to the private secretary's office one day, he observed the door ajar, and the President standing near it, in the act of taking down a book from the bookcase. Catching a glimpse of him, Mr. Lincoln said, " Come in ; you are the very man I want to see." Mr. Bowen entered the office, and the President, laying aside other business, said: "I have been thinking a great deal lately about Fremont; and I want to ask you, as an old friend of his, what is thought about his continuing inactive?" "Mr. President," returned Mr. Bowen, "I will say to you frankly, that a large class of people feel that General Fremont has been badly treated, and nothing would give more satisfaction, both to him and to his friends, than his re-appointment to a command commensurate, in some degree, with his rank and ability." "Do you think he would accept an inferior position to that he occupied in Missouri?" asked the President. "I have that confidence in General Fremont's patriotism, that I venture to promise for him in advance," was the earnest reply. "Well," rejoined Mr. Lincoln, thoughtfully, "I have had it on my mind for some time that Fremont should be given a chance to redeem himself. The great hue and cry about him has been concerning his expenditure of the public money. I have looked into the matter a little, and I can't see as he has done any worse or any more, in that line, than our *Eastern* commanders. At any rate, he shall have another trial!" The result, close upon this interview, was the appointment of Fremont to the "Mountain Department of Western Virginia."

While Mr. Bowen was in Washington, he drove out, by invitation one evening, with one or two friends, to the Soldier's Home, where the Presi-

áent spent the nights of midsummer. More at leisure there than at the "shop," as he was in the habit
of calling his official chamber at the White House,
Mr. Lincoln sat down with the party for a leisurely
conversation. "I know," he said to Mr. Bowen,
"that you are a great admirer of Mr. Chase and
Mr. Seward. Now, I will tell you a circumstance
that may please you. Before sunset of election-day,
in 1860, I was pretty sure, from the despatches I
received, that I was elected. The very first thing
that I settled in my mind, after reaching this conclusion, was that these two great leaders of the
party should occupy the two first places in my
cabinet."

LXIV.

"The Soldier's Home," writes a California
lady,* who visited Mr. Lincoln there, "is a few miles
out of Washington on the Maryland side. It is situa-
ted on a beautifully wooded hill, which you ascend by
a winding path, shaded on both sides by wide-spread
branches, forming a green arcade above you. When
you reach the top you stand between two mansions,
large, handsome, and substantial, but with nothing
about them indicative of the character of either.
That on your left is the Presidential country-house;
that directly before you, the ' Rest ' for soldiers who
are too old for further service. . . . . The
' Home' only admitted soldiers of the regular army ;
but in the graveyard near at hand there are num-

* *San Francisco Bulletin.*

perless graves — some without a spear of grass to hide their newness — that hold the bodies of volunteers.

"While we stood in the soft evening air, watching the faint trembling of the long tendrils of waving willow, and feeling the dewy coolness that was flung out by the old oaks above us, Mr. Lincoln joined us, and stood silent, too, taking in the scene.

> " ' How sleep the brave, who sink to rest
> By all their country's wishes blest,' —

he said, softly.

"There was something so touching in the picture opened before us, — the nameless graves, the solemn quiet, the tender twilight air, but more particularly our own feminine disposition to be easily melted, I suppose, — that it made us cry as if we stood beside the tomb of our own dead, and gave point to the lines which he afterwards quoted : —

> " ' And women o'er the graves shall weep,
> Where nameless heroes calmly sleep.' "

. . . .

"Around the 'Home' grows every variety of tree, particularly of the evergreen class. Their branches brushed into the carriage as we passed along, and left with us that pleasant, woody smell belonging to leaves. One of the ladies, catching a bit of green from one of these intruding branches, said it was cedar, and another thought it spruce.

" ' Let me discourse on a theme I understand,' said the President. ' I know all about trees in

right of being a backwoodsman. I 'll show you
the difference between spruce, pine, and cedar, and
this shred of green, which is neither one nor the
other, but a kind of illegitimate cypress.' He then
proceeded to gather specimens of each, and explain the distinctive formation of foliage belonging
to every species. ' Trees,' he said, ' are as decep-
tive in their likeness to one another as are certain
classes of men, amongst whom none but a physiog-
nomist's eye can detect dissimilar moral features
until events have developed them. Do you know
it would be a good thing if in all the schools proposed and carried out by the improvement of modern thinkers, we could have a school of events ? '

" ' A school of events ? ' repeated the lady he
addressed.

" ' Yes,' he continued, ' since it is only by that
active development that character and ability can
be tested. Understand me, I now mean men, not
trees ; *they* can be tried, and an analysis of their
strength obtained less expensive to life and human
interests than man's. What I say now is a mere
whimsey, you know ; but when I speak of a school
of events, I mean one in which, before entering
real life, students might pass through the mimic
vicissitudes and situations that are necessary to
bring out their powers and mark the calibre to
which they are assigned. Thus, one could select
from the graduates an invincible soldier, equal to
any position, with no such word as fail ; a martyr

15

to Right, ready to give up life in the cause ; a politician too cunning to be outwitted ; and so on. These things have all to be tried, and their some-time failure creates confusion as well as disappoint-ment.   There is no more dangerous or expensive analysis than that which consists of trying a man.'

" ' Do you think all men are tried ? ' was asked.

" ' Scarcely,' said Mr. Lincoln, ' or so many would not fit their place so badly.   Your friend, Mr. Beecher, being an eloquent man, explains this well in his quaint illustration of people out of their sphere, — the clerical faces he has met with in gay, rollicking life, and the natural wits and good brains that have by a freak dropped into ascetic robes.'

" ' Some men seem able to do what they wish in any position, being equal to them all,' said some one.

" ' Versatility,' replied the President, ' is an inju-rious possession, since it never can be greatness.   It misleads you in your calculations from its very agree-ability, and it inevitably disappoints you in any great trust from its want of depth.   A versatile man, to be safe from execration, should never soar ; medioc-rity is sure of detection.'

" On our return to the city we had reached that street — I forget its name — crossing which you find yourself out of Maryland and in the District of Columbia.   Wondering at this visible boundary that made certain laws and regulations apply to one side of a street that did not reach the other, I lost the conversation, till I found it consisted of a dis-

cursive review of General McClellan's character, in
which I was directly appealed to to know if we had
not at one time considered him the second Napoleon
in California.

" I hastened to say that I had found, in travelling
in the New England States, more fervent admirers
of the Unready than I had ever known to expend
speculative enthusiasm upon him among us.

" ' So pleasant and scholarly a gentleman can
never fail to secure personal friends,' said the President.   ' In fact,' he continued, kindly,

' " Even his failings lean to virtue's side."

A keen sense of genius in another, and a reverence for it that forced expression, was out of place
at Seven Oaks, as beautiful things sometimes will
be. He was lost in admiration of General Lee, and
filled with that feeling, forebore to conquer him.
The quality that would prove noble generosity in a
historian, does not fit the soldier. Another instance
of the necessity for my suggestion being carried into
effect,' he added, smiling.

" When in New York a few months afterwards,
I heard the regular dinner-table conversation turn
on the ' Nero who cracked jokes while Rome was
burning,' and the hundred and one wicked things
the McClellanites said of Mr. Lincoln, I recalled
the gentle verdict I had heard, and acknowledged
how bitterly a noble Christian gentleman may be
belied. It was after McClellan's speech at West

Point, and his admirers were wild with enthusiasm
ver the learning and classic taste it displayed.
The word ' scholarly ' rang from mouth to mouth in
characterizing it, — the very word Mr. Lincoln had
used months before in finding a merciful excuse for
his inefficiency.

" There is one little incident connected with this
visit to the Soldier's Home that remains with me as
connected with my home here. I had always noticed that the bare mention of our California cemetery filled the minds of those who heard it with a solemn sense of awe and sorrow, — ' Lone Mountain ! '
It seemed to rise before them out of the quiet sea, a
vast mausoleum from the hand of God, wherein to
lay the dead. I was not astonished, therefore, when
Mr. Lincoln alluded to it in this way, and gave, in
a few deep-toned words, a eulogy on one of its most
honored dead, Colonel Baker. Having witnessed
the impressive spectacle of that glorious soldier's
funeral, I gave him the meagre outline one can
convey in words, of something which, having been
once seen, must remain a living picture in the
memory forever. I tried to picture the solemn hush
that lay like a pall on the spirit of the people while
the grand procession wound its mournful length
through the streets of the city out on that tear-
stained road to the gate of the cemetery, where the
body passed beneath the prophetic words of California's most eloquent soul, ' Hither in future ages they
shall bring,' etc. When I spoke of 'Starr King,' I saw

how strong a chord I had touched in the great
appreciative heart I addressed ; and giving a weak
dilution of that wondrous draught of soul-lit eloquence, that funeral hymn uttered by the priest of
God over the sacred ashes of the advocate and soldier of liberty, whose thrilling threnody seems yet
to linger in the sighing wind that waves the grass
upon the soil made sacred by the treasure it received
that day, I felt strangely impressed as to the power
and grandeur of that mind, whose thoughts, at sec-
ond-hand and haltingly given from memory, could
move and touch the soul of such a man as Abraham
Lincoln as I saw it touched when he listened.   It
is the electric chain with which all genius and
grandeur of soul whatsoever is bound, — the free-
masonry by which spirit hails spirit, though unseen.
Now they all three meet where it is not seeing
through a glass darkly, but in the light of a perfect
day."

LXV.

On the morning of Mr. Lincoln's arrival in
Washington, just before his inauguration, it will
be remembered that the Peace Convention was in
session.   Among those who were earliest to call
upon him was a gentleman from Pennsylvania, who
had been in Congress with him, and who was a
member of the Peace Convention.   He at once
commenced plying the President elect with urgent reasons for *compromising* matters in dispute,

saying, " It must be done sooner or later, and that this seemed the propitious moment." Listening attentively to all that was said, Mr. Lincoln finally replied: " Perhaps your reasons for compromising the alleged difficulties are correct, and that now is the favorable time to do it; still, if I remember correctly, *that* is not what *I* was elected for ! "

The same day, at Willard's Hotel, a gentleman from Connecticut was introduced, who said he wanted nothing but to take the incoming President by the hand. Mr. Lincoln surveyed him from head to foot, and giving him a cordial grasp, replied: " You are a *rare* man."

During the brief period that the Rev. Henry Ward Beecher was editor-in-chief of the " Independent," in the second year of the war, he felt called upon to pass some severe strictures upon the course of the administration. For several weeks the successive leaders of the editorial page were like bugle-blasts, waking the echoes throughout the country. Somebody cut these editorials out of the different numbers of the paper, and mailed them all to the President under one envelop. One rainy Sunday he took them from his drawer, and read them through to the very last word. One or two of the articles were in Mr. Beecher's strongest style, and criticized the President in no measured terms. As Mr. Lincoln finished reading them, his face flushed up with indignation. Dashing the package to the floor, he exclaimed, " Is thy servant a *dog*, that he should do this thing ? "

The excitement, however, soon passed off, leaving no trace behind of ill-will toward Mr. Beecher ; and the impression made upon his mind by the criticism was lasting and excellent in its effects.

Mr. Lincoln's popularity with the soldiers and the people is well illustrated in the following incidents.

Just after the presidential nominations had been made in 1864, a discussion arose in a certain regiment in the Army of the Potomac as to the merits of the two candidates.   Various opinions had been warmly expressed, when at length a German spoke. " I goes," said he, " for Fader Abraham.   Fader Abraham, he likes the soldier-boy.   Ven he serves tree years he gives him four hundred tollar, and reënlists him von veteran.   Now Fader Abraham, he serve four years.   We reënlist him four years more, and make *von veteran of him*."

The night following the election, a clergyman of Middletown, Conn., at a torchlight display, exhibited a transparency over his door, with a quotation from Genesis xxii. 15, — " The angel of the Lord called unto Abraham out of heaven a second time."

A few days before the reinauguration of Mr. Lincoln, my picture was placed temporarily on exhibition in the Rotunda of the Capitol.   As the workmen were raising it to its place, over the northern door leading to the Senate Chamber, a group gathered in front of it, among whom was policeman R——, of the Capitol squad.   As the painting reached its position, a wandering sunbeam crept in from the top of the great dome and settled full upon

the head of Mr. Lincoln, leaving all the rest of the
picture in shadow. The effect was singular and
wonderful. " Look ! " exclaimed the enthusiastic
R——, pointing to the canvas; " that is as it
should be. God bless him; may the sun shine
upon his head forever."

LXVI.

The 22d of February, 1865, Lieutenant Cushing
of the Navy reached Washington, from the fleet
at Wilmington, with the news of the capture of
Fort Anderson. This gallant officer, only twenty
or twenty-one years of age, had greatly distinguished himself by planning and successfully accomplishing the destruction of the rebel ram *Savannah*,
also in the construction of the " bogus " monitor
which played so effectual a part in the capture of
Fort Anderson. He was introduced to the President by the Secretary of the Navy, and was received in the most cordial manner. Sitting down
for an hour's talk, Mr. Lincoln, who was in high
spirits over the late military successes, sparkled
with humor. Temporarily upon the wall of the
room was a portrait of himself recently painted for
Secretary Welles by a Connecticut artist friend.
Turning to the picture, Mr. Welles remarked that
he thought it a successful likeness. " Yes," returned the President, hesitatingly ; and then came
a story of a western friend whose wife pronounced

her husband's portrait, painted secretly for a birth
day present, " horridly like ; " " and that," said he,
" seems to me a just criticism of *this !* "   The liability to " mistakes," so many instances of which had
occurred during the war, both on land and sea, was
illustrated by reference to a charitably disposed
woman, with a very indifferent face, who, while
visiting the rooms of the Young Men's Christian
Association, or a similar institution, caught sight of
her own reflection in a concealed looking-glass,
upon which she retired in great confusion, saying
she would have nothing more to do with an institution which one could not visit without meeting dis-
reputable characters.

Lieutenant Cushing related a circumstance showing the estimation in which General Sherman was
held by the rebel privates.   A deserter of this
class had lately fallen into his hands.   " Our boys,"
said he, speaking of the Rebels, " say General Sherman never makes but one speech.   When ready for
a movement, he says : ' Now boys, let 's get ready
to go ; ' and they get ready," said the deserter,
" on both sides."

" There is a good deal of mother-wit in some
of those fellows," rejoined Mr. Lincoln, much
amused.   " That puts me in mind of a conversation between two opposing pickets, just after Hooker
fell back across the Rappahannock, after the battle
of Chancellorville.   ' Where 's Old Joe ? ' called
out a ' butternut ' one frosty morning.   ' Gone to

Stonewall Jackson's funeral,' was the ready reply. 'What is the reason you " Johnnies " never have any decent clothes?' hallooed the ' Union' boy back. 'We-uns don't put on our best to kill hogs in,' was the retort."

I was sitting in the President's office with Mr G. B. Lincoln, of Brooklyn, and the Hon. John A. Bingham, of Ohio, — who were there by appointment of the President, — the Sunday evening before the reinauguration, when Mr. Lincoln came in through the side passage which had lately been constructed, holding in his hand a roll of manuscripts.

" Lots of wisdom in that document, I suspect," said he; " it is what will be called my 'second inaugural,' containing about six hundred words. I will put it away here in this drawer until I want it."

Seating himself by the open grate, he commenced conversation in a familiar and cheerful mood, referring to his early life in Illinois. Nothing, he said, had ever gratified him so much as his first election to the legislature of that State, just after his return from the Black-Hawk war. In the election district a large majority were Democrats, and he was known as a " talking Whig." Nevertheless, he said, in a vote of two hundred, he received all but three.

LXVII.

" The world," writes one who knew Mr. Lincoln well, " will never hear the last of the ' little stories ' with which the President garnished or illustrated his conversation and his early stump-speeches. He once said, however, that as near as he could reckon, about one sixth only of those credited to him were old acquaintances, — all the rest were the productions of other and better story-tellers than himself. ' I remember a good story when I hear it,' he continued ; ' but I never invented anything original ; I am only a retail-dealer.' " *

" Mr. Lincoln's jocoseness," wrote another, " though sometimes grim and sarcastic, was *never* abusive, and seldom wounded. Often nicely adapted to the place and the occasion, it was used, as the case might be, either as a shield or a weapon." †

Humor and shrewdness, together with a certain nameless individuality, were combined in his stories in a degree that will secure for many of them enduring interest. These characteristics, marked and prominent as they were, are directly traceable to the powerful effect produced upon the plastic mind of the pioneer boy, by the early study of Æsop's Fables, and the " Pilgrim's Progress." His lightest as well as his most powerful thought almost invariably took on the form of a figure in speech,

* Noah Brooks, *Harper's Monthly*, July, 1865.
† *Boston Watchman and Reflector.*

which drove the point *home*, and *clinched* it, as few abstract reasoners are able to do.

The character of this volume, necessarily rambling and fragmentary, seems to present a legitimate field for the incorporation and preservation of some of the best of Mr. Lincoln's "little stories" and quaint sayings, other than those which came within my own personal observation. Beside these, there has accumulated in my possession a variety of incidents, many of which have never been published, throwing light not only upon the character of the man, but upon many events and circumstances connected with the war and the administration.

Believing everything of this kind to have more than a temporary interest and value, I devote the following section to their embodiment.

LXVIII.

Mr. Lincoln made his first political speech in 1832, at the age of twenty-three, when he was a candidate for the Illinois Legislature. His opponent had wearied the audience by a long speech, leaving him but a short time in which to present his views. He condensed all he had to say into a few words, as follows : —

"Gentlemen, Fellow-citizens : I presume you know who I am. I am humble Abraham Lincoln. I have been solicited by many friends to become a candidate for the legislature. My politics can be briefly stated. I am in favor of a national bank. I am in favor of the internal improvement system, and a high protective tariff. These are my sentiments and political principles. If elected, I shall be thankful. If not, it will be all the same."

The contrast between Mr. Lincoln and Senator Douglas is well brought out in the following extract from a speech by Hon. I. N. Arnold of Illinois, in 1863. Speaking of their great contest for the senatorship, Mr. Arnold said : —

" Douglas went through this campaign like a conquering hero. He had his special train of cars, his band of music, his body-guard of devoted friends, a cannon carried on the train, the firing from which announced his approach to the place of meeting. Such a canvass involved, necessarily, very large expenditures ; and it has been said that Douglas did not expend less than $50,000 in this canvass. Some idea of the plain, simple, frugal habits of Mr. Lincoln may be gathered, when I tell you that at its close, having occupied several months, Mr. Lincoln said, with the idea, apparently, that he had been somewhat extravagant: ' I do not believe I have spent a cent less than five hundred dollars in this canvass.' "

Soon after Mr. Lincoln entered upon the practice of his profession at Springfield, he was engaged in a criminal case in which it was thought there was little chance of success. Throwing all his powers into it, he came off victorious, and promptly received for his services five hundred dollars. A legal friend calling upon him the next morning found him sitting before a table, upon which his money was spread out, counting it over and over. " Look here, Judge," said he; " see what a heap of money I 've got from the —— case. Did you ever see anything like it ? Why, I never had so much money in my life before, put it all together!" Then crossing his arms upon the table, his manner sobering down, he added, " I have got just five hundred dollars: if it was only seven hundred and fifty, I would go directly and purchase a quarter section of land, and settle it upon my old step-mother." His friend said that if the deficiency was all he needed, he would loan him the amount, taking his note, to which Mr. Lincoln instantly acceded.

His friend then said: " Lincoln, I would not do just what you have indicated. Your step-mother is getting old, and will not probably live many years. I would settle the property upon her for her use during her lifetime, to revert to you upon her death."

With much feeling, Mr. Lincoln replied: " I shall do no such thing. It is a poor return, at the best, for all the good woman's devotion and fidelity to me, and there is not going to be any half-way business about it;" and so saying, he gathered up his money, and proceeded forthwith to carry his long-cherished purpose into execution.

SIX MONTHS AT THE WHITE HOUSE.   239

Among the numerous delegations which thronged
Washington in the early part of the war was one
from New York, which urged very strenuously the
sending of a fleet to the southern cities, — Charleston, Mobile, and Savannah, — with the object of
drawing off the rebel army from Washington.
Mr. Lincoln said the project reminded him of the
case of a girl in New Salem, who was greatly
troubled with a " singing " in her head.   Various
remedies were suggested by the neighbors, but
nothing tried afforded any relief.   At last a man
came along, — "a common-sense sort of man," said
he, inclining his head towards the gentleman com-
plimentarily, — " who was asked to prescribe for the
difficulty.   After due inquiry and examination, he
said the cure was very simple.   ' What is it ? ' was
the anxious question.   ' Make a plaster of *psalm-
tunes*, and apply to her feet, and draw the " singing " *down*,' was the rejoinder."

On another occasion, an antislavery delegation,
also from New York, were pressing the adoption of
the emancipation policy.   During the interview the
" chairman," the Rev. Dr. C——, made a characteristic and powerful appeal, largely made up of
quotations from the Old Testament Scriptures.   Mr.
Lincoln received the " bombardment " in silence.
As the speaker concluded, he continued for a moment in thought, and then, drawing a long breath,
responded : " Well, gentlemen, it is not often one
is favored with a delegation *direct* from the Almighty ! "

One of Mr. Lincoln's Springfield neighbors, a clergyman, visiting Washington early in the administration, asked the President what was to be his policy on the slavery question. "Well," said he, "I will answer by telling you a story. You know Father B., the old Methodist preacher? and you know Fox River and its freshets? Well, once in the presence of Father B., a young Methodist was worrying about Fox River, and expressing fears that he should be prevented from fulfilling some of his appointments by a freshet in the river. Father B. checked him in his gravest manner. Said he: 'Young man, I have always made it a rule in my life not to cross Fox River till I get to it!' And," added Mr. Lincoln, "I am not going to worry myself over the slavery question till I get to it."

General Garfield, of Ohio, received from the President an account of the capture of Norfolk, similar to that recorded on a previous page, with the following preface: —

" By the way, Garfield," said Mr. Lincoln, "you never heard, did you, that Chase, Stanton, and I, had a campaign of our own? We went down to Fortress Monroe in Chase's revenue cutter, and consulted with Admiral Goldsborough as to the feasibility of taking Norfolk by landing on the north shore and making a march of eight miles. The Admiral said, very positively, there was no landing on that shore, and we should have to double the cape and appioach the place from the south side, which would be a long and difficult journey. I thereupon asked him if he had ever tried to find a landing, and he replied that he had not. 'Now,' said I, 'Admiral, that reminds me of a chap out West who had studied law, but had never tried a case. Being sued, and not having confidence in his ability to manage his own case, he employed a fellow-lawyer to manage it for him. He had only a confused idea of the meaning of law terms, but was anxious to make a display of learning, and on the trial constantly made suggestions to his lawyer, who paid no attention to him. At last, fearing that his lawyer was not handling the opposing counsel very well, he lost all patience, and springing to his feet cried out, " Why don't you go at him with a *capias*, or a *surre-butter*, or something, and not stand there like a confounded old *nudum-pactum?*" ' "

An officer of the Government called one day at the White House, and introduced a clerical friend. " Mr. President," said he, " allow me to present to you my friend, the Rev. Mr. F., of ———. Mr. F. has expressed a desire to see you and have some conversation with you, and I am happy to be the means of introducing him." The President shook hands with Mr. F., and desiring him to be seated took a seat himself. Then, his countenance having assumed an air of patient waiting, he said: " I am now ready to hear what you have to say." " Oh, bless you, sir," said Mr. F., " I have nothing special to say ; I merely called to pay my respects to you, and, as one of the million, to assure you of my hearty sympathy and support." "My dear sir," said the President, rising promptly, his face showing instant relief, and with both hands grasping that of his visitor, "I am very glad to see you, indeed. *I thought you had come to preach to me !*"

On the way to the cemetery dedication at Gettysburg, Mr. Lincoln said to his friend, McVeagh, of Pennsylvania, speaking of Governor Gamble and the administration troubles in Missouri : — " I do not understand the spirit of those men who, in such a time as this, because they cannot have a whole loaf will take no bread. For my part, I am willing to receive any man, or class of men, who will help us even a *little*."

On the same occasion, when the Presidential party reached Hanover Junction they found a large concourse of people assembled to greet them. Mr. Lincoln and Secretary Seward, an hour previous, had gone into the sleeping-car attached to the train, for some rest. In response to the clamor of the crowd, a friend intruded upon them, saying to the President that he was " expected to make a speech."

" No ! " he rejoined, very emphatically ; " I had enough of that sort of thing all the way from Springfield to Washington. Seward," said he, turning over in his berth, " you go out and repeat some of your '*poetry*' to the people ! "

Upon the betrothal of the Prince of Wales to the Princess Alexandra, Queen Victoria sent a letter to each of the European sovereigns, and also to President Lincoln, announcing the fact. Lord Lyons, her ambassador at Washington, — a " bachelor," by the way, — requested an audience of Mr. Lincoln, that he might present this important document in person. At the time appointed he was received at the White House, in company with Mr. Seward.

" May it please your Excellency," said Lord Lyons, " I hold in my hand an autograph letter from my royal mistress, Queen Victoria, which I have been commanded to present to your Excellency. In it she informs your Excellency that her son, his Royal Highness the Prince of Wales, is about to contract a matrimonial alliance with her Royal Highness the Princess Alexandra of Denmark."

After continuing in this strain for a few minutes, Lord Lyons tendered the letter to the President and awaited his reply. It was short, simple, and expressive, and consisted simply of the words : —

" Lord Lyons, go thou and do likewise."

It is doubtful if an English ambassador was ever addressed in this manner before, and it would be interesting to learn what success he met with in putting the reply in diplomatic language when he reported it to her Majesty.

The antagonism between the northern and south-

ern sections of the Democratic party, which cul-
minated in the nomination of two separate tickets
in 1860, was a subject to draw out one of Mr. Lincoln's hardest hits.

"I once knew," said he, "a sound churchman
by the name of Brown, who was a member of a
very sober and pious committee having in charge
the erection of a bridge over a dangerous and rapid
river.   Several architects failed, and at last Brown
said he had a friend named Jones, who had built
several bridges and undoubtedly could build that
one.   So Mr. Jones was called in.   'Can you build
this bridge?' inquired the committee.   'Yes,' replied Jones, 'or any other.   I could build a bridge
to the infernal regions, if necessary!'   The committee were shocked, and Brown felt called upon
to defend his friend.   'I know Jones so well,' said
he, 'and he is so honest a man and so good an
architect, that if he states soberly and positively
that he can build a bridge to — to ——, why, I
believe it; but I feel bound to say that I have my
doubts about the abutment on the infernal side.'
So," said Mr. Lincoln, "when politicians told me
that the northern and southern wings of the Dem-
ocracy could be harmonized, why, I believed them,
of course; but I always had my doubts about the
'abutment' on the *other* side." *

About the time Mr. Lincoln began to be known
as a successful lawyer, he was waited upon by a

* Abbott's *History of the Civil War.*

lady, who held a real-estate claim which she desired to have him prosecute, — putting into his hands, with the necessary papers, a check for two hundred and fifty dollars, as a retaining fee. Mr. Lincoln said he would look the case over, and asked her to call again the next day. Upon presenting herself, Mr. Lincoln told her that he had gone through the papers very carefully, and he must tell her frankly that there was not a " peg " to hang her claim upon, and he could not conscientiously advise her to bring an action. The lady was satisfied, and, thanking him, rose to go. " Wait," said Mr. Lincoln, fumbling in his vest pocket ; " here is the check you left with me." " But, Mr. Lincoln," returned the lady, " I think you have earned *that*." " No, no," he responded, handing it back to her; " that would not be right. I can't take *pay* for doing my duty."

Mr. Lincoln liked to feel himself the attorney of the people, not their ruler. Speaking once of the probability of his renomination, he said : " If the people think I have managed their ' case ' for them well enough to trust me to carry it up to the next term, I am sure I shall be glad to take it."

" Judge Baldwin of California, being in Washington, called one day on General Halleck, and, presuming upon a familiar acquaintance in California a few years before, solicited a pass outside of our lines to see a brother in Virginia, not thinking that he would meet with a refusal, as both his brother and himself were good Union men. " We have been deceived too often," said General Hal-leck, " and I regret I can't grant it." Judge B. then went to Stanton, and was very briefly disposed of, with the same result. Finally, he obtained an interview with Mr. Lincoln, and stated his case. " Have you applied to General Halleck ? " inquired the President. " Yes, and met with a flat refusal," said Judge B. " Then you must see Stanton," continued the President. " I have, and with the same result," was the reply. " Well, then," said Mr. Lincoln, with a smile, " I can do nothing ; for you must know *that I have very little influence with this Administration.*"

Mr. Colfax told me of a gentleman's going to the President, one day, with a bitter denunciation of Secretary Stanton and his management of the War Department. " Go home, my friend," inter-rupted Mr. Lincoln, " and read attentively the tenth verse of the thirtieth chapter of Proverbs ! " *

A lieutenant, whom debts compelled to leave his father-land and service, succeeded in being admitted to President Lincoln, and, by reason of his com-mendable and winning deportment and intelligent appearance, was promised a lieutenant's commission m a cavalry regiment. He was so enraptured with his success, that he deemed it a duty to inform the President that he belonged to one of the oldest noble houses in Germany. " Oh, never mind that,'

* " Accuse not a servant to his master, lest he curse thee, and then be found guilty."

said Mr. Lincoln; "you will not find that to be an obstacle to your advancement."

Just previous to the fall of Vicksburg, a self-constituted committee, solicitous for the *morale* of our armies, took it upon themselves to visit the President and urge the removal of General Grant. In some surprise Mr. Lincoln inquired, "For what reason?" "Why," replied the spokesman, "he drinks too much whiskey." "Ah!" rejoined Mr. Lincoln, dropping his lower lip. "By the way, gentlemen, can either of you tell me where General Grant procures his whiskey? because, if I can find out, I will send every general in the field a barrel of it!"

When the telegram from Cumberland Gap reached Mr. Lincoln that "firing was heard in the direction of Knoxville," he remarked that he was "glad of it." Some person present, who had the perils of Burnside's position uppermost in his mind, could not see *why* Mr. Lincoln should be *glad* of it, and so expressed himself. "Why, you see," responded the President, "it reminds me of Mistress Sallie Ward, a neighbor of mine, who had a very large family. Occasionally one of her numerous progeny would be heard crying in some out-of-the-way place, upon which Mrs. Ward would exclaim, 'There's one of my children that is n't dead yet.'"

A gentleman once complimented the President on having no vices, neither drinking nor smoking.

" That is a doubtful compliment," answered the President ; " I recollect once being outside a stage-coach, in Illinois, and a man sitting by me offered me a cigar. I told him I had no vices. He said nothing, but smoked for some time, and then growled out : ' It 's my experience that folks who have no vices have generally very few virtues.' "

Mr. Lincoln's aversion to calls for a speech that must be merely " off-hand," was decided ; yet, unwilling altogether to disappoint the crowds, who perhaps too often made such demands of him, he seldom excused himself altogether from speaking. One evening a friend was conversing with him in his room, when his quick ear caught the sound of approaching music, and his countenance suddenly changed, as he inquired its meaning, though readily divining it. A serenade was presently announced by an usher, and Mr. Lincoln, as he arose to go forward to the front window, lingered a moment, and said : —

" These ' serenade ' speeches bother me a good deal, they are so hard to make. I feel very much like the steam doctor, who said he could get along very well in his practice with almost every case, but he was always a little puzzled when it came to mending a broken leg."

It has been repeatedly said that Mr. Lincoln lacked imagination and poetic sensibility. Surely, the soul which could conceive the last inaugural, or indite the closing sentence of the first, was not wanting in these elements : —

" The mystic chords of memory, stretching from every battle-field and patriot grave to every living heart and hearthstone all over this broad land, will yet swell the chorus of the Union, when again touched, as surely they will be, by the better angels of our nature."

Neither was the mind deficient in enthusiasm, which could prophesy : —

" There are already those among us, who, if the Union be preserved, will live to see it contain two hundred and fifty millions.   The struggle *of* to-day is not altogether *for* to-day ; it is for a vast future also."

" The President," said a leading member of the Cabinet, on one occasion, " is his own War-Minister.   He directs personally the movements of the armies, and is fond of strategy ; but pays much less attention to official details than is generally supposed."

Mr. Lincoln's wit was never malicious nor rudely personal.   Once when Mr. Douglas had attempted to parry an argument by impeaching the veracity of a senator whom Mr. Lincoln had quoted, he answered that the question was not one of veracity, but simply one of argument.   " By a course of reasoning, Euclid proves that all the angles in a triangle are equal to two right angles.   Now, if vou undertake to disprove that proposition, would you prove it to be false by calling Euclid a liar ? " *

* Speech at Charleston, September 18th, 1858.

A couple of well-known New York gentlemen called upon the President one day to solicit a pardon for a man who, while acting as mate of a sailing vessel, had struck one of his men a blow which resulted in his death. Convicted and sentenced for manslaughter, a powerful appeal was made in his behalf, as he had previously borne an excellent character. Giving the facts a hearing, Mr. Lincoln responded : —

" Well, gentlemen, leave your papers, and I will have the Attorney-General, Judge Bates, look them over, and we will see what can be done. Being both of us ' *pigeon-hearted* ' fellows, the chances are that, if there is any ground whatever for interference, the scoundrel will get off ! "

Attorney-General Bates was once remonstrating with the President against the appointment to a judicial position of considerable importance of a western man, who, though once on the " bench," was of indifferent reputation as a lawyer.

" Well now, Judge," returned Mr. Lincoln, " I think you are rather too hard on ——. Besides that, I must tell you, he did me a good turn long ago. When I took to the law, I was going to court one morning, with some ten or twelve miles of bad road before me, when —— overtook me in his wagon. ' Hallo, Lincoln ! ' said he ; ' going to the court-house ? come in and I will give you a seat.' Well, I got in, and —— went on reading his papers. Presently the wagon struck a stump on one side of the road; then it hopped off to the other. I looked out and saw the driver was jerking from side to side in his seat: so said I, ' Judge, I think your coachman has been taking a drop too much this morning.' ' Well, I declare, Lincoln,' said he, ' I should not much wonder if you are right, for he has nearly upset me half-a-dozen times since starting.' So, putting his head out of the window, he shouted, ' Why, you infernal scoundrel, you are drunk!' Upon which, pulling up his horses and turning round with great gravity, the coachman said : ' Bedad! but that 's the first rightful decision your honor has given for the last twelve months.' "

Some gentlemen fresh from a western tour, during a call at the White House, referred in the course of conversation to a body of water in Nebraska which bore an Indian name signifying " weeping water." Mr. Lincoln instantly responded : " As ' laughing water,' according to Longfellow, is ' Minnehaha,' this evidently should be ' Minneboohoo.' "

A farmer from one of the border counties went to the President on a certain occasion with the complaint that the Union soldiers in passing his farm had helped themselves not only to hay but to his horse; and he hoped the proper officer would be required to consider his claim immediately.

" Why, my good sir," replied Mr. Lincoln, " If I should attempt to consider every such individual case, I should find work enough for twenty Presidents! In my early days, I knew one Jack Chase, who was a lumberman on the Illinois, and, when steady and sober, the best raftsman on the river. It was quite a trick twenty-five years ago to take the logs over the rapids, but he was skilful with a raft, and always kept her straight in the channel. Finally a steamer was put on, and Jack — he's dead now, poor fellow! — was made captain of her. He always used to take the wheel going through the rapids. One day, when the boat was plunging and wallowing along the boiling current, and Jack's utmost vigilance was being exercised to keep her in the narrow channel, a boy pulled his coat-tail and hailed him with: 'Say, Mister Captain! I wish you would just stop your boat a minute — I've lost my apple overboard!'"

At a time of financial difficulty, a committee of New York bankers waited upon the Secretary of the Treasury and volunteered a loan to the government, which was gratefully accepted. Mr. Chase subsequently accompanied the gentlemen to the White House and introduced them to the President, saying they had called to have a talk with him about money. " Money," replied Mr. Lincoln; " I don't know anything about ' *money*.' I never had enough of my own to fret me, and I have no opin-'on about it any way."

" It is considered rather necessary to the carrying on of a war, however," returned the Secretary.

" Well, I don't know about that," rejoined Mr.

Lincoln, turning crosswise in his chair, swinging both legs backward and forward.   "We don't read that ' Hannibal ' had any ' *money* ' to prosecute his wars with."

The President was one day speaking of a visit he had just received from another delegation of bankers, from New York and Boston, who had been urging the removal of General Cameron from the Cabinet.

" They talked very glibly," said he, " especially a man named G —— from Boston ; and I finally told them as much — adding, nevertheless, that I was not convinced.   ' Now,' said I, 'gentlemen, if you want General Cameron removed, you have only to bring me *one proved* case of dishonesty, and I promise you his " head " ; but I assure you I am not going to act on what seems to me the most unfounded gossip.' "

The Hon. Mr. Hubbard of Connecticut once called upon the President in reference to a newly invented gun, concerning which a committee had been appointed to make a report.

The " report " was sent for, and when it came in was found to be of the most voluminous description. Mr. Lincoln glanced at it, and said : " I should want a new lease of life to read this through ! " Throwing it down upon the table, he added : " Why can't a committee of this kind occasionally exhibit a grain of common sense ?   If I send a man to buy a horse for me, I expect him to tell me his '*points*'— not how many *hairs* there are in his tail."

Late one evening, the President brought in to see my picture his friend and biographer, the Hon. J. H. Barrett, and a Mr. M ——, of Cincinnati. An allusion to a question of law in the course of conversation suggesting the subject, Mr. Lincoln said: " The strongest example of ' rigid government ' and 'close construction ' I ever knew, was that of Judge ——. It was once said of him that he would *hang* a man for blowing his nose in the street, but that he would *quash* the indictment if it failed to specify which *hand* he blew it with ! "

A new levy of troops required, on a certain occasion, the appointment of a large additional number of brigadier and major-generals. Among the immense number of applications, Mr. Lincoln came upon one wherein the claims of a certain worthy (not in the service at all) for a generalship were glowingly set forth. But the applicant did n't specify whether he wanted to be brigadier or major-general. The President observed this difficulty, and solved it by a lucid indorsement. The clerk, on receiving the paper again, found written across its back : " Major-General, I reckon. A. Lincoln."

A juvenile " Brigadier " from New York, with a small detachment of cavalry, having imprudently gone within the Rebel lines near Fairfax Court House, was captured by " guerillas." Upon the fact being reported to Mr. Lincoln, he said that he was very sorry to lose the horses !

" What do you mean ? " inquired his informant.

" Why," rejoined the President, " I can make a better ' brigadier ' any day ; but those horses cost the government a hundred and twenty-five dollars a head ! "

Mr. Lincoln sometimes had a very effective way of dealing with men who troubled him with questions. A visitor once asked him how many men the Rebels had in the field. The President replied, very seriously, " Twelve hundred thousand, according to the best authority." The interrogator blanched in the face, and ejaculated, " Good Heavens ! " " Yes sir, twelve hundred thousand — no doubt of it.   You see, all of our generals, when they get whipped, say the enemy outnumbers them from three or five to one, and I must believe them. We have four hundred thousand men in the field, and three times four make twelve.   Don't you see it ? "

Some gentlemen were discussing in Mr. Lincoln's presence on a certain occasion General McClellan's military capacity.   " It is doubtless true that he is a good ' engineer,' said the President ; but he seems to have a special talent for developing a ' *stationary*' ingine."

When Mr. Lincoln handed to his friend Gilbert his appointment as assessor in the Wall Street district, New York, he said : " Gilbert, from what I can learn, I judge that you are going upon good missionary ' ground. Preach God and Liberty to the ' bulls ' and ' bears,' and get all the money you can for the government ! "

A gentleman calling at the White House **one**
evening carried a cane, which, in the course of conversation, attracted the President's attention. Taking it in his hand, he said : "I always used a cane
when I was a boy. It was a freak of mine. My
favorite one was a knotted beech stick, and I carved
the head myself. There's a mighty amount of
character in sticks. Don't you think so? You
have seen these fishing-poles that fit into a cane?
Well that was an old idea of mine. Dogwood clubs
were favorite ones with the boys. I suppose they
use them yet. Hickory is too heavy, unless you get
it from a young sapling. Have you ever noticed
how a stick in one's hand will change his appearance? Old women and witches wouldn't look so
without sticks. Meg Merrilies understands that."

One of Mr. Lincoln's "illustrations" in my hearing, on one occasion, was of a man who, in driving
the hoops of a hogshead to "head" it up, was
much annoyed by the constant falling in of the top.
At length the bright idea struck him of putting his
little boy inside to "hold it up." This he did; it
never occurring to him till the job was done, how
he was to get his child out. "This," said he, "is
a fair sample of the way some people always do
business."

In a time of despondency, some visitors were telling the President of the "breakers" so often seen
ahead — "this time surely coming." "That,"
said he, "suggests the story of the school-boy,

who never could pronounce the names 'Sha-
drach,' 'Meshach,' and 'Abednego.' He had been
repeatedly whipped for it without effect. Some-
time afterwards he saw the names in the regular
lesson for the day. Putting his finger upon the
place, he turned to his next neighbor, an older boy,
and whispered, 'Here come those "tormented He-
brews" again.'"

Referring to the divisions upon the Missouri
Compromise, Mr. Lincoln once said: "It used to
amuse me to hear the slave-holders talk about
wanting more territory, because they had not
room enough for their slaves; and yet they com-
plained of not having the slave-trade, because they
wanted more slaves for their room."

Speaking on a certain occasion, of a prominent
man who had the year before been violent in his
manifestations of hostility to the Administration,
but was then ostensibly favoring the same policy
previously denounced, Mr. Lincoln expressed his
entire readiness to treat the past as if it had not
been, saying, "I choose always to make my 'stat-
ute of limitations' a short one."

At the White House one day some gentlemen
were present from the West, excited and troubled
about the commissions or omissions of the Administration. The President heard them patiently,
and then replied: "Gentlemen, suppose all the
property you were worth was in gold, and you had
put it in the hands of Blondin to carry across the

17

Niagara River on a rope, would you shake the cable, or keep shouting out to him, ' Blondin, stand up a little straighter — Blondin, stoop a little more — go a little faster — lean a little more to the north — lean a little more to the south.' No, you would hold your breath as well as your tongue, and keep your hands off until he was safe over. The Government are carrying an immense weight. Untold treasures are in their hands. They are doing the very best they can. Don't badger them. Keep silence, and we 'll get you safe across."

The President was once speaking of an attack made on him by the Committee on the Conduct of the War, for a certain alleged blunder, or some thing worse, in the Southwest — the matter involved being one which had fallen directly under the observation of the officer to whom he was talking, who possessed official evidence completely upsetting all the conclusions of the Committee.

" Might it not be well for me," queried the officer, " to set this matter right in a letter to some paper, stating the facts as they actually transpired ? "

" Oh, no," replied the President, " at least, not now. If I were to try to read, much less answer, all the attacks made on me, this shop might as well be closed for any other business. I do the very best I know how — the very best I can ; and I mean to keep doing so until the end. If the end brings me out all right, what is said against me won't amount to anything. If the end brings me out wrong, ten angels swearing I was right would make no difference."

" I shall ever cherish among the brightest memories of my life," says the Rev. J. P. Thompson, of New York, " the recollection of an hour in Mr. Lincoln's working-room in September, '64, which was one broad sheet of sunshine. . . . . I spoke of the rapid rise of Union feeling since the promulgation of the Chicago Platform, and the victory at Atlanta; and the question was started, which had contributed the most to the reviving of Union sentiment — the victory or the platform. 'I guess,' said the President, 'it was the victory; at any rate, I'd rather have that repeated.' "

Being informed of the death of John Morgan, he said: " Well, I would n't crow over anybody's death; but I can take this as *resignedly* as any dispensation of Providence."

The celebrated case of Franklin W. Smith and brother, was one of those which most largely helped to bring military tribunals into public contempt. Those two gentlemen were arrested and kept in confinement, their papers seized, their business destroyed, their reputation damaged, and a naval court-martial, " organized to convict," pursued them unrelentingly till a wiser and juster hand arrested the malice of their persecutors. It is known that President Lincoln, after full investigation of the case, annulled the whole proceed-

ings, but it is remarkable that the actual record of
his decision could never be obtained from the Navy
Department.   An exact copy being withheld, the
following was presented to the Boston Board of
Trade as being very nearly the words of the late
President : —

"*Whereas*, Franklin W. Smith had transactions with
the Navy Department to the amount of one million and
a quarter of a million of dollars ; and *whereas*, he had
the chance to steal a quarter of a million, and was only
charged with stealing twenty-two hundred dollars —
and the question now is about his stealing a hundred —
I don't believe he stole anything at all.   Therefore, the
record and findings are disapproved — declared null and
void, and the defendants are fully discharged."

"It would be difficult," says the New York
"Tribune," "to sum up the rights and wrongs of
the business more briefly than that, or to find a
paragraph more characteristically and unmistakably
Mr. Lincoln's."

A gentleman was pressing very strenuously the
promotion of an officer to a "Brigadiership." "But
we have already more generals than we know
what to do with," replied the President.   "But,"
persisted the visitor, "my friend is very strongly
recommended."   "Now, look here," said Mr. Lincoln, throwing one leg over the arm of his chair,
"you are a farmer, I believe ; if not, you will understand me.   Suppose you had a large cattle-
yard full of all sorts of cattle, — cows, oxen, bulls,

— and you kept killing and selling and disposing of your cows and oxen, in one way and another, — taking good care of your bulls. By-and-by you would find that you had nothing but a yard full of old bulls, good for nothing under heaven. Now, it will be just so with the army, if I don't stop making brigadier-generals."

Captain Mix, the commander, at one period, of the President's body-guard, told me that on their way to town one sultry morning, from the " Soldiers' Home," they came upon a regiment marching into the city. A " straggler," very heavily loaded with camp equipage, was accosted by the President with the question : " My lad, what is that ? " referring to the designation of his regiment. " It 's a regiment," said the soldier, curtly, plodding on, his gaze bent steadily upon the ground. " Yes, I see that," rejoined the President, " but I want to know *what* regiment." " —— Pennsylvania," replied the man in the same tone, looking neither to the right nor the left. As the carriage passed on, Mr. Lincoln turned to Captain Mix and said, with a merry laugh, " It is very evident that chap smells no blood of ' *royalty* ' in this establishment."

Captain Mix was frequently invited to breakfast with the family at the " Home " residence. " Many times," said he, " have I listened to our most eloquent preachers, but *never* with the same feeling of awe and reverence, as when our Christian Presi-

dent, his arm around his son, with his deep, earnest tone, each morning read a chapter from the
Bible."

Some one was discussing, in the presence of Mr.
Lincoln, the character of a time-serving Washington clergyman.   Said Mr. Lincoln to his visitor: —

"I think you are rather hard upon Mr. ——.
He reminds me of a man in Illinois, who was tried
for passing a counterfeit bill.   It was in evidence
that before passing it he had taken it to the cashier
of a bank and asked his opinion of the bill, and he
received a very prompt reply that it was a counterfeit.   His lawyer, who had heard of the evidence
to be brought against his client, asked him, just
before going into court, 'Did you take the bill to
the cashier of the bank and ask him if it was good?'
'I did,' was the reply.   'Well, what was the reply
of the cashier?'   The rascal was in a corner, but
he got out of it in this fashion: 'He said it was a
pretty tolerable, respectable sort of a bill.'"

Mr. Lincoln thought the clergyman was "a pretty
tolerable, respectable sort of a clergyman."

A visitor, congratulating Mr. Lincoln on the
prospects of his reëlection, was answered with an
anecdote of an Illinois farmer who undertook to
blast his own rocks.   His first effort at producing
an explosion proved a failure.   He explained the
cause by exclaiming, "Pshaw, this powder has been
shot before!"

An amusing, yet touching instance of the President's preoccupation of mind, occurred at one of his levees, when he was shaking hands with a host of visitors passing him in a continuous stream. An intimate acquaintance received the usual conventional hand-shake and salutation, but perceiving that he was not recognized, kept his ground instead of moving on, and spoke again; when the President, roused to a dim consciousness that something unusual had happened, perceived who stood before him, and seizing his friend's hand, shook it again heartily, saying, "How do you do? How do you do? Excuse me for not noticing you. I was thinking of a man down South." He afterward privately acknowledged that the "man down South" was Sherman, then on his march to the sea.

Mr. Lincoln may not have expected death from the hand of an assassin, but he had an impression, amounting to a "presentiment," that his life would end with the war. This was expressed not only to Mr. Lovejoy, as stated on a previous page, but to Mrs. Stowe and others.

"He told me, in July, 1864," says a correspondent of the Boston "Journal," "that he was certain he should not outlast the rebellion.

"It was a time of dissension among the Republican leaders. Many of his best friends had deserted him, and were talking of an opposition convention to nominate another candidate; and universal gloom was among the people.

"The North was tired of the war, and supposed

an honorable peace attainable. Mr. Lincoln knew
it was not, — that any peace at that time would be
only disunion. Speaking of it, he said : ' I have
faith in the people. They will not consent to disunion. The danger is, in their being misled. Let
them know the truth, and the country is safe.' He
looked haggard and careworn ; and further on in
the interview I remarked on his appearance, ' You
are wearing yourself out with work.' ' I can't
work less,' he answered ; ' but it isn't that, —
work never troubled me. Things look badly, and
I can't avoid anxiety. Personally, I care nothing
about a reëlection ; but if our divisions defeat us, I
fear for the country.' When I suggested that
right must eventually triumph, that I had never
despaired of the result, he said : —

" ' Neither have I, but I may never live to see
it. I feel a presentiment that I shall not outlast
the Rebellion. When it is over, my work will be
done.' "

" The Freedmen," once said the President to the
Secretary of War, " are the ' wards ' of the nation."

" Yes," replied Stanton, " wards in chancery."

A few days before the President's death, Secretary Stanton tendered his resignation of the War
Department. He accompanied the act with a heart-
felt tribute to Mr. Lincoln's constant friendship
and faithful devotion to the country ; saying, also,
that he as Secretary had accepted the position to

hold it only until the war should end, and that now he felt his work was done, and his duty was to resign.

Mr. Lincoln was greatly moved by the Secretary's words, and tearing in pieces the paper containing the resignation, and throwing his arms about the Secretary, he said : "Stanton, you have been a good friend and a faithful public servant, and it is not for you to say when you will no longer be needed here." Several friends of both parties were present on the occasion, and there was not a dry eye that witnessed the scene.

"On the night of the 3rd of March, the Secretary of War, with others of the Cabinet, were in the company of the President, at the Capitol, awaiting the passage of the final bills of Congress. In the intervals of reading and signing these documents, the military situation was considered, — the lively conversation tinged by the confident and glowing account of General Grant, of his mastery of the position, and of his belief that a few days more would see Richmond in our possession, and the army of Lee either dispersed utterly or captured bodily, — when the telegram from Grant was received, saying that Lee had asked an interview with reference to peace. Mr. Lincoln was elated, and the kindness of his heart was manifest in intimations of favorable terms to be granted to the conquered Rebels.

"Stanton listened in silence, restraining his emo-

tion, but at length the tide burst forth. 'Mr. President,' said he, 'to-morrow is inauguration day. If
you are not to be the President of an obedient and
united people, you had better not be inaugurated.
Your work is already done, if any other authority
than yours is for one moment to be recognized. or
any terms made that do not signify you are the
supreme head of the nation. If generals in the
field are to negotiate peace, or any other chief mag-
istrate is to be acknowledged on this continent, then
you are not needed, and you had better not take
the oath of office.'

"'Stanton, you are right!' said the President,
his whole tone changing. 'Let me have a pen.'

"Mr. Lincoln sat down at the table, and wrote
as follows : —

"'The President directs me to say to you that
he wishes you to have no conference with General
Lee, unless it be for the capitulation of Lee's army,
or on some minor or purely military matter. He
instructs me to say that you are not to decide, discuss, or confer upon any political question. Such
questions the President holds in his own hands, and
will submit them to no military conferences or conventions. In the mean time you are to press to the
utmost your military advantages.'

"The President read c7er what he had written,
and then said : —

"'Now Stanton, date and sign this paper, and
send it to Grant. We'll see about this peace business.'

" The duty was discharged only too gladly by the energetic and far-sighted Secretary; with what effect and renown the country knows full well." *

Governor Yates, of Illinois, in a speech at Springfield, quoted one of Mr. Lincoln's early friends — W. T. Greene — as having said that the first time he ever saw Mr. Lincoln, he was in the Sangamon River with his trousers rolled up five feet, more or less, trying to pilot a flat-boat over a mill-dam. The boat was so full of water that it was hard to manage. Lincoln got the prow over, and then, instead of waiting to bail the water out, bored a hole through the projecting part and let it run out; affording a forcible illustration of the ready ingenuity of the future President in the quick invention of moral expedients.

" Some two years ago," said Colonel Forney, in a speech at Weldon, Pennsylvania, before the "Soldiers' Aid Society," in 1865, " a deputation of colored people came from Louisiana, for the purpose of laying before the President a petition asking certain rights, not including the right of universal suffrage. The interview took place in the presence of a number of distinguished gentlemen. After reading their memorial, he turned to them and said: ' I regret, gentlemen, that you are not able to secure all your rights, and that circumstances will not permit the government to confer them upon you. I wish you would amend your petition, so as to

* *Boston Commonwealth.*

include several suggestions which I think will give more effect to your prayer, and after having done so please hanc it to me.' The leading colored man said: 'If you will permit me, I will do so here.' 'Are you, then, the author of this eloquent production?' asked Mr. Lincoln. 'Whether eloquent or not,' was the reply, 'it is my work;' and the Louisiana negro sat down at the President's side and rapidly and intelligently carried out the suggestions that had been made to him. The Southern gentlemen who were present at this scene did not hesitate to admit that their prejudices had just received another shock.

"To show the magnanimity of Mr. Lincoln, I may mention that on one occasion, when an editorial article appeared in my newspaper, the Washington 'Chronicle,' speaking well of the bravery and the mistaken sincerity of Stonewall Jackson, the news of whose death had been just received, the President wrote me a letter thanking me warmly for speaking kindly of a fallen foe. These were his words: —

"'I honor you for your generosity to one who, though contending against us in a guilty cause, was nevertheless a gallant man. Let us forget his sins over his fresh-made grave.'

"Again, I happened to be in the Executive Chamber when a number of Kentuckians insisted that troops should not be sent through that State for the purpose of putting down the rebel spirit in

Tennessee.   The President was hesitating what to
do, and they were pressing immediate action.

"'I am,' he said, 'a good deal like the farmer
who, returning to his home one winter night, found
his two sweet little boys asleep with a hideous ser··
pent crawling over their bodies.   He could not
strike the serpent without wounding or killing the
children, so he calmly waited until it had moved
away.   Now I do not want to act in a hurry about
this matter; I don't want to hurt anybody in Kentucky; but I will get the serpent out of Tennessee.'

"And he did march through Kentucky, to the
aid of Andrew Johnson's mountaineers."

"The roll containing the Emancipation Proclamation was taken to Mr. Lincoln at noon on the
first day of January, 1863, by Secretary Seward
and his son Frederick.   As it lay unrolled before
him, Mr. Lincoln took a pen, dipped it in ink,
moved his hand to the place for the signature, held
it a moment, and then removed his hand and dropped
the pen.   After a little hesitation he again took up
the pen and went through the same movement as
before.   Mr. Lincoln then turned to Mr. Seward,
and said : —

"'I have been shaking hands since nine o'clock
this morning, and my right arm is almost paralyzed.
If my name ever goes into history it will be for
this act, and my whole soul is in it.   If my hand
trembles when I sign the Proclamation, all who
examine the document hereafter will say, "He hes
itated."'"

" He then turned to the table, took up the pen again, and slowly, firmly wrote that ' Abraham Lincoln ' with which the whole world is now familiar. He looked up, smiled, and said : ' That will do.' " *

What Mr. Lincoln's policy on the subject of " reconstruction " would have been, had he lived, is clearly foreshadowed in the following extract from a letter to General Wadsworth, who was killed in one of the battles of the Wilderness. Few sentences from Mr. Lincoln's lips or pen are more worthy the profound consideration and remembrance of his countrymen.

" You desire to know, in the event of our complete success in the field, the same being followed by a loyal and cheerful submission on the part of the South, if universal amnesty should not be accompanied with universal suffrage.

" Now, since you know my private inclinations as to what terms should be granted to the South in the contingency mentioned, I will here add, that if our success should thus be realized, followed by such desired results, I cannot see, if universal amnesty is granted, how, under the circumstances, I can avoid exacting in return universal suffrage, or at least suffrage on the basis of intelligence and military service.

" How to better the condition of the colored race has long been a study which has attracted my serious and careful attention ; hence I think I am clear

* *Rochester* (New York) *Express.*

and decided as to what course I shall pursue in the premises, regarding it a religious duty, as the nation's guardian of these people who have so heroically vindicated their manhood on the battle-field, where, in assisting to save the life of the Republic, they have demonstrated in blood their right to the ballot, which is but the humane protection of the flag they have so fearlessly defended."

When Mr. Lincoln was in Congress, General Cass was nominated by the Democratic party for President. In a speech on the floor of the House shortly afterward, Mr. Lincoln subjected the political course of the candidate to scathing criticism. Quoting extracts from the speeches of General Cass, to show his vacillation in reference to the Wilmot Proviso, he added : " These extracts show that in 1846 General Cass was for the Proviso at once ; that in March, 1847, he was still for it, but not just then ; and that in December, he was against it altogether. This is a true index of the whole man. When the question was raised in 1846, he was in a blustering hurry to take ground for it, . . . but soon he began to see glimpses of the great Democratic ox-gad waving in his face, and to hear indistinctly a voice saying : ' Back ! back, sir ! back a little ! ' He shakes his head, and bats his eyes, and blunders back to his position of March, 1847 ; but still the ' gad ' waves, and the voice grows more distinct and sharper still : ' Back, sir ! back, I say ! further back ! ' and back he goes to the position of

December, 1847, at which the 'gad' is still, and the voice soothingly says: 'So! stand still at that!'"

A party of gentlemen, among whom was a doctor of divinity of much dignity of manner, calling at the White House one day, was informed by the porter that the President was at dinner, but that he would present their cards. The doctor demurred to this, saying that he would call again. "Edward" assured them that he thought it would make no difference, and went in with the cards. In a few minutes the President walked into the room, with a kindly salutation, and a request that the friends would take seats. The doctor expressed his regret that their visit was so ill-timed, and that his Excellency was disturbed while at dinner. "Oh! no consequence at all," said Mr. Lincoln, good-naturedly. "Mrs. Lincoln is absent at present, and when she is away, I generally '*browse*' around."

"Upon entering the President's office one afternoon," says a Washington correspondent, "I found Mr. Lincoln busily counting greenbacks. 'This, sir,' said he, 'is something out of my usual line; but a President of the United States has a multiplicity of duties not specified in the Constitution or acts of Congress. This is one of them. This money belongs to a poor negro who is a porter in the Treasury Department, at present very bad with the small-pox. He is now in hospital, and could not draw his pay because he could not sign his name. 1 have been at considerable trouble to overcome the difficulty and get it for him, and have at length succeeded in cutting red tape, as you newspaper men say. I am now dividing the money and putting by a portion labelled, in an envelope, with my own hands, according to his wish;' and he proceeded to indorse the package very carefully." No one witnessing the transaction could fail to appreciate the goodness of heart which prompted the President of the United States to turn aside for a time from his weighty cares to succor one of the humblest of his fellow-creatures in sickness and sorrow.

When General Phelps took possession of Ship Island, near New Orleans, early in the war, it will be remembered that he issued a proclamation, somewhat bombastic in tone, freeing the slaves. To the surprise of many people, on both sides, the President took no official notice of this movement. Some time had elapsed, when one day a friend took him to task for his seeming indifference on so important a matter.

" Well," said Mr. Lincoln, " I feel about that a good deal as a man whom I will call ' Jones,' whom I once knew, did about his wife. He was one of your meek men, and had the reputation of being badly henpecked. At last, one day his wife was seen switching him out of the house. A day or two afterward a friend met him in the street, and said : ' Jones, I have always stood up for you, as you

18

know; but I am not going to do it any longer
Any man who will stand quietly and take a switch
ing from his wife, deserves to be horsewhipped.
' Jones ' looked up with a wink, patting his friend
on the back. ' Now *don't*,' said he : ' why, it did n't
hurt me any ; and you 've no idea what a *power* of
good it did Sarah Ann ? ' "

The Rev. Dr. Bellows, of New York, as President of the Sanitary Commission, backed by powerful influences, had pressed with great strenuousness
upon the President the appointment of Dr. Hammond as Surgeon-General. For some unexplained
reason, there was an unaccountable delay in making
the appointment. One stormy evening — the rain
falling in torrents — Dr. Bellows, thinking few visitors likely to trouble the President in such a storm,
determined to make a final appeal, and stepping
into a carriage, he was driven to the White House.
Upon entering the Executive Chamber, he found Mr.
Lincoln alone, seated at the long table, busily engaged in signing a heap of congressional documents,
which lay before him. He barely nodded to Dr.
Bellows as he entered, having learned what to expect, and kept straight on with his work. Standing
opposite to him, Dr. B. employed his most powerful
arguments, for ten or fifteen minutes, to accomplish
the end sought, the President keeping steadily on
signing the documents before him. Pausing, at
length, to take breath, the clergyman was greeted
in the most unconcerned manner, the pen still at

work, with, — " Should n't wonder if Hammond was at this moment ' Surgeon-General,' and had been for some time."

" You don't mean to say, Mr. President," asked Dr. B. in surprise, " that the appointment has been made ? "

" I may say to you," returned Mr. Lincoln, for the first time looking up, " that it *has ;* only you need n't *tell* of it just yet."

In August, 1864, the prospects of the Union party, in reference to the Presidential election, became very gloomy.   A friend, the private secretary of one of the cabinet ministers, who spent a few days in New York at this juncture, returned to Washington with so discouraging an account of the political situation, that after hearing it, the Secretary told him to go over to the White House and repeat it to the President.   My friend said that he found Mr. Lincoln alone, looking more than usually careworn and sad.   Upon hearing the statement, he walked two or three times across the floor in silence.   Returning, he said with grim earnestness of tone and manner : " Well, I cannot run the political machine ; I have enough on my hands without *that.*   It is the *people's* business, — the election is in their hands.   If they turn their backs to the fire, and get *scorched* in the rear, they 'll find they have got to ' *sit* ' on the ' blister ' ! "

Mr. Lincoln came to have an almost morbid dread of office-seekers, from whose importunity the executive of a republican government can neces-sarily never be free. Harassed with applications of every description, he once said that it sometimes seemed as if every visitor "darted at him, and with thumb and finger carried off a portion of his vitality."

As the day of his reinauguration approached, he said to Senator Clark, of New Hampshire, " Can't you and others start a public sentiment in favor of making no changes in offices except for good and sufficient cause ?   It seems as though the bare thought of going through again what I did the first year here, would *crush* me."   To another he said, " I have made up my mind to make very few changes in the offices in my gift for my second term.   I think now that I will not remove a sin-gle man, except for delinquency.   To remove a man is very easy, but when I go to fill his place, there are *twenty* applicants, and of these I must make *nineteen* enemies."   " Under these circum-stances," says one of his friends, " Mr. Lincoln's natural charity for all was often turned into an unwonted suspicion of the motives of men whose selfishness cost him so much wear of mind.   Once he said, 'Sitting here, where all the avenues to public patronage seem to come together in a knot, it does seem to me that our people are fast ap-proaching the point where it can be said that seven eighths of them are trying to find how to live at the expense of the other eighth.'"

A year or more before Mr. Lincoln's death, a delegation of clergymen waited upon him in reference to the appointment of the army chaplains. The delegation consisted of a Presbyterian, a Baptist, and an Episcopal clergyman. They stated that the character of many of the chaplains was notoriously bad, and they had come to urge upon the President the necessity of more discretion in these appointments. "But, gentlemen," said the President, "that is a matter which the Governmer t has nothing to do with; the chaplains are chosen by the regiments." Not satisfied with this, the clergymen pressed, in turn, a change in the system. Mr. Lincoln heard them through without remark, and then said, "Without any disrespect, gentlemen, I will tell you a 'little story.' Once, in Springfield, I was going off on a short journey, and reached the depot a little ahead of time. Leaning against the fence just outside the depot was a little darkey boy, whom I knew, named 'Dick,' busily digging with his toe in a mud-puddle. As I came up, I said, '"Dick," what are you about?' 'Making a " church,"' said he. 'A church?' said I; 'what do you mean?' 'Why, yes,' said 'Dick,' pointing with his toe, 'don't you see? there is the shape of it; there's the " steps " and " front-door " — here the " pews," where the folks set — and there's the " pulpit."' 'Yes, I see,' said I, 'but why don't you make a " minister?"' 'Laws,' answered 'Dick,' with a grin, 'I hain't got *mud* enough!'"

Mr. Lincoln had a dread of people who could not appreciate humor. He once instanced a member of his own cabinet, of whom he quoted the saying of Sydney Smith, that " it required a surgical operation to get a joke into his head." The light trifles of conversation diverted his mind, or, as he said of his theatre-going, gave him " a refuge from himself and his weariness."

One of the last stories I heard from Mr. Lincoln was concerning John Tyler, for whom it was to be expected, as an old Henry Clay Whig, he would entertain no great respect. " A year or two after Tyler's accession to the Presidency," said he, " contemplating an excursion in some direction, his son went to order a special train of cars. It so happened that the railroad superintendent was a very strong Whig. On 'Bob's' making known his errand, that official bluntly informed him that his road did not run any special trains for the President. 'What!' said 'Bob,' 'did you not furnish a special train for the funeral of General Harrison ?' 'Yes,' said the superintendent, stroking his whiskers ; 'and if you will only bring your father here in *that* shape, you shall have the best train on the road . '

" Once — on what was called a 'public day,' when Mr. Lincoln received all applicants in their turn — the writer * was struck by observing, as he passed through the corridor, the heterogeneous crowd of

* Colonel Charles G. Halpine, *New York Citizen.*

men and women, representing all ranks and classes, who were gathered in the large waiting-room outside the Presidential suite of offices.

" Being ushered into the President's chamber by Major Hay, the first thing he saw was Mr. Lincoln bowing an elderly lady out of the door, — the President's remarks to her being, as she still lingered and appeared reluctant to go: 'I am really very sorry, madam; very sorry. But your own good sense must tell you that I am not here to collect small debts. You must appeal to the courts in regular order.'

" When she was gone, Mr. Lincoln sat down, crossed his legs, locked his hands over his knees, and commenced to laugh, — this being his favorite attitude when much amused.

" 'What odd kinds of people come to see me,' he said; 'and what odd ideas they must have about my office! Would you believe it, Major, that old lady who has just left, came in here to get from me an order for stopping the pay of a treasury clerk, who owes her a board-bill of about seventy dollars?' And the President rocked himself backward and forward, and appeared intensely amused.

" 'She may have come in here a loyal woman,' continued Mr. Lincoln; 'but I 'll be bound she has gone away believing that the worst pictures of me in the Richmond press only lack truth in not being half black and bad enough.'

"This led to a somewhat general conversation, in which I expressed surprise that he did not adopt the plan in force at all military head-quarters, under which every applicant to see the general commanding had to be filtered through a sieve of officers, — assistant adjutant-generals, and so forth, — who allowed none in to take up the general's time save such as they were satisfied had business of sufficient importance, and which could be transacted in no other manner than by a personal interview.

"'Of every hundred people who come to see the general-in-chief daily,' I explained, 'not ten have any sufficient business with him, nor are they admitted. On being asked to explain for what purpose they desire to see him, and stating it, it is found, in nine cases out of ten, that the business properly belongs to some one or other of the subordinate bureaus. They are then referred, as the case may be, to the quartermaster, commissary, medical, adjutant-general, or other departments, with an assurance that even if they saw the general-in-chief he could do nothing more for them than give the same direction. With these points courteously explained,' I added, 'they go away quite content, although refused admittance.'

"'Ah, yes!' said Mr. Lincoln, gravely, — and his words on this matter are important as illustrating a rule of his action, and to some extent, perhaps, the essentially representative character of his mind and of his administration, — 'ah, yes, such things do very well for you military people, with your arbitrary rule, and in your camps. But the office of President is essentially a civil one, and the affair is very different. For myself, I feel — though the tax on my time is heavy — that no hours of my day are better employed than those which thus bring me again within the direct contact and atmosphere of the average of our whole people. Men moving only in an official circle are apt to become merely official — not to say arbitrary — in their ideas, and are apter and apter, with each passing day, to forget that they only hold power in a representative capacity. Now this is all wrong. I go into these promiscuous receptions of all who claim to have business with me twice each week, and every applicant for audience has to take his turn, as if waiting to be shaved in a barber's shop. Many of the matters brought to my notice are utterly frivolous, but others are of more or less importance, and all serve to renew in me a clearer and more vivid image of that great popular assemblage out of which I sprung, and to which at the end of two years I must return. I tell you, Major,' he said, — appearing at this point to recollect I was in the room, for the former part of these remarks had been made with half-shut eyes, as if in soliloquy, — 'I tell you that I call these receptions my "*public-opinion baths;*" for I have but little time to read the papers and gather public

opinion that way; and though they may not be
pleasant in all their particulars, the effect, as a
whole, is renovating and invigorating to my per
ceptions of responsibility and duty.'"

No nobler reply ever fell from the lips of ruler,
than that uttered by President Lincoln in response
to the clergyman who ventured to say, in his presence, that he *hoped* "the LORD was on our side."

"I am not at all concerned about that," replied
Mr. Lincoln, "for I know that the LORD is *always*
on the side of the *right*. But it is my constant anxiety and prayer that *I* and *this nation* should be on
the LORD's *side*."

In the midst of the despondency produced by the
raid on Washington, in the summer of 1864, and
the successful return of the Rebel force to Richmond, the President's Proclamation of July 18th
appeared, calling for five hundred thousand more
men.

In view of the impending presidential canvass,
Mr. Lincoln's strongest friends looked upon this
step, at this time, as calculated to utterly defeat his
chances of reëlection. Commissioner Dole ventured
to say as much upon the President's announcement
to him of his contemplated purpose.

"It matters not what becomes of me," replied
Mr. Lincoln; "we must have the men! If I go
down, I intend to go like the *Cumberland*, with
my colors flying!"

Upon Mr. Lincoln's return to Washington, after

the capture of Richmond, a member of the Cabinet asked him if it would be proper to permit Jacob Thompson to slip through Maine in disguise, and embark from Portland. The President, as usual, was disposed to be merciful, and to permit the arch-rebel to pass unmolested, but the Secretary urged that he should be arrested as a traitor. " By permitting him to escape the penalties of treason," persistently remarked the Secretary, " you sanction it." "Well," replied Mr. Lincoln, " let me tell you a story. There was an Irish soldier here last summer, who wanted something to drink stronger than water, and stopped at a drug-shop, where he espied a soda-fountain. ' Mr. Doctor,' said he, ' give me, plase, a glass of soda-wather, an' if yees can put in a few drops of whiskey unbeknown to any one, I 'll be obleeged.' Now," continued Mr. Lincoln, " if Jake Thompson is permitted to go through Maine unbeknown to any one, what 's the harm ? So don't have him arrested."

I asked the President, during the progress of the battles of the Wilderness, how General Grant personally impressed him as compared with other officers of the army, and especially those who had been in command.

" The great thing about Grant," said he, " I take it, is his perfect coolness and persistency of purpose. I judge he is not easily excited, — which .s a great element in an officer, — and he has the *grit* of a bull-dog ! Once let him get his ' teeth ' *in*, and nothing can shake him off."

One of the latest of Mr. Lincoln's stories was told to a party of gentlemen, who, amid the tum bling ruins of the 'Confederacy,' anxiously asked " what he would do with ' Jeff. Davis ' ? "

" There was a boy in Springfield," rejoined Mr. Lincoln, " who saved up his money and bought a ' coon,' which, after the novelty wore off, became a great nuisance. He was one day leading him through the streets, and had his hands full to keep clear of the little vixen, who had torn his clothes half off of him. At length he sat down on the curb-stone, completely fagged out. A man passing was stopped by the lad's disconsolate appearance, and asked the matter. ' Oh,' was the reply, ' this coon is such a *trouble* to me ! ' ' Why don't you get rid of him, then ? ' said the gentleman. ' Hush ! ' said the boy ; ' don't you see he is gnawing his rope off ? I am going to let him do it, and then I will go home and tell the folks *that he got away from me ?* ' "

LXIX.

The last story told by Mr. Lincoln was drawn out by a circumstance which occurred just before the interview with Messrs. Colfax and Ashmun, on the evening of his assassination.

Marshal Lamon of Washington had called upon him with an application for the pardon of a soldier. After a brief hearing the President took the appli cation, and when about to write his name upon the back of it, he looked up and said: "Lamon, have you ever heard how the Patagonians eat oysters? They open them and throw the shells out of the window until the pile gets higher than the house, and then they move;" adding: "I feel to-day like commencing a new pile of pardons, and I may as well begin it just here."

At the subsequent interview with Messrs. Colfax and Ashmun, Mr. Lincoln was in high spirits. The uneasiness felt by his friends during his visit to Richmond was dwelt upon, when he sportively replied that he "supposed he should have been uneasy also, had any other man been President and gone there; but as it was, he felt no apprehension of danger whatever." Turning to Speaker Colfax, he said: "Sumner has the 'gavel' of the Confederate Congress, which he got at Richmond, and intended to give to the Secretary of War, but I insisted he must give it to you, and you tell him from me to hand it over."

Mr. Ashmun, who was the presiding officer of the Chicago Convention in 1860, alluded to the "gavel" used on that occasion, saying he had preserved it as a valuable memento.

Mr. Ashmun then referred to a matter of business connected with a cotton claim, preferred by a client of his, and said that he desired to have a "commission" appointed to examine and decide upon the merits of the case. Mr. Lincoln replied, with considerable warmth of manner, " I have done with ' commissions.' I believe they are contrivances to *cheat* the Government out of every pound of cotton they can lay their hands on." Mr. Ashmun's face flushed, and he replied that he hoped the President meant no personal imputation.

Mr. Lincoln saw that he had wounded his friend, and he instantly replied : " You did not understand me, Ashmun. I did not mean what you inferred. I take it all back." Subsequently he said : " I apologize to you, Ashmun."

He then engaged to see Mr. Ashmun early the next morning, and taking a card, he wrote :

" Allow Mr. Ashmun and friend to come in at 9 A. M. to-morrow.   A. Lincoln."

These were his last written words. Turning to Mr. Colfax he said : " You will accompany Mrs. Lincoln and me to the theatre, I hope ? " Mr. Colfax pleaded other engagements, — expecting to start on his Pacific trip the next morning. The party passed out on the portico together, the President saying at the very last, " Colfax, don't forget to tell the people of the mining regions what I told you this morning about the development when peace comes ; " then shaking hands with both gentlemen, he followed Mrs. Lincoln into the carriage, leaning forward, at the last moment, to say as they were driven off, " I will telegraph you, Colfax, at

San Francisco," — passing thus forth for the last
time from under that roof into the creeping shad-
ows which were to settle before another dawn into
a funeral pall upon the orphaned heart of the
nation.

·   ·   ·   ·   ·   ·

LXX.

" On the Monday before the assassination,*
when the President was on his return from Richmond, he stopped at City Point.   Calling upon
the head surgeon at that place, Mr. Lincoln told
him that he wished to visit all the hospitals under
his charge, and shake hands with every soldier.
The surgeon asked if he knew what he was
undertaking, there being five or six thousand
soldiers at that place, and it would be quite a
tax upon his strength to visit all the wards and
shake hands with every soldier.   Mr. Lincoln answered with a smile, he ' guessed he was equal to
the task; at any rate he would try, and go as far
as he could; he should never, probably, see the
boys again, and he wanted them to know that he
appreciated what they had done for their country.'
" Finding it useless to try to dissuade him, the
surgeon began his rounds with the President, who
walked from bed to bed, extending his hand to all,
saying a few words of sympathy to some, making

* Correspondence of the *N. Y. Independent.*

kind inquiries of others, and welcomed by all with the heartiest cordiality.

" As they passed along, they came to a ward in which lay a Rebel who had been wounded and was a prisoner. As the tall figure of the kindly visitor appeared in sight he was recognized by the Rebel soldier, who, raising himself on his elbow in bed, watched Mr. Lincoln as he approached, and extending his hand exclaimed, while tears ran down his cheeks : ' Mr. Lincoln, I have long wanted to see you, to ask your forgiveness for ever raising my hand against the old flag.'   Mr. Lincoln was moved to tears.   He heartily shook the hand of the repentant Rebel, and assured him of his good-will, and with a few words of kind advice passed on.

" After some hours the tour of the various hospitals was made, and Mr. Lincoln returned with the surgeon to his office.   They had scarcely entered, however, when a messenger came saying that one ward had been omitted, and ' the boys ' wanted to see the President.   The surgeon, who was thoroughly tired, and knew Mr. Lincoln must be, tried to dissuade him from going ; but the good man said he must go back ; he would not knowingly omit one, ' the boys ' would be so disappointed.   So he went with the messenger, accompanied by the surgeon, and shook hands with the gratified soldiers, and then returned again to the office.

" The surgeon expressed the fear that the President's arm would be lamed with so much hand-

sbaking, saying that it certainly must ache. **Mr.**
Lincoln smiled, and saying something about his
' strong muscles,' stepped out at the open door,
took up a very large, heavy axe which lay there by
a log of wood, and chopped vigorously for a few
moments, sending the chips flying in all directions;
and then, pausing, he extended his right arm to its
full length, holding the axe out horizontally, without its even quivering as he held it. Strong men
who looked on — men accustomed to manual labor
— could not hold the same axe in that position for
a moment. Returning to the office, he took a glass
of lemonade, for he would take no stronger beverage; and while he was within, the chips he had
chopped were gathered up and safely cared for by
a hospital steward, because they were ' the chips
that Father Abraham chopped.' In a few hours
more the beloved President was at home in Wash
ington; in a few days more he had passed **away**
and a bereaved nation was in mourning."

LXXI.

Mr. Lincoln returned from Richmond with a
heart-full purpose to issue immediately a proclamation for a day of National Thanksgiving. " Baby-
lon " had fallen, and with his own eyes, as from
another Pisgah, he had looked over into the promised land of Peace, — a land which, like his **great**
prototype, his feet were not to tread!

19

During his absence from Washington, Secretary Seward met with the serious accident by which his arm and jaw were broken. Mr. Lincoln's first visit was to the house of the Secretary, who was confined to his bed by his injuries. After a few words of sympathy and condolence, with a countenance beaming with joy and satisfaction, he entered upon an account of his visit to Richmond, and the glorious success of Grant, — throwing himself, in his almost boyish exultation, at full length across the bed, supporting his head upon one hand, and in this manner reciting the story of the collapse of the Rebellion. Concluding, he lifted himself up and said: " And now for a day of Thanksgiving ! " Mr. Seward entered fully into his feelings, but observed, with characteristic caution, that the issue between Sherman and Johnston had not yet been decided, and a premature celebration might have the effect to nerve the remaining army of the Confederacy to greater desperation. He advised, therefore, no official designation of a day " until the result of Sherman's combinations was known." Admitting the force of the Secretary's view, Mr. Lincoln reluctantly gave up the purpose, and three days later suffered in his own person the last, most atrocious, but culminating act of the most wicked of all rebellions recorded on the pages of history ! It was the last interview on earth between the President and his Secretary of State.

This incident, related by Mr. Seward to a friend *

* J. C. Derby, Esq., of New York.

while slowly recovering from the murderous attack upon himself, was followed by an interesting account of his personal relations with Mr. Lincoln. " No knife was ever sharp enough to divide us upon any question of public policy," said the Secretary; " though we frequently arrived at the same conclusion through different processes of thought." " Once only," he continued, musingly, " did we disagree in sentiment." Mr. D. inquired the subject of dissent. " His ' colonization ' scheme," was the reply, " which I opposed on the self-evident principle that all *natives* of a country have an *equal* right in its soil."

The knowledge of the terrible calamity which had befallen the nation was rigidly withheld from Mr. Seward at the time, his physician fearing that the shock would be too great for him to bear. The Sunday following, he had his bed wheeled around so that he could see the tops of the trees in the park opposite his residence, — just putting on their spring foliage, — when his eyes caught sight of the Stars and Stripes at half-mast on the War Department, on which he gazed awhile, then turning to his attendant, said: " The President is dead ! " The confused attendant stammered as he tried to say nay ; but the Secretary could not be deceived. " If he had been alive, he would have been the first to call on me," he continued ; " but he has not been here, nor has he sent to know how I am ; and there is the flag at half-mast." The statesman's inductive reason had discerned the truth, and in silence the great tears coursed down his gashed cheeks, as it sank into his heart.

LXXII.

At the Cabinet meeting held the morning of the day of the assassination, it was afterward remembered, a remarkable circumstance occurred. General Grant was present, and during a lull in the discussion the President turned to him and asked if he had heard from General Sherman. General Grant replied that he had not, but was in hourly expectation of receiving despatches from him announcing the surrender of Johnston.

"Well," said the President, "you will hear very soon now, and the news will be important."

"Why do you think so?" said the General.

"Because," said Mr. Lincoln, "I had a dream last night; and ever since the war began, I have invariably had the same dream before any important military event occurred." He then instanced Bull Run, Antietam, Gettysburg, etc., and said that before each of these events, he had had the same dream; and turning to Secretary Welles, said: "It is in your line, too, Mr. Welles. The dream is, that I saw a ship sailing very rapidly; and I am sure that it portends some important national event."

Later in the day, dismissing all business, the

carriage was ordered for a drive. When asked by Mrs. Lincoln if he would like any one to accompany them, he replied, " No ; I prefer to ride by ourselves to-day." Mrs. Lincoln subsequently said that she never saw him seem so supremely happy as on this occasion. In reply to a remark to this effect, the President said : " And well I may feel so, Mary, for I consider this day the war has come to a close." And then added : " We must both be more cheerful in the future ; between the war and the loss of our darling Willie, we have been very miserable."

.   .   .   .

Little " Tad's " frantic grief upon being told that his father had been shot was alluded to in the Washington correspondence of the time. For twenty-four hours the little fellow was perfectly inconsolable. Sunday morning, however, the sun rose in unclouded splendor, and in his simplicity he looked upon this as a token that his father was happy. " Do you think my father has gone to heaven ? " he asked of a gentleman who had called upon Mrs. Lincoln. " I have not a doubt of it," was the reply. " Then," he exclaimed, in his broken way, " I am glad he has gone there, for he never was happy after he came here. This was not a good place for him ! "

LXXIII.

"President Lincoln," says the Hon. W. D. Kelly,* "was a large and many-sided man, and yet so simple that no one, not even a child, could approach him without feeling that he had found in him a sympathizing friend. I remember that I apprised him of the fact that a lad, the son of one of my townsmen, had served a year on board the gunboat *Ottawa*, and had been in two important engagements; in the first as a powder-monkey, when he had conducted himself with such coolness that he had been chosen as captain's messenger in the second; and I suggested to the President that it was in his power to send to the Naval School, annually, three boys who had served at least a year in the navy.

"He at once wrote on the back of a letter from the commander of the *Ottawa*, which I had handed him, to the Secretary of the Navy· 'If the appointments for this year have not been made, let this boy be appointed.' The appointment had not been made, and I brought it home with me. It directed the lad to report for examination at the school in July. Just as he was ready to start, his father, looking over the law, discovered that he could not report until he was fourteen years of age, which he would not be until September following. The poor child sat down and wept. He

* Address in Philadelphia upon the death of Mr. Lincoln.

feared that he was not to go to the Naval School.
He was, however, soon consoled by being told that
'the President could make it right.' It was my
fortune to meet him the next morning at the door
of the Executive Chamber with his father.

" Taking by the hand the little fellow, — short
for his age, dressed in the sailor's blue pants and
shirt, — I advanced with him to the President, who
sat in his usual seat, and said : ' Mr. President,
my young friend, Willie Bladen, finds a difficulty
about his appointment. You have directed him to
appear at the school in July ; but he is not yet
fourteen years of age.' But before I got half of
this out, Mr. Lincoln, laying down his spectacles,
rose and said : ' Bless me ! is that the boy who did
so gallantly in those two great battles ? Why, I
feel that I should bow to him, and not he to me.'

" The little fellow had made his graceful bow.
The President took the papers at once, and as soon
as he learned that a postponement till September
would suffice, made the order that the lad should
report in that month. Then putting his hand on
Willie's head, he said : ' Now, my boy, go home
and have good fun during the two months, for they
are about the last holiday you will get.' The little
fellow bowed himself out, feeling that the President of the United States, though a very great
man, was one that he would nevertheless like to
have a game of romps with."

There was not unfrequently a curious mingling

of humor and pathos exhibited in Mr. Lincoln's exercise of the pardoning power. Lieutenant-Governor Ford, of Ohio, had an appointment with him one evening at six o'clock. As he entered the vestibule of the White House his attention was attracted by a poorly clad young woman who was violently sobbing. He asked her the cause of her distress. She said that she had been ordered away by the servants, after vainly waiting many hours to see the President about her only brother, who had been condemned to death. Her story was this: She and her brother were foreigners, and orphans. They had been in this country several years. Her brother enlisted in the army, but, through bad influences, was induced to desert. He was captured, tried, and sentenced to be shot — the old story. The poor girl had obtained the signatures of some persons who had formerly known him to a petition for a pardon, and, alone, had come to Washington to lay the case before the President. Thronged as the waiting-rooms always were, she had passed the long hours of two days trying in vain to get an audience, and had at length been ordered away.

Mr. Ford's sympathies were at once enlisted. He said that he had come to see the President, but did not know as *he* should succeed. He told her, however, to follow him up-stairs, and he would see what could be done. Just before reaching the door, Mr. Lincoln came out, and meeting his friend, said good-humoredly, " are you not ahead of time ? " Mr. Ford showed his watch, with the pointers upon the hour of six. " Well," replied Mr. Lincoln, " I have been so busy to-day that I have not had time to get a lunch. Go in and sit down ; I will be back directly."

Mr. Ford made the young woman accompany him into the office, and when they were seated, said to her : " Now, my good girl, I want you to muster all the courage you have in the world. When the President comes back he will sit down in that arm-chair. I shall get up to speak to him, and as I do so you must force yourself between us, and insist upon his examination of your papers, telling him it is a case of life and death, and admits of no delay." These instructions were carried out to the letter. Mr. Lincoln was at first somewhat surprised at the apparent forwardness of the young woman, but observing her distressed appearance, he ceased conversation with his friend, and com‐ menced an examination of the document she had placed in his hands. Glancing from it to the face of the petitioner, whose tears had broken forth afresh, he studied its expression for a moment, and then his eye fell upon her scanty but neat dress. Instantly his face lighted up. " My poor girl," said he, " you have come here with no governor, or senator, or member of congress, to plead your cause. You seem honest and truthful; and " — with much emphasis — " you don't wear ' *hoops;*

and I will be whipped but I will pardon your brother ! ''

Among the applicants received on another occasion by the President, was a woman who had also met with considerable difficulty and delay in getting admission to him. She said that her husband had been arrested some months before and sent to the " Old Capitol" prison; that he had not been " tried," and could not learn as he was likely to be ; and she appealed to the President as a husband and father to interfere and order an immediate trial. Mr. Lincoln said he was sorry this could not be done, — adding that such cases were much like the different sacks of grain at a country grist-mill, all " waiting their turn to be ground," and that it would be unfair for the " *miller* " to show any " partiality." The woman left, but the next day appeared again before him. Recognizing her, Mr. Lincoln asked if anything " new " had happened. " No," replied the woman ; " but I have been thinking, sir, about what you said concerning the ' grists,' and I am afraid *mine* will get ' mouldy' and 'spoil' before its turn comes around, so I have come to ask, Mr. President, that it may be taken to some other ' mill' to be ground."

Mr. Lincoln was so much amused at the wit and shrewdness of the request, that he instantly gave the woman an unconditional discharge for her husband.

LXXIV.

"Good morning, Abe!" was the greeting addressed to the President, as we sat together in his
office one morning, — he absorbed at his desk, and
I with my pencil. I looked up in astonishment at
the unaccustomed familiarity.

"Why, Dennis," returned Mr. Lincoln, "is this
you?"

"Yes, Abe," was the rejoinder; "I made up my
mind I must come down and see you once while
you were President, anyhow. So here I am, all the
way from Sangamon."

Sitting down, side by side, it would have been
difficult for one unfamiliar with democratic institutions to tell, by the appearance or conversation,
which was the President and which the back-coun-
tryman, save that from time to time I overheard the
man addressed as "Dennis" refer to family trials
and hardships, and intimate that one object of his
journey so far, was to see if his old friend "could
not do something for one of his boys?"

The response to this was: "Now, Dennis, sit
down and write out what you want, so that I can
have it before me, and I will see what can be done."

I have always supposed that this was "Dennis
Hanks," the early companion and friend of Mr.
Lincoln; but my attention at the time being diverted, the matter passed out of my mind, and I
neglected subsequently to inquire.

About this period — it may have been the following evening — the house was thrown into an
uproar by a performance of little " Tad's." I was
sitting in Mr. Nicolay's room, about ten o'clock
when Robert Lincoln came in with a flushed face.
" Well," said he, " I have just had a great row
with the President of the United States ! "

" What ? " said I.

" Yes," he replied, " and very good cause there is
for it, too. Do you know," he continued, " ' Tad'
went over to the War Department to-day, and
Stanton, for the fun of the thing, — putting him a
peg above the ' little corporal ' of the French Government, — commissioned him ' lieutenant.' On the
strength of this, what does ' Tad ' do but go off and
order a quantity of muskets sent to the house ! To-
night he had the audacity to discharge the guard,
and he then mustered all the gardeners and servants, gave them the guns, drilled them, and put
them on duty in their place. I found it out an hour
ago," continued Robert, " and thinking it a great
shame, as the men had been hard at work all day, I
went to father with it ; but instead of punishing
' Tad,' as I think he ought, he evidently looks upon
it as a good joke, and won't do anything about it ! "

" Tad," however, presently went to bed, and then
the men were quietly discharged. And so it happened that the presidential mansion was unguarded
one night, at least, during the war !

The second week in July the whole country, and

Washington in particular, was thrown into a fever of anxiety by the rebel raid upon that city under Early and Breckinridge. The night of Sunday, the 10th, I have always believed the city might have been captured had the enemy followed up his advantage. The defences were weak, and there were comparatively but few troops in the city or vicinity. All day Monday the excitement was at the highest pitch. At the White House the cannonading at Fort Stevens was distinctly heard throughout the day. During Sunday, Monday, and Tuesday, the President visited the forts and outworks, part of the time accompanied by Mrs. Lincoln. While at Fort Stevens on Monday, both were imprudently exposed, — rifle - balls coming, in several instances, alarmingly near!

The almost defenceless condition of the city was the occasion of much censure. Some blamed General Halleck; others General Augur, the commander of the Department; others the Secretary of War; and still others the President.

Subsequently the rebel force returned to Richmond almost unharmed. I saw no one who appeared to take this more to heart than Mrs. Lincoln, who was inclined to lay the responsibility at the door of the Secretary of War.

Two or three weeks later, when tranquillity was perfectly restored, it was said that Stanton called upon the President and Mrs. Lincoln one evening at the "Soldiers' Home." In the course of conversation the Secretary said, playfully, "Mrs. Lincoln, I intend to have a full-length portrait of you painted, standing on the ramparts at Fort Stevens overlooking the fight!"

"That is very well," returned Mrs. Lincoln, very promptly; "and I can assure you of one thing, Mr. Secretary, if I had had a few *ladies* with me the Rebels would not have been permitted to get away as they did!"

LXXV.

It was not generally known before the publication of Dr. Holland's biography of Mr. Lincoln, that he was once engaged in a "duel," although a version of the affair had been published previous to his biographer's account of it, which, however, the few who saw it were disposed to regard as a fabrication.

One evening, at the rooms of the Hon. I. N. Arnold, of Illinois, I met Dr. Henry, of Oregon, an early and intimate friend of Mr. Lincoln's. Mr. Arnold asked me in the course of conversation if I had ever heard of the President's "duel" with General Shields? I replied that I might have seen a statement of the kind, but did not suppose it to be true. "Well," said Mr. Arnold, "we were all young folks together at the time in Springfield. In some way a difficulty occurred between Shields and Lincoln, resulting in a challenge from Shields, which was at length accepted, Mr. Lincoln nam-

ing '*broadswords*' for weapons, and the two opposite banks of the Mississippi, where the river was
about a *mile* wide, for the '*ground.*' "

Dr. Henry, who had listened quietly to this, here
broke in, " That will do for a ' story,' Arnold,"
said he, " but it will hardly pass with me, for I
happened to be Lincoln's ' *second* ' on the occasion .
The facts are these.   You will bear me witness
that there was never a more spirited circle of young
folks in one town than lived in Springfield at that
period.   Shields, you remember, was a great '*beau.*'
For a bit of amusement one of the young ladies
wrote some verses, taking him off sarcastically,
which were abstracted from her writing-desk by
a mischievous friend, and published in the local
newspaper.   Shields, greatly irritated, posted at
once to the printing-office and demanded the name
of the author.   Much frightened, the editor re
quested a day or two to consider the matter, and
upon getting rid of Shields went directly to Mr.
Lincoln with his trouble.

" ' Tell Shields,' was the chivalric rejoinder, ' that
I hold myself responsible for the verses.'   The
next day Mr. Lincoln left for a distant section to
attend court.   Shields, boiling over with wrath,
followed and ' challenged' him.   Scarcely knowing what he did, Mr. Lincoln accepted the challenge, seeing no alternative.   The choice of weapons being left to him, he named ' broadswords,'
intending to act only on the defensive, and think-

ing his long arms would enable him to keep clear of his antagonist.

" I was then a young surgeon," continued Dr. Henry, " and Mr. Lincoln desired me accompany him to the point chosen for the contest, — ' Bloody Island,' in the Mississippi, near St. Louis, — as his ' second.' To this I at length consented, hoping to prevent bloodshed. On our way to the ground we met Colonel Hardin, a friend of both parties, and a cousin of the lady who was the real offender. Suspecting something wrong, Hardin subsequently followed us, coming in upon the party just as Lincoln was clearing up the underbrush which covered the ground. Entering heartily upon an attempt at pacification, he at length succeeded in mollifying Shields, and the whole party returned harmoniously to Springfield, and thus the matter ended."

This version of the affair coming from an eye-witness is undoubtedly in all respects correct. It subsequently came in my way to know that Mr. Lincoln himself regarded the circumstance with much regret and mortification, and hoped it might be forgotten. In February preceding his death a distinguished officer of the army called at the White House, and was entertained by the President and Mrs. Lincoln for an hour in the parlor. During the conversation the gentleman said, turning to Mrs. Lincoln, " Is it true, Mr. President, as I have heard, that you once went out to fight a ' duel ' for the sake of the lady by your side ? "

"I do not deny it," replied Mr. Lincoln, with a flushed face; "but if you desire my friendship you will never mention the circumstance again!"

LXXVI.

In August following the rebel raid, Judge J. T. Mills, of Wisconsin, in company with ex-Governor Randall, of that State, called upon the President at the "Soldiers' Home."

Judge Mills subsequently published the following account of the interview, in the "Grant County (Wisconsin) Herald":—

.   .   .   .

"The Governor addressed him: 'Mr. President this is my friend and your friend Mills, from Wisconsin.'

"'I am glad to see my friends from Wisconsin; they are the hearty friends of the Union.'

"'I could not leave the city, Mr. President, without hearing words of cheer from your own lips. Upon you, as the representative of the loyal people, depend, as we believe, the existence of our government and the future of America.'

"'Mr. President,' said Governor Randall, 'why can't you seek seclusion, and play hermit for a fortnight? it would reinvigorate you.'

"'Aye,' said the President, 'two or three weeks would do me good, but I cannot fly from my thoughts; my solicitude for this great country fol

20

lows me wherever I go. I don't think it is personal vanity or ambition, though I am not free from these infirmities, but I cannot but feel that the weal or woe of this great nation will be decided in November. There is no programme offered by any wing of the Democratic party but that must result in the permanent destruction of the Union.'

" ' But Mr. President, General McClellan is in favor of crushing out the rebellion by force. He will be the Chicago candidate.'

" ' Sir,' said the President, ' the slightest knowledge of arithmetic will prove to any man that the rebel armies cannot be destroyed by democratic strategy. It would sacrifice all the white men of the North to do it. There are now in the service of the United States near two hundred thousand able-bodied colored men, most of them under arms, defending and acquiring Union territory. The democratic strategy demands that these forces should be disbanded, and that the masters be conciliated by restoring them to slavery. The black men who now assist Union prisoners to escape are to be converted into our enemies, in the vain hope of gaining the good-will of their masters. We shall have to fight two nations instead of one.

" ' You cannot conciliate the South if you guarantee to them ultimate success; and the experience of the present war proves their success is inevitable if you fling the compulsory labor of millions of black men into their side of the scale. Will you give tar enemies such military advantages as insure **success**, and then depend on coaxing, flattery, and **concession**, to get them back into the Union? Abandon all the posts now garrisoned by black men; take two hundred thousand men from our side and put them in the battle-field or cornfield against us, and we would be compelled to abandon the war in three weeks.

" 'We have to hold territory in inclement and sickly places; where are the Democrats to do this? It was a free fight, and the field was open to the War Democrats to put down this rebellion by fighting against both master and slave long before the present policy was inaugurated.

" 'There have been men base enough to propose to me to return to slavery the black warriors of Port Hudson and Olustee, and thus win the respect of the masters they fought. Should I do so, I should deserve to be damned in time and eternity. Come what will, I will keep my faith with friend and foe. My enemies pretend I am now carrying on this war for the sole purpose of Abolition. So long as I am President, it shall be carried on for the sole purpose of restoring the Union. But no human power can subdue this rebellion without the use of the emancipation policy, and every other policy calculated to weaken the moral and physical forces of the rebellion.

" 'Freedom has given us two hundred thousand men raised on Southern soil. It will give us more

yet.   Just so much it has subtracted from the enemy, and instead of alienating the South, there are
now evidences of a fraternal feeling growing up between our men and the rank and file of the rebel
soldiers.   Let my enemies prove to the country
that the destruction of slavery is not necessary
to a restoration of the Union.   I will abide the
issue.'

"I saw that the President was a man of deep
convictions, of abiding faith in justice, truth, and
Providence.   His voice was pleasant, his manner
earnest and emphatic.   As he warmed with his
theme, his mind grew to the magnitude of his body.
I felt I was in the presence of the great guiding intellect of the age, and that those 'huge Atlantean
shoulders were fit to bear the weight of mightiest
monarchies.'   His transparent honesty, republican
simplicity, his gushing sympathy for those who offered their lives for their country, his utter forget-
fulness of self in his concern for its welfare, could
not but inspire me with confidence that he was
Heaven's instrument to conduct his people through
this sea of blood to a Canaan of peace and freedom."

LXXVII.

No reminiscence of the late President has been
given to the public more thoroughly valuable and
characteristic than a sketch which appeared in the
New York "Independent" of September 1st, 1864,

from the pen of the Rev. J. P. Gulliver, of Norwich, Connecticut : —

"It was just after his controversy with Douglas, and some months before the meeting of the Chicago Convention of 1860, that Mr. Lincoln came to Norwich to make a political speech. It was in substance the famous speech delivered in New York, commencing with the noble words : ' There is but one political question before the people of this country, which is this, *Is slavery right, or is it wrong ?* ' and ending with the yet nobler words : ' Gentlemen, it has been said of the world's history hitherto that " might makes right ; " it is for us and for our times to reverse the maxim, and to show that *right makes might !* '

"The next morning I met him at the railroad station, where he was conversing with our Mayor, every few minutes looking up the track and inquiring, half impatiently and half quizzically, ' Where's that ' wagon ' of yours ? Why don't the ' wagon ' come along ? ' On being introduced to him, he fixed his eyes upon me, and said : ' I have seen you before, sir ! ' ' I think not,' I replied ; ' you must mistake me for some other person.' ' No, I don't ; I saw you at the Town Hall, last evening.' ' Is it possible, Mr. Lincoln, that you could observe individuals so closely in such a crowd ? ' ' Oh, yes ! ' he replied, laughing ; ' that is my way. I don't forget faces. Were you not there ? ' ' I was, sir, and I was well paid for going ; ' adding, somewhat

in the vein of pleasantry he had started, ' I consider it one of the most extraordinary speeches I
ever heard.'

"As we entered the cars, he beckoned me to
take a seat with him, and said, in a most agreeably
frank way, ' Were you sincere in what you said
about my speech just now ?' 'I meant every
word of it, Mr. Lincoln. Why, an old dyed-in-
the-wool Democrat, who sat near me, applauded
you repeatedly ; and, when rallied upon his con-
version to sound principles, answered, "I don't believe a word he says, but I can't help clapping
him, he is so *pat!*" That I call the triumph of
oratory, —

> " When you convince a man against his will,
>   Though he is of the same opinion still."

Indeed, sir, I learned more of the art of public
speaking last evening than I could from a whole
course of lectures on Rhetoric.'

"'Ah! that reminds me,' said he, ' of a most
extraordinary circumstance which occurred in New
Haven the other day.   They told me that the Professor of Rhetoric in Yale College, — a very learned
man, is n't he ?'

"' Yes, sir, and a fine critic too.'

"' Well, I suppose so ; he ought to be, at any
rate, — they told me that he came to hear me, and
took notes of my speech, and gave a lecture on it
to his class the next day; and, not satisfied with
that, he followed me up to Meriden the next even-

ing, and heard me again for the same purpose. Now, if this is so, it is to my mind very extraordinary. I have been sufficiently astonished at my success in the West. It has been most unexpected. But I had no thought of any marked success at the East, and least of all that I should draw out such commendations from literary and learned men. Now,' he continued, 'I should like very much to know what it was in my speech you thought so remarkable, and what you suppose interested my friend, the Professor, so much.'

" 'The clearness of your statements, Mr. Lincoln ; the unanswerable style of your reasoning, and especially your illustrations, which were romance and pathos, and fun and logic all welded together. That story about the snakes, for example, which set the hands and feet of your Democratic hearers in such vigorous motion, was at once queer and comical, and tragic and argumentative. It broke through all the barriers of a man's previous opinions and prejudices at a crash, and blew up the very citadel of his false theories before he could know what had hurt him.'

" 'Can you remember any other illustrations,' said he, ' of this peculiarity of my style ? '

" I gave him others of the same sort, occupying some half-hour in the critique, when he said : ' I am much obliged to you for this. I have been wishing for a long time to find some one who would make this analysis for me. It throws light on a

su'ject which has been dark to me. I can under▪
stand very readily how such a power as you have
ascribed to me will account for the effect which
seems to be produced by my speeches. I hope you
have not been too flattering in your estimate. Certainly, I have had a most wonderful success, for a
man of my limited education.'

" ' That suggests, Mr. Lincoln, an inquiry which
has several times been upon my lips during this
conversation. I want very much to know how
you got this unusual power of " putting things."
It must have been a matter of education. No man
has it by nature alone. What has your education
been ? '

" ' Well, as to education, the newspapers are correct ; I never went to school more than six months
in my life. But, as you say, this must be a product
of culture in some form. I have been putting the
question you ask me to myself, while you have
been talking. I can say this, that among my earliest recollections I remember how, when a mere
child, I used to get irritated when any body talked
to me in a way I could not understand. I don't
think I ever got angry at anything else in my life.
But that always disturbed my temper, and has ever
since. I can remember going to my little bed-
room, after hearing the neighbors talk of an evening with my father, and spending no small part of
the night walking up and down, and trying to
make out what was the exact meaning of some of

their, to me, dark sayings. I could not sleep, though I often tried to, when I got on such a hunt after an idea, until I had caught it ; and when I thought I had got it, I was not satisfied until I had repeated it over and over, until I had put it in language plain enough, as I thought, for any boy I knew to comprehend. This was a kind of passion with me, and it has stuck by me ; for I am never easy now, when I am handling a thought, till I have bounded it North, and bounded it South, and bounded it East, and bounded it West. Perhaps that accounts for the characteristic you observe in my speeches, though I never put the two things together before.'

" 'Mr. Lincoln, I thank you for this. It is the most splendid educational fact I ever happened upon. This is *genius*, with all its impulsive, inspiring, dominating power over the mind of its possessor, developed by education into *talent*, with its uniformity, its permanence, and its disciplined strength, — always ready, always available, never capricious, — the highest possession of the human intellect. But, let me ask, did you prepare for your profession ? '

" 'Oh, yes ! I " read law," as the phrase is that is, I became a lawyer's clerk in Springfield, and copied tedious documents, and picked up what I could of law in the intervals of other work. But your question reminds me of a bit of education I had, which I am bound in honesty to mention. In the course of my law-reading, I constantly came upon the word *demonstrate*. I thought at first that I understood its meaning, but soon became satisfied that I did not. I said to myself, " What do I mean when I *demonstrate* more than when I *reason* or *prove?* How does *demonstration* differ from any other proof? " I consulted Webster's Dictionary. That told of " certain proof," " proof beyond the possibility of doubt ; " but I could form no idea what sort of proof that was. I thought a great many things were proved beyond a possibility of doubt, without recourse to any such extraordinary process of reasoning as I understood " demonstration " to be. I consulted all the dictionaries and books of reference I could find, but with no better results. You might as well have defined *blue* to a blind man. At last I said, " Lincoln, you can never make a lawyer if you do not understand what *demonstrate* means ; " and I left my situation in Springfield, went home to my father's house, and stayed there till I could give any proposition in the six books of Euclid at sight. I then found out what " demonstrate " means, and went back to my law-studies.'

" I could not refrain from saying, in my admiration at such a development of character and genius combined : ' Mr. Lincoln, your success is no longer a marvel. It is the legitimate result of adequate causes. You deserve it all, and a great deal more. If you will permit me, I would like to use this fact publicly. It will be most valuable in inciting our young men to that patient classical and mathematical culture which most minds absolutely require. No man can talk well unless he is able first of all to define to himself what he is talking about. Euclid, well studied, would free the world of half its calamities, by banishing half the nonsense which now deludes and curses it. I have often thought that Euclid would be one of the best books to put on the catalogue of the Tract Society, if they could only get people to read it. It would be a means of grace.'

" 'I think so,' said he, laughing; 'I vote for Euclid.'

" Just then a gentleman entered the car who was well known as a very ardent friend of Douglas. Being a little curious to see how Mr. Lincoln would meet him, I introduced him after this fashion: — 'Mr. Lincoln, allow me to introduce Mr. L——, a very particular friend of your particular friend, Mr. Douglas.' He at once took his hand in a most cordial manner, saying: 'I have no doubt you think you are right, sir.' This hearty tribute to the honesty of a political opponent, with the manner of doing it, struck me as a beautiful exhibition of a large-hearted charity, of which we see far too little in this debating, fermenting world.

" As we neared the end of our journey, Mr. Lincoln turned to me very pleasantly, and said : 'I want to thank you for this conversation. I have enjoyed it very much.' I replied, referring to some stalwart denunciations he had just been uttering of the demoralizing influences of Washington upon Northern politicians in respect to the slavery question, ' Mr. Lincoln, may I say one thing to you before we separate ? '

" ' Certainly, anything you please.'

" ' You have just spoken of the tendency of political life in Washington to debase the moral convictions of our representatives there by the admixture of considerations of mere political expediency. You have become, by the controversy with Mr. Douglas, one of our leaders in this great struggle with slavery, which is undoubtedly *the* struggle of the nation and the age. What I would like to say is this, and I say it with a full heart, *Be true to your principles and we will be true to you, and God will be true to us all!* ' His homely face lighted up instantly with a beaming expression, and taking my hand warmly in both of his, he said: ' I say *Amen* to that — AMEN to that ! '

" There is a deep excavation in the rock shown to visitors, among the White Mountains, into which one of the purest of the mountain streams pours itself, known as ' The Pool.' As you stand by its side at an ordinary time you look down upon a mass of impenetrable green, lying like a rich emerald in a setting of granite upon the bosom of the mountain. But occasionally the noon-day sun darts through it a vertical ray which penetrates to its

rery bottom, and shows every configuration of the
varied interior I felt at that moment that a ray
had darted down to the bottom of Abraham Lincoln's heart, and that I could see the whole. It
seemed to me as beautiful as that emerald pool, and
as pure. I have never forgotten that glimpse.
When the strange revocation came of the most
rational and reasonable proclamation of Fremont, —
' The slaves of Rebels shall be set free,' — I remembered that hearty ' *Amen*,' and stifled my rising
apprehensions. I remembered it in those dark
days when McClellan, Nero-like, was fiddling on
James River, and Pope was being routed before
Washington, and the report came that a prominent
Cabinet Minister had boasted that he had succeeded
in preventing the issue of the Emancipation Proclamation ; I said : ' Abraham Lincoln will prove
true yet.' *And he has !* God bless him ! *he has.*
Slow, if you please, but *true.* Unimpassioned, if
you please, but *true.* Jocose, trifling, if you please,
but *true.* Reluctant to part with unworthy official
advisers, but *true* himself — *true as steel !* I could
wish him less a man of facts, and more a man of
deas. I could wish him more stern and more vigorous : but every man has his faults, and still I
say : *Amen to Abraham Lincoln !* " *

* This article was written and first published some months previous
to Mr. Lincoln's reëlection, during the depression of the public mind
following the " raid " on Washington.

LXXVIII.

The Hon. Orlando Kellogg, of New York, was sitting in his room at his boarding-house one evening, when one of his constituents appeared, — a white-headed old man, — who had come to Washington in great trouble, to seek the aid of his representative in behalf of his son. His story was this: "The young man had formerly been very dissipated. During an absence from home a year or two previous to the war, he enlisted in the regular army, and, after serving six months, deserted. Returning to his father, who knew nothing of this, he reformed his habits, and when the war broke out, entered heart and soul into the object of raising a regiment in his native county, and was subsequently elected one of its officers. He had proved an efficient officer, distinguishing himself particularly on one occasion, in a charge across a bridge, when he was severely wounded, — his colonel being killed by his side. Shortly after this, he came in contact with one of his old companions in the 'regular' service, who recognized him, and declared his purpose of informing against him. Overwhelmed with mortification, the young man procured a furlough and returned home, revealing the matter to his father, and declaring his purpose never to submit to an arrest, — 'he would die first.'" In broken tones the old man finished his statement, saying: "Can you do anything for us,

Judge? — it is a hard, hard case!" "I will see about that," replied the representative, putting on his hat; "wait here until I return." He went immediately to the White House, and fortunately finding Mr. Lincoln alone, they sat down together, and he repeated the old man's story. The President made no demonstration of particular interest until the Judge reached the description of the charge across the bridge, and the wound received. "Do you say," he interrupted, "that the young man was wounded?" "Yes," replied the congressman, "badly." "Then he has shed his blood for his country," responded Mr. Lincoln, musingly. "Kellogg," he continued, brightening up, "is n't there something in Scripture about the ' shedding of blood' being ' the remission of sins ?' " " Guess you are about right there," replied the Judge. "It is a good 'point,' and there is no going behind it," rejoined the President; and taking up his pen, another "pardon" — this time without "oath," condition, or reserve — was added to the records of the War Office.

"Among a large number of persons waiting in the room to speak with Mr. Lincoln, on a certain day in November, '64, was a small, pale, delicate-looking boy about thirteen years old. The President saw him standing, looking feeble and faint, and said : ' Come here, my boy, and tell me what you want.' The boy advanced, placed his hand on the arm of the President's chair, and with bowed

head and timid accents said : 'Mr. President, I
have been a drummer in a regiment for two years,
and my colonel got angry with me and turned me
off. I was taken sick, and have been a long time
in hospital. This is the first time I have been out,
and I came to see if you could not do something
for me.' The President looked at him kindly and
tenderly, and asked him where he lived. 'I have
no home,' answered the boy. 'Where is your
father?' 'He died in the army,' was the reply.
'Where is your mother?' continued the President.
'My mother is dead also. I have no mother, no
father, no brothers, no sisters, and,' bursting into
tears, 'no friends — nobody cares for me.' Mr.
Lincoln's eyes filled with tears, and he said to him,
'Can't you sell newspapers?' 'No,' said the boy,
'I am too weak; and the surgeon of the hospital
told me I must leave, and I have no money, and no
place to go to.' The scene was wonderfully affecting. The President drew forth a card, and addressing on it certain officials to whom his request
was law, gave special directions 'to care for this
poor boy.' The wan face of the little drummer lit
up with a happy smile as he received the paper,
and he went away convinced that he had one good
and true friend, at least, in the person of the
President." *

No incident of this character related of the late
President, is more profoundly touching in its ten-

* Rev. Mr. Henderson, Louisville, Ky.

derness and simplicity than that given to me the last evening I passed at the White House, in the office of the private secretary, by a resident of Washington,* who witnessed the scene.

"I was waiting my turn to speak to the President one day, some three or four weeks since," said Mr. M——, "when my attention was attracted by the sad patient face of a woman advanced in life, who in a faded hood and shawl was among the applicants for an interview.

" Presently Mr. Lincoln turned to her, saying in his accustomed manner, ' Well, my good woman, what can I do for you this morning?' ' Mr. President,' said she, ' my husband and three sons all went into the army. My husband was killed in the fight at ——. I get along very badly since then, living all alone, and I thought I would come and ask you to release to me my oldest son.' Mr. Lincoln looked into her face a moment, and in his kindest accents responded, ' Certainly! certainly! If you have given us *all*, and your prop has been taken away, you are justly entitled to one of your boys!' He immediately made out an order discharging the young man, which the woman took, and thanking him gratefully, went away.

" I had forgotten the circumstance," continued M ——, " till last week, when happening to be here again, who should come in but the same

---

* Mr. Murtagh, of the *W shington Republican.*

21

woman. It appeared that she had gone herself to the front, with the President's order, and found the son she was in search of had been mortally wounded in a recent engagement, and taken to a hospital. She found the hospital, but the boy was dead, or died while she was there. The surgeon in charge made a memorandum of the facts upon the back of the President's order, and almost broken-hearted, the poor woman had found her way again into Mr. Lincoln's presence. He was much affected by her appearance and story, and said: ' I know what you wish me to do now, and I shall do it without your asking; I shall release to you your second son.' Upon this, he took up his pen and commenced writing the order. While he was writing the poor woman stood by his side, the tears running down her face, and passed her hand softly over his head, stroking his rough hair, as I have seen a fond mother caress a son. By the time he had finished writing, his own heart and eyes were full. He handed her the paper : ' Now,' said he, '*you* have one and *I* one of the other two left : that is no more than right.' She took the paper, and reverently placing her hand again upon his head, the tears still upon her cheeks, said : ' The Lord bless you, Mr. Lincoln. May you live a thousand years, and may you always he the head of this great nation ! ' "

LXXIX.

The Hon. W. H. Herndon, of Springfield, Illinois, for more than twenty years the law-partner of Mr. Lincoln, delivered an address in that city, December 12th, 1865, upon the life and character of the lamented President, which, for masterly analysis, has scarcely an equal in the annals of biographical literature. Quaint and original in style and construction, this description — an imperfect abstract of which I subjoin — is in singular harmony with the character it depicts. To those who knew Mr. Lincoln personally, so thorough a dissection of his nature and traits will need no indorsement; while to the multitude who knew him not, it may be commended as probably more complete and exhaustive in its treatment of the subject, than anything which has been given to the world.

" Abraham Lincoln was born in Hardin County, Kentucky, February 12th, 1809. He moved to Indiana in 1816; came to Illinois in March, 1830; to old Sangamon County in 1831, settling in New Salem, and from this last place to this city in April, 1837: coming as a rude, uncultivated boy, without polish or education, and having no friends. He was about six feet four inches high, and when he left this city was fifty-one years old, having good health and no gray hairs, or but few on his head. He was thin, wiry, sinewy, raw-boned; thin through the breast to the back, and narrow across the shoul-

ders ; standing, he leaned forward — was what **may**
be called stoop-shouldered, inclining to the consump-
tive by build.   His usual weight was one hundred
and sixty pounds.   His organization — rather his
structure and functions — worked slowly.   His blood
had to run a long distance from his heart to the ex-
tremities of his frame, and his nerve-force had **to**
travel through dry ground a long distance before his
muscles were obedient to his will.   His structure
was loose and leathery ; his body was shrunk and
shrivelled, having dark skin, dark hair, — looking
woe-struck.   The whole man, body and mind,
worked slowly, creakingly, as if it needed oiling.
Physically, he was a very powerful man, lifting
with ease four hundred or six hundred pounds.   His
mind was like his body, and worked slowly **but**
strongly.   When he walked, he moved cautiously
but firmly, his long arms and hands on them, hanging like giant's hands, swung down by his side.   **He**
walked with even tread, the inner sides of his feet
being parallel.   He put the whole foot flat down **on**
the ground at once, not landing on the heel ; he likewise lifted his foot all at once, not rising from **the**
toe, and hence he had no spring to his walk.   **He**
had economy of fall and lift of foot, though he **had**
no spring or apparent ease of motion in his tread.
He walked undulatory, up and down, catching **and**
pocketing tire, weariness, and pain, all up and down
his person, preventing them from locating.   **The**
first opinion of a stranger, or a man who did **not**

observe closely, was that his walk implied shrewdness, cunning, — a tricky man ; but his was the
walk of caution and firmness.   In sitting down on
a common chair he was no taller than ordinary men.
His legs and arms were, abnormally, unnaturally
long, and in undue proportion to the balance of his
body.   It was only when he stood up that he loomed
above other men.

  " Mr. Lincoln's head was long and tall from the
base of the brain and from the eyebrows.   His
head ran backwards, his forehead rising as it ran
back at a low angle, like Clay's, and, unlike Webster's, almost perpendicular.   The size of his hat,
measured at the hatter's block, was 7⅛, his head
being, from ear to ear, 6½ inches, and from the front
to the back of the brain 8 inches.   Thus measured,
it was not below the medium size.   His forehead
was narrow but high ; his hair was dark, almost
black, and lay floating where his fingers or the
winds left it, piled up at random.   His cheek-bones
were high, sharp, and prominent ; his eyebrows
heavy and prominent ; his jaws were long, upcurved, and heavy ; his nose was large, long, and
blunt, a little awry towards the right eye ; his
chin was long, sharp, and upcurved ; his eyebrows
cropped out like a huge rock on the brow of a hill
his face was long, sallow, and cadaverous, shrunk,
shrivelled, wrinkled, and dry, having here and there
a hair on the surface ; his cheeks were leathery ;
his ears were large, and ran out almost at right an-

gles from his head, caused partly by heavy hats and partly by nature; his lower lip was thick, hanging, and undercurved, while his chin reached for the lip upcurved; his neck was neat and trim, his head being well balanced on it; there was the lone mole on the right cheek, and Adam's apple on his throat.

"Thus stood, walked, acted, and looked Abraham Lincoln. He was not a pretty man by any means, nor was he an ugly one; he was a homely man, careless of his looks, plain-looking and plain-acting. He had no pomp, display, or dignity, so-called. He appeared simple in his carriage and bearing. He was a sad-looking man; his melancholy dripped from him as he walked. His apparent gloom impressed his friends, and created a sympathy for him, — one means of his great success. He was gloomy, abstracted, and joyous, — rather humorous, — by turns. I do not think he knew what real joy was for many years.

"Mr. Lincoln sometimes walked our streets cheerily, — good-humoredly, perhaps joyously, — and then it was, on meeting a friend, he cried ' How d' y ? ' clasping one of his friend's hands in both of his, giving a good hearty soul-welcome. Of a winter's morning, he might be seen stalking and stilting it towards the market-house, basket on arm, his old gray shawl wrapped around his neck, his little Willie or Tad running along at his heels, asking a thousand little quick questions, which his father heard not, not even then knowing that little Willie

or Tad was there, so abstracted was he. When he
thus met a friend, he said that something put him
in mind of a story which he heard in Indiana or
elsewhere, and tell it he would, and there was no
alternative but to listen.

"Thus, I say, stood and walked and looked this
singular man. He was odd, but when that gray
eye and face and every feature were lit up by the
inward soul in fires of emotion, *then* it was that all
these apparently ugly features sprang into organs
of beauty, or sunk themselves into a sea of inspiration that sometimes flooded his face. Sometimes it
appeared to me that Lincoln's soul was just fresh
from the presence of its Creator.

.   .   .   .

"I have asked the friends and foes of Mr. Lincoln alike, what they thought of his perceptions.
One gentleman of undoubted ability and free from
all partiality or prejudice, said, ' Mr. Lincoln's perceptions are slow, a little perverted, if not somewhat distorted and diseased.' If the meaning of
this is that Mr. Lincoln saw things from a peculiar
angle of his being, and from this was susceptible to
Nature's impulses, and that he so expressed himself, then I have no objection to what is said. Otherwise, I dissent. Mr. Lincoln's perceptions were
slow, cold, precise, and exact. Everything came to
him in its precise shape and color. To some men
the world of matter and of man comes ornamented
with beauty, life, and action, and hence more or less

false and inexact. No lurking illusion or other
error, false in itself, and clad for the moment in
robes of splendor, ever passed undetected or un-
challenged over the threshold of his mind, — that
point that divides vision from the realm and home
of thought.   Names to him were nothing, and titles
naught, — assumption always standing back abashed
at his cold, intellectual glare.   Neither his perceptions nor intellectual vision were perverted, distorted,
or diseased.   He saw all things through a perfect
mental lens.   There was no diffraction or refraction
there.   He was not impulsive, fanciful, or imagina-
tive, but cold, calm, precise, and exact.   He threw
his whole mental light around the object, and in
time, substance, and quality stood apart ; form and
color took their appropriate places, and all was clear
and exact in his mind.   His fault, if any, was that
he saw things less than they really were ; less beautiful and more frigid.   In his mental view he crushed
the unreal, the inexact, the hollow, and the sham.
He saw things in rigidity rather than in vital action.
Here was his fault.   He saw what no man could
dispute ; but he failed to see what might have been
seen.   To some minds the world is all life, a soul
beneath the material ; but to Mr. Lincoln no life
was individual or universal that did not manifest itself to him.   His mind was his standard.   His perceptions were cool, persistent, pitiless in pursuit of
the truth.   No error went undetected, and no false-
hood unexposed, if he once was aroused in search

of truth. If his perceptions were perverted, distorted, and diseased, would to Heaven that more minds were so.

. . . .

"The true peculiarity of Mr. Lincoln has not been seen by his various biographers; or, if seen, they have failed wofully to give it that prominence which it deserves. It is said that Newton saw an apple fall to the ground from a tree, and beheld the law of the universe in that fall; Shakspeare saw human nature in the laugh of a man; Professor Owen saw the animal in its claw; and Spencer saw the evolution of the universe in the growth of a seed. Nature was suggestive to all these men. Mr. Lincoln no less saw philosophy in a story, and a schoolmaster in a joke. No man, no men, saw nature, fact, thing, or man from his stand-point. His was a new and original position, which was always suggesting, hinting something to him. Nature, insinuations, hints, and suggestions were new, fresh, original, and odd to him. The world, fact, man, principle, all had their powers of suggestion to his susceptible soul. They continually put him in mind of something. He was odd, fresh, new, original, and peculiar for this reason, that he was a new, odd, and original creation and fact. He had keen susceptibilities to the hints and suggestions of nature, which always put him in mind of something known or unknown. Hence his power and tenacity of what is called association of ideas must have been great.

His memory was tenacious and strong. His sus-
ceptibility to all suggestions and hints enabled him
at will to call up readily the associated and classified
fact and idea.

"As an evidence of this, especially peculiar to Mr
Lincoln, let me ask one question. Were Mr. Lincoln's expression and language odd and original,
standing out peculiar from those of all other men?
What does this imply? Oddity and originality of
vision as well as expression; and what is expression
in words and human language, but a telling of what
we see, defining the idea arising from and created
by vision and view in us. Words and language
are but the counterparts of the idea, — the other
half of the idea; they are but the stinging, hot,
heavy, leaden bullets that drop from the mould;
and what are they in a rifle with powder stuffed
behind them and fire applied, but an embodied force
pursuing their object. So are words an embodied
power feeling for comprehension in other minds.
Mr. Lincoln was often perplexed to give expression
to his ideas: first, because he was not master of
the English language; and, secondly, because there
were no words in it containing the coloring, shape,
exactness, power, and gravity of his ideas. He
was frequently at a loss for a word, and hence was
compelled to resort to stories, maxims, and jokes to
embody his idea, that it might be comprehended.
So true was this peculiar mental vision of his, that
though mankind has been gathering, arranging, and

classifying facts for thousands of years, Lincoln's
peculiar stand-point could give him no advantage
of other men's labor.   Hence he tore up to the
deep foundations all arrangements of facts, and
coined and arranged new plans to govern himself.
He was compelled, from his peculiar mental organization, to do this.   His labor was great, continuous,
patient, and all-enduring.

  " The truth about this whole matter is that Mr.
Lincoln read *less* and thought *more* than any man
in his sphere in America.   No man can put his
finger on any great book written in the last or present century that he read.   When young he read
the Bible, and when of age he read Shakspeare.
This latter book was scarcely ever out of his mind.
Mr. Lincoln is acknowledged to have been a great
man, but the question is what made him great.   I
repeat, that he read less and thought more than any
man of his standing in America, if not in the world.
He possessed originality and power of thought in
an eminent degree.   He was cautious, cool, con-
centrated, with continuity of reflection ; was patient
and enduring.   These are some of the grounds of
his wonderful success.

  " Not only was nature, man, fact, and principle
suggestive to Mr. Lincoln, not only had he accurate
and exact perceptions, but he was causative, *i. e.*,
his mind ran back behind all facts, things, and principles to their origin, history, and first cause,— to
that point where forces act at once as effect and

cause. He would stop and stand in the street and analyze a machine. He would whittle things to a point, and then count the numberless inclined planes, and their pitch, making the point. Mastering and defining this, he would then cut that point back, and get a broad transverse section of his pine stick, and peel and define that. Clocks, omnibuses, and language, paddle-wheels, and idioms, never escaped his observation and analysis. Before he could form any idea of anything, before he would express his opinion on any subject, he must know it in origin and history, in substance and quality, in magnitude and gravity. He must know his subject inside and outside, upside and downside. He searched his own mind and nature thoroughly, as I have often heard him say. He must analyze a sensation, an idea, and words, and run them back to their origin, history, purpose, and destiny. He was most emphatically a remorseless analyzer of facts, things, and principles. When all these processes had been well and thoroughly gone through, he could form an opinion and express it, but no sooner. He had no faith 'Say so's' he had no respect for, coming though they might from tradition, power, or authority.

"All things, facts, and principles had to run through his crucible and be tested by the fires of his analytic mind; and hence, when he did speak his utterances rang out gold-like, quick, keen, and current upon the counters of the understanding. He reasoned logically, through analogy and comparison. All opponents dreaded him in his originality of idea, condensation, definition, and force of expression, and woe be to the man who hugged to his bosom a secret error if Mr. Lincoln got on the chase of it. I say, woe to him! Time could hide the error in no nook or corner of space in which he would not detect and expose it.

.   .   .   .

"Though Mr. Lincoln had accurate perceptions, though nature was extremely suggestive to him, though he was a profound thinker as well as analyzer, still his judgments and opinions formed upon minor matters were often childish. I have sometimes asked prominent, talented, and honest men in this and other States for their manly opinion of Mr. Lincoln's judgments. I did this to confirm or overthrow my own opinions on this point. Their answers were that his judgments were poor. But now what do we understand by the word 'judgments?' It is not reason, it is not will, nor is it understanding; but it is the judging faculty, — that capacity or power that forms opinions and decides on the fitness, beauty, harmony, and appropriateness of things under all circumstances and surroundings, quickly, wisely, accurately. Had Mr. Lincoln this quality of mind? I think not. His mind was like nis body, and worked slowly.

.   .   .   .

"One portion of mankind maintained that Mr.

Lincoln was weak-minded, and they look at him
only from the stand-point of his judgments. Another class maintain that he was a great, deep, profound man in his judgments. Do these two classes
understand themselves? Both views cannot be
correct. Mr. Lincoln's mind was slow, angular, and
ponderous, rather than quick and finely discriminat-
ing, and *in time* his great powers of reason on cause
and effect, on creation and relation, on substance
and on truth, would form a proposition, an opinion
wisely and well, — *that* no human being can deny.
When his mind could not grasp premises from
which to argue he was weaker than a child, because he had none of the child's intuitions, — the
soul's quick, bright flash over scattered and unar-
ranged facts.

" Mr. Lincoln was a peculiar man, having a peculiar mind ; he was gifted with a peculiarity,
namely, a new lookout on nature. Everything had
to be newly created for him, — facts newly gathered, newly arranged, and newly classed. He had
no faith, as already expressed. In order to believe
he must see and feel, and thrust his hand into the
place. He must taste, smell, and handle before he
had faith, *i. e.*, belief. Such a mind as this must
act slowly, — must have its time. His forte and
power lay in his love of digging out for himself and
hunting up for his own mind its own food, to be
assimilated unto itself; and then in time he could
and would form opinions and conclusions that no

human power could overthrow. They were as irresistible as iron thunder, as powerful as logic embodied in mathematics.

"I have watched men closely in reference to their approaches to Mr. Lincoln. Those who approached him on his judgment side treated him tenderly — sometimes respectfully, but always as a weak-minded man. This class of men take the judgment as the standard of the mind. I have seen another class approach him on his reason-side, and they always crouched low down and truckled, as much as to say, ' great,' 'grand,' ' omnipotent.' Both these classes were correct. One took judgment as the standard of the man, and the other took reason. Yet both classes were wrong in this, — they sunk out of view one side of Mr. Lincoln. A third class knew him well, and always treated him with human respect: not that awe and reverence with which we regard the Supreme Being; not that supercilious haughtiness which greatness shows to littleness. Each will please to examine itself, and then judge of what I say. I have approached Mr. Lincoln on all sides, and treated him according to the angle approached.

.   .   .   .

"An additional question naturally suggests itself here, and it is this: Had Mr. Lincoln great, good common sense? Different persons, of equal capacity and honesty, hold different views on this question, — one class answering in the affirmative, and the other in the negative.

These various opinions necessarily spring out of the question just discussed. If the true test is that a man shall quickly, wisely, and well judge the rapid rush and whirl of human transactions, as accurately as though indefinite time and proper conditions were at his disposal, then I am compelled to follow the logic of things, and say that Mr. Lincoln had no more than ordinary common sense. The world, men and their actions, must be judged as they rush and pass along. They will not wait on us ; will not stay for our logic and analysis ; they must be seized as they run. We all our life act on the moment. Mr. Lincoln knew himself, and never trusted his dollar or his fame on his casual opinions; he never acted hastily on great matters.

.   .   .   .

" Mr. Lincoln very well knew that the great leading law of human nature was *motive*. He reasoned all ideas of a disinterested action from my mind. I used to hold that an action could be pure, disinterested, and holy, free from all selfishness, but he divested me of that delusion. His idea was that all human actions were caused by *motives*, and that at the bottom of those motives was *self*. He defied me to act without a motive and unselfishly ; and when I did the act and told him of it, he analyzed and sifted it, and demonstrated beyond the possibility of controversy that it was altogether selfish. Though he was a profound analyzer of the laws of human nature, still he had no idea of the peculiar motives

of the particular individual.   He could not well
discriminate in human nature.   He knew but little
of the play of the features as seen in 'the human
face divine.'   He could not distinguish between the
paleness of anger and the crimson tint of modesty.
He could not determine what each play of the features indicated.

.   .   .   .

"The great predominating elements of Mr. Lincoln's peculiar character, were : First, his great capacity and *power of reason ;* secondly, his excellent
understanding ; thirdly, an exalted idea of the sense
of *right and equity ;* and, fourthly, his intense ven-
eration of what was *true and good.*   His reason
ruled despotically all other faculties and qualities of
his mind.   His conscience and heart were ruled
by it.   His conscience was ruled by one faculty —
reason.   His heart was ruled by two faculties —
reason and conscience.   I know it is generally
believed that Mr. Lincoln's heart, his love and
kindness, his tenderness and benevolence, were his
ruling qualities ; but this opinion is erroneous in
every particular.   First, as to his *reason.*   He dwelt
in the mind, not in the conscience, and not in the
heart.   He lived and breathed and acted from
his reason, — the throne of logic and the home of
principle, the realm of Deity in man.   It is from
this point that Mr. Lincoln must be viewed.   His
views were correct and original.   He was cautious
not to be deceived ; he was patient and endur-

22

ing. He had concentration and great continuity of thought; he had a profound analytic power; his visions were clear, and he was emphatically the master of statement. His pursuit of the truth was indefatigable, terrible. He reasoned from his well-chosen principles with such clearness, force, and compactness, that the tallest intellects in the land bowed to him with respect. He was the strongest man I ever saw, looking at him from the stand-point of his reason, — the throne of his logic. He came down from that height with an irresistible and crushing force. His printed speeches will prove this; but his speeches before courts, especially before the Supreme Courts of the State and Nation, would demonstrate it: unfortunately none of them have been preserved. Here he demanded time to think and prepare. The office of reason is to determine the truth. Truth is the power of reason — the child of reason. He loved and idolized truth for its own sake. It was reason's food.

"Conscience, the second great quality and forte of Mr. Lincoln's character, is that faculty which loves the just: its office is justice; right and equity are its correlatives. It decides upon all acts of all people at all times. Mr. Lincoln had a deep, broad, living conscience. His great reason told him what was true, good, and bad, right, wrong, just or unjust, and his conscience echoed back its decision; and it was from this point that he acted and spoke and wove his character and fame among us. His

conscience ruled his heart; he was always just before he was gracious. This was his motto, his glory:
and this is as it should be. It cannot be truthfully
said of any mortal man that he was always just.
Mr. Lincoln was not always just; but his great general life was. It follows that if Mr. Lincoln had
great reason and great conscience, he was an honest man. His great and general life was honest,
and he was justly and rightfully entitled to the ap-
pellation, 'Honest Abe.' Honesty was his great
polar star.

" Mr. Lincoln had also a good understanding;
that is, the faculty that understands and compre-
hends the exact state of things, their near and re-
mote relation. The understanding does not necessarily inquire for the reason of things. I must here
repeat that Mr. Lincoln was an odd and original
man; he lived by himself and out of himself. He
could not absorb. He was a very sensitive man,
unobtrusive and gentlemanly, and often hid himself
in the common mass of men, in order to prevent
the discovery of his individuality. He had no in-
sulting egotism, and no pompous pride; no haughtiness, and no aristocracy. He was not indifferent,
however, to approbation and public opinion. He
was not an upstart, and had no insolence. He
was a meek, quiet, unobtrusive gentleman. These
qualities of his nature merged somewhat his iden-
tities. Read Mr. Lincoln's speeches, letters, messages, and proclamations, read his whole record in

his actual life, and you cannot fail to perceive that
he had good understanding. He understood and
fully comprehended himself, and what he did and
why he did it, better than most living men.

.   .   .   .

" There are contradictory opinions in reference to
Mr. Lincoln's *heart and humanity*. One opinion is
that he was cold and obdurate, and the other opinion is that he was warm and affectionate. I have
shown you that Mr. Lincoln first lived and breathed
upon the world from his head and conscience. I have
attempted to show you that he lived and breathed
upon the world through the tender side of his heart,
subject at all times and places to the logic of his
reason, and to his exalted sense of right and equity,
namely, his conscience. He always held his conscience subject to his head ; he held his heart always
subject to his head and conscience. His heart was
the lowest organ, the weakest of the three. Some
men would reverse this order, and declare that his
heart was his ruling organ ; that always manifested
itself with love, regardless of truth and justice,
right and equity. The question still is, was Mr.
Lincoln a cold, heartless man, or a warm, affectionate man ? Can a man be a warm-hearted man who
is all head and conscience, or nearly so ? What, in
the first place, do we mean by a warm-hearted man ?
Is it one who goes out of himself and reaches for
others spontaneously, because of a deep love of humanity, apart from equity and truth, and does what

it does for love's sake? If so, Mr. Lincoln was a
cold man. Or, do we mean that when a human
being, man or child, approached him in behalf
of a matter of right, and that the prayer of such
an one was granted, that this is an evidence of
his love? The African was enslaved, his rights
were violated, and a principle was violated in them.
Rights imply obligations as well as duties. Mr.
Lincoln was President; he was in a position that
made it his duty through his sense of right, his
love of principle, his constitutional obligations imposed upon him by oath of office, to strike the blow
against slavery. But did he do it for love? He
himself has answered the question: ' I would not
free the slaves if I could preserve the Union without it.' I use this argument against his too enthusiastic friends. If you mean that this is love for
love's sake, then Mr. Lincoln was a warm-hearted
man — not otherwise. To use a general expression, his general life was cold. He had, however,
a strong latent capacity to love; but the object must
first come as principle, second as right, and third as
lovely. He loved abstract humanity when it was
oppressed. This was an abstract love, not concrete
in the individual, as said by some. He rarely used
the term love, yet was he tender and gentle. He
gave the key-note to his own character, when he
said, ' with malice toward none, and with charity for
all,' he did what he did. He had no intense loves,
and hence no hates and no malice. He had a broad

charity for imperfect man, and let us imitate his great life in this.

"'But was not Mr. Lincoln a man of great humanity?' asks a friend at my elbow, a little angrily; to which I reply, 'Has not that question been answered already?' Let us suppose that it has not. We must understand each other. What do you mean by humanity? Do you mean that he had much of human nature in him? If so, I will grant that he was a man of humanity. Do you mean, if the above definition is unsatisfactory, that Mr. Lincoln was tender and kind? Then I agree with you. But if you mean to say that he so loved a man that he would sacrifice truth and right for him, for love's sake, then he was not a man of humanity. Do you mean to say that he so loved man, for love's sake, that his heart led him out of himself, and compelled him to go in search of the objects of his love, for their sake? He never, to my knowledge, manifested this side of his character. Such is the law of human nature, that it cannot be all head, all conscience, and all heart at one and the same time in one and the same person. Our Maker made it so, and where God through reason blazed the path, walk therein boldly. Mr. Lincoln's glory and power lay in the just combination of head, conscience, and heart, and it is here that his fame must rest, or not at all.

" Not only were Mr. Lincoln's perceptions good not only was nature suggestive to him; not only

was he original and strong ; not only had he great
reason, good understanding ; not only did he love
the true and good — the eternal *right ;* not only was
he tender and kind, — but, in due proportion and
in legitimate subordination, had he a glorious combination of them all.   Through his perceptions, —
the suggestiveness of nature, his originality and
strength ; through his magnificent reason, his understanding, his conscience, his tenderness, and
kindness, his heart, rather than love, — he approx-
imated as nearly as most human beings in this
imperfect state to an embodiment of the great moral
principle, ' Do unto others as ye would they should
do unto you.'

.   .   .   .

"There are two opinions — radically different opinions — expressed about Mr. Lincoln's will, by men
of equal and much capacity.   One opinion is, that
he had *no* will ; and the other is, that he was *all* will
— omnipotently so.   These two opinions are loudly
and honestly affirmed.   Mr. Lincoln's mind loved
the true, the right, and good, all the great truths
and principles in the mind of man.   He loved the
true, first ; the right, second ; and the good, the
least.   His mind struggled for truths and his soul
for substances.   Neither in his head nor in his soul
did he care for forms, methods, ways, — the *non-
substantial* facts or things.   He could not, by his
very structure and formation in mind and body,
care anything about them.   He did not intensely

or much care for particular individual man, — the dollar, property, rank, order, manners, or such like things. He had no avarice in his nature, or other like vice. He despised, somewhat, all technical rules in law and theology and other sciences, — mere forms everywhere, — because they were, as a general rule, founded on arbitrary thoughts and ideas, and not on reason, truth, right, and the good. These things were without substance, and he disregarded them because they cramped his original nature. What suited a little, narrow, critical mind did not suit Mr. Lincoln's, any more than a child's clothes did his body. Generally, Mr. Lincoln could not take any interest in little local elections — town meetings. He attended no gatherings that pertained to local or other such interests, saving general political ones. He did not care (because he could not, in his nature) who succeeded to the presidency of this or that Christian Association or Railroad Convention; who made the most money; who was going to Philadelphia, when and for what, and what were the costs of such a trip. He could not care who, among friends, got this office or that — who got to be street inspector or alley commissioner. No principle of goodness, of truth, or right was here. How could he be moved by such things as these? He could not understand why men struggled for such things. He made this remark to me one day, I think at Washington, ' If ever this free people — if this Government itself is ever

utterly demoralized, it will come from this human
wriggle and struggle for office — a way to live without work ; from which nature I am not free myself.'
It puzzled him a good deal, at Washington, to know
and to get at the root of this dread desire, — this
contagious disease of national robbery in the nation's
death-struggle.

" Because Mr. Lincoln could not feel any interest
in such little things as I have spoken of, nor feel
any particular interest in the success of those who
were thus struggling and wriggling, he was called
indifferent — nay, ungrateful — to his friends.   Especially is this the case with men who have aided
Mr. Lincoln all their life.   Mr. Lincoln always and
everywhere wished his friends well ; he loved his
friends and clung to them tenaciously, like iron to
iron welded ; yet he could not be actively and
energetically aroused to the true sense of his friends'
particularly strong feelings of anxiety for office,
From this fact Mr. Lincoln has been called ungrateful.   He was not an ungrateful man by any
means.   He may have been a cool man — a passive
man in his general life ; yet he was not ungrateful.
Ingratitude is too positive a word — it does not convey the truth.   Mr. Lincoln may not have measured
his friendly duties by the applicant's hot desire ; I
admit this.   He was not a selfish man, — if by selfishness is meant that Mr. Lincoln would do any
act, even to promote himself to the Presidency, if
by that act any human being was wronged.   If it

is said that Abraham Lincoln preferred Abraham Lincoln to any one else, in the pursuit of his ambitions; and that, because of this, he was a selfish man, then I can see no objections to such an idea, for this is universal human nature.

"It must be remembered that Mr. Lincoln's mind acted logically, cautiously, and slowly. Now, having stated the above facts, the question of his will and its power is easily solved. Be it remembered that Mr. Lincoln cared nothing for simple facts, manners, modes, ways, and such like things. Be it remembered that he *did* care for truth, right, for principle, for all that pertains to the good. In relation to simple facts, unrelated to substance, forms, rules, methods, ways, manners, he cared nothing; and if he could be aroused, he would do anything for any body at any time, as well foe as friend. As a politician he would courteously grant all facts and forms — all non-essential things — to his opponent. He did so because he did not care for them; they were rubbish, husks, trash. On the question of substance, he hung and clung with all his might. On questions of truth, justice, right, the good, on principle his will was as firm as steel and as tenacious as iron. It was as firm, solid, real, vital, and tenacious as an idea on which the world hinges or hangs. Ask Mr. Lincoln to do a wrong thing, and he would scorn the request; ask him to do an unjust thing, and he would cry, 'Begone!' ask him to sacrifice his convictions of the truth, and his soul would indignantly exclaim, 'The world perish first!'

" Such was Mr. Lincoln's will. On manners **and**
such like things, he was pliable. On questions **of**
right and substance, he was as firm as a rock. One
of these classes of men look at Mr. Lincoln from
the stand-point of things non-essential, and the other
looks at him from the stand-point of substance, rejecting forms. Hence the difference. Mr. Lincoln was a man of firm, unyielding will, when, in
human transactions, it was necessary to be so, and
not otherwise. At one moment Mr. Lincoln was
as pliable and expansive as gentle air, and at the
next moment he was as biting, firm, tenacious, and
unyielding as gravity itself.

"Thus I have traced Mr. Lincoln through his
perceptions, his suggestiveness, his judgments, and
his four great predominant qualities, namely, — his
powers of reason, his great understanding, his conscience, and his heart. I assert that Mr. Lincoln
lived in the head. He loved the truth ; he loved
the eternal right and the good, — never yielding the
fundamental conceptions of these to any man **for**
any end.

" All the follies and wrong Mr. Lincoln ever **fell**
into, or committed, sprang or came out of his **weak**
points, namely, his want of quick, sagacious, **intu-**
itive judgment, — his want of quick, sagacious, intuitive knowledge of the play and meaning of the
features of men as written on the face, — his tenderness and mercy, and, lastly, his utterly unsuspecting
nature. He was deeply and seriously honest him-

self, and assumed that others were so organized. He never suspected men. These, with other defects of his nature, caused all his follies and wrongs, if he ever had any of either.

"All the wise and good things Mr. Lincoln ever did, sprang or came out of his great reason, his conscience, his understanding, and his heart, his love of truth, right, and the good. I am speaking now of his particular and individual faculties and qualities, *not their combination*, nor the result of wise or unwise combinations. Each man and woman must form his or her own estimate of the man in the mind. Run out these facts, qualities, and faculties, and see what they must produce. For instance, a tender heart; a wise, strong reason; a good understanding, an exalted conscience, a love of the good, must, in such combination, practically applied, produce a man of great humanity.

"Take another illustration in the combination of his faculties and qualities. Mr. Lincoln's eloquence lay, 1st, in the strength of his logical faculty, his supreme power of reasoning, his great understanding, and his love of principle; 2d, in his clear, exact, and very accurate vision; 3d, in his cool and masterly statement of his principles, around which the issues gather; in the statement of those issues, and the grouping of the facts that are to carry conviction, aided by his logic, to the minds of men of every grade of intelligence. He was so clear that he could not be misunderstood nor misrepresented.

He stood square and bolt upright to his convictions, and formed by them his thoughts and utterances Mr. Lincoln's mind was not a wide, deep, broad, generalizing, and comprehensive mind, nor versatile quick, bounding here and there, as emergencies demanded it. His mind was deep, enduring, and strong, running in deep iron grooves, with flanges on its wheels. His mind was not keen, sharp, and subtile ; it was deep, exact, and strong.

" Whatever of life, vigor, force, and power of eloquence the whole of the above qualities, or a wise combination will give ; whatever there is in a fair, manly, honest, and impartial administration of justice, under law, to all men at all times, — through these qualities and capabilities given, never deviating ; whatever there is in a strong will in the right, governed by tenderness and mercy ; whatever there is in toil and a sublime patience ; whatever there is in particular faculties, or a wise combination of them, — not forgetting his weak points, — working wisely, sagaciously, and honestly, openly and fairly ; — I say, whatever there is in these, or a combination of them, that Mr. Lincoln is justly entitled to in all the walks of life. These limit, bound, and define him as statesman, orator, as an executive of the nation, as a man of humanity, a good man, and a gentleman. These limit, bound, and define him every way, in all the ways and walks of life. He is under his law and his nature, and he never can get out of it.

"This man, this long, bony, wiry, sad man, floated into our county in 1831, in a frail canoe, down the north fork of the Sangamon River, friendless, pennyless, powerless, and alone, — begging for work in this city, — ragged, struggling for the common necessaries of life. This man, this peculiar man, left us in 1861, the President of the United States, backed by friends and power, by fame, and all human force ; and it is well to inquire *how*.

"To sum up, let us say, here is a sensitive, diffident, unobtrusive, natural-made gentleman. His mind was strong and deep, sincere and honest, patient and enduring ; having no vices, and having only negative defects, with many positive virtues. His is a strong, honest, sagacious, manly, noble life. He stands in the foremost rank of men in all ages, — their equal, — one of the best types of this Christian civilization."

LXXX.

At the end of six months' incessant labor, my task at the White House drew near completion. On the 22d of July, the President and Cabinet, at the close of the regular session, adjourned in a body to the State Dining-room, to view the work, at last in a condition to receive criticism. Sitting in the midst of the group, the President expressed his "unschooled" opinion, as he called it, of the result, in terms which could not but have afforded the deepest gratification to any artist.

The curiosity of the public to see the picture was so great that during the last two days of my stay in Washington, by the kind permission of the President, it was placed in the East Room, and thrown open to the public. During this time the house was thronged with visitors, the porters estimating their number each day at several thousands.

Towards the close of the second day's exhibition, intending to have the canvas taken down and rolled up during the night for transportation to New York, I watched for an opportunity to say a last word to Mr. Lincoln previous to his leaving for the Soldiers' Home, where the family were then staying, At four o'clock the carriage drove up to the door, accompanied by the " Black-Horse Cavalry " escort. Knowing the President would soon appear, I stepped out under the portico to wait for him. Presently I caught sight of his unmistakable figure standing half-way between the portico and the gateway leading to the War Department leaning against the iron fence, — one arm thrown over the railing, and one foot on the stone coping which supports it, evidently having been intercepted, on his way in from the War Department, by a plain-looking man, who was giving him, very diffidently, an account of a difficulty which he had been unable to have rectified. While waiting, I walked out leisurely to the President's side. He said very little to the man, but was intently studying the expression of his face while he was narrating his trouble. When he had finished, Mr. Lincoln said to him, " Have you a blank card?" The man searched his pockets, but finding none, a gentleman standing near, who had overheard the question, came forward and said, " Here is one, Mr. President." Several persons had in the mean time gathered around. Taking the card and a pencil, Mr. Lincoln sat down upon the low stone coping, presenting almost the appearance of sitting upon the pavement itself, and wrote an order upon the card to the proper official to " examine this man's case." While writing this, I observed several persons passing down the promenade smiling, at what I presume they thought the undignified appearance of the head of the nation, who, however, seemed utterly unconscious, either of any impropriety in the action, or of attracting any attention. To me it was not only another picture of the native goodness of the man, but of true nobility of character, exemplified not so much by a disregard of conventionalities, as in unconsciousness that there *could* be any breach of etiquette or dignity in the manner of an honest attempt to serve or secure justice to a citizen of the Republic, however humble he might be. Rising to his feet he handed the man the card, with a word of direction, and then turning to me said : " Well C——, I must go in and take one more look at the picture before you leave us." So saying, he accompanied me to the East Room, and sitting down in front of it, remained for some time in silence. I said that

I nad at length worked out my idea, as he ex·
pressed it at our first interview, and would now be
glad to hear his final suggestions and criticism.

" There is little to find fault with," he replied ;
" the portraiture is the main thing, and that seems
to me absolutely perfect."

I then called his attention afresh to the accessories of the picture, stating that these had been
selected from the objects in the Cabinet chamber
with reference solely to their bearing upon the subject. " Yes," said he, " there are the war-maps,
the portfolios, the *slave*-map, and all; but the book
in the corner, leaning against the chair-leg, — you
have changed the title of that, I see." " Yes," I
replied; " at the last moment I learned that you
frequently consulted, during the period you were
preparing the Proclamation, Solicitor Whiting's
work on the ' War Powers of the President,' and
as Emancipation was the result in fact of a military necessity, the book seemed to me just the
thing to go in there ; so I simply changed the
title, leaving the old sheepskin cover as it was."
" Now," said he, " Whiting's book is not a regular law-book. It is all very well that it should
be there; but I would suggest that as you have
changed the title, you change also the character of
the binding. It now looks like an old volume of
United States Statutes." I thanked him for this
criticism, and then said: " Is there anything else
that you wculd like changed or added ? "   " No,"

he replied, and then repeated very emphatically the expression he used when the design was first sketched upon the canvas: "It is as good as it can be made."

I then referred at some length, to the enthusiasm in which the picture was conceived and had been executed, concluding with an expression of my profound appreciation of the very unusual opportunities afforded me in the prosecution of the work, and his unvarying kindness and consideration through the many weeks of our intercourse.

He listened pensively, — almost passively, to me, — his eyes fastened upon the picture. As I finished he turned, and in his simple-hearted, earnest way, said: "C——, I believe I am about as glad over the success of this work as you are." And with these words in my ear, and a cordial "good-bye" grasp of the hand, President and painter separated: the one to gather into and around himself more and more the affections of a mighty people, till in the culmination and attainment of all his heart's desires he should be called from "glory to glory;" the other, in his humble sphere, to garner as a precious legacy to him and his these fragments of leaves from the daily life of one whose name and fame — inseparably bound up with devotion to freedom and reverence for law, fragrant with the tender memories and sweet humanities of life — are to grow brighter and stronger with God's eternal years, as men learn to appreciate and emulate a true Christian manhood.

INDEX.

THE END.